MANAGEMENT PRINCIPLES FOR ASSET PROTECTION

MANAGEMENT PRINCIPLES FOR ASSET PROTECTION

Understanding the Criminal Equation

PHILIP KROPATKIN

RICHARD P. KUSSEROW

A Ronald Press Publication
JOHN WILEY & SONS
New York · Chichester · Brisbane · Toronto · Singapore

Library of Congress Cataloging in Publication Data:

Kropatkin, Philip.
    Management principles for asset protection.

   "A Ronald Press publication."
   Bibliography: p.
   Includes index.
   1. Fraud.   2. White collar crimes—Prevention.
3. Computer crimes—Prevention.   I. Kusserow, Richard P.
II. Title.

HV6691.K7   1986   364.1'68   85-22736

ISBN 0-471-80938-1

Printed in the United States of America

10 9 8 7 6 5 4 3 2 1

PREFACE

The economic and social implications of crime are tightly woven throughout the fabric of our society. Losses from white collar crime coupled with those from waste and abuse can best be described as staggering. We discuss in considerable detail all of the factors that, when present, fit together to form high opportunity for a criminal act. An individual who understands and appreciates the implications of these factors can take positive measures to reduce the chance of a crime being committed by budding or active criminals.

White Collar Crimes consist of activities that are considered to be crimes only because the law says they are. While there is no generally accepted single definition, White Collar Crime can be defined as:

> Wrongful activity or some aspect of a wrongful pattern of activity committed by the use of misrepresentation, guile, or deception (nonphysical means) to obtain something of value, prevent loss, or obtain personal or business advantage, and often in violation of a fiduciary relationship.

Who are its perpetrators? As this book will illustrate, it can be anyone if all of the variables necessary for a criminal equation are present.

We have employed the principles and approaches discussed herein in our work at the Office of Inspector General in the federal Department of Health and Human Services (HHS). HHS, with fiscal year 1985 program expenditures of some

$316.5 billion, has *the world's third largest budget.* These principles have worked well for the Inspector General's office which was set up to promote economy and efficiency in HHS' programs and reduce the incidence of fraud, waste, and abuse. For fiscal year 1985, this office reported that their work culminated in 1005 successful prosecutions, a 500 percent increase since 1981. Administrative sanctions were taken against 390 health care providers and suppliers who were "kicked out" of the Medicare and Medicaid programs, a 900 percent increase since 1981. Over $4.9 billion in settlements, fines, restitutions, recoveries, and savings were realized due to management and congressional action on HHS Inspector General recommendations. (Savings include those attributable to legislative changes, predicated on findings calculated over a five year budget cycle; and management commitments to not expend funds or to more efficiently use resources.) This represents a 30 fold increase since 1981.

The principles for asset protection outlined in this book apply to the whole ADP arena as well. To illustrate, one of the authors (the HHS Inspector General) has testified on a number of occasions as an expert witness before congressional committees on such issues as computer security, computer related fraud and abuse, and computer record matching.

This book provides managers with a broad understanding of the ways in which they can protect their property from criminal attack. The principles illustrated have been tested and found valid. We can thus recommend them for use.

PHILIP KROPATKIN
RICHARD P. KUSSEROW

Mill Creek, Washington
Bethesda, Maryland

January 1986

ACKNOWLEDGMENT

We wish to thank Charles L. Johnson for his invaluable assistance in reviewing, editing, and providing perceptive and practical contributions to this book.

R.K.
P.K.

CONTENTS

PART ONE   INTRODUCTION

1   The Criminal Equation   3

PART TWO   THE TARGETS

2   Protecting Your Targets   19

PART THREE   MOTIVATION

3   Motive: Examining the Why Factor Behind
    Wrongful Acts   49
4   Motive: The Internal Forces   57
5   The External Forces   73
6   The Corporate Mind   95

PART FOUR   ACCESS

7   Denying Access: Promoting Security   105
8   The Insiders: Allowing Access to Employees   119
9   Physical Security   135

10   Controlling Access by Mechanical Means   145
11   The Problem of False Identification   159

PART FIVE   OPPORTUNITY

12   Denying Opportunity Through Using Proper Sets
     of Rules and Controls   175
13   Denying Opportunity: By Utilizing Auditors,
     Inspectors General, and Others   199
14   Testing Controls Through Auditing   213
15   Indicators of Criminal Activities in the Business
     World   229

PART SIX   APPLYING THE FORMULA FOR FRAUD TO
THE WORLD OF COMPUTERS

16   The Problems of Rising Technology   259
17   Basic Computer Security Measures: Denying Access
     and Opportunities   287
18   Insuring System Integrity   299
19   Insuring Data Integrity: Using the Computer to Tame
     the Computer   313

APPENDICES

Appendix I   Theory of Differential Association   329
Appendix II   Convicted Providers in Medicare and
                Medicaid—Report of Inspector
                General, HHS   331
Appendix III   Preventing Sexual Abuse in Day Care
                Programs—Report of Inspector
                General, HHS   345
Appendix IV   Computer-Related Fraud and Abuse in
                Government Agencies—PCIE Report   379

Appendix V   Computer Related Fraud in Government
               Agencies: Perpetrator Interviews—Report
               of Inspector General, HHS   403
Appendix VI   Report of the Task Force on the
               Criminal Implications of False
               Identification   441

Bibliography   453
Index   455

MANAGEMENT PRINCIPLES FOR ASSET PROTECTION

PART ONE

INTRODUCTION

CHAPTER ONE

THE CRIMINAL EQUATION

For many years the authors were involved as Federal auditors and investigators in dealing with wrongful or inappropriate behavior after it was committed and manifested. Our most recent experiences have been connected with managing the audit and investigative resources of the largest government agency in the world, the U.S. Department of Health and Human Services. Its outlays exceed $300 billion a year.

From conducting audits and inspections we found questionable management practices, inappropriate expenditures, disallowable costs, and occasionally crime. From engaging in the investigation of crimes we uncovered other crimes, identified wrongdoing, and built a chain of evidence leading to judicial sanctioning. Many years of experience in dealing with the consequences and failures of systemic weaknesses caused by poor management and internal controls gave us insight into principles and techniques that can be used to detect fraud after the fact and to anticipate and prevent fraud. For example an investigator who is called to the scene of a crime follows essentially the same routine or procedure each time whether the crime is robbery, rape, arson, embezzlement, burglary, murder, assault or something else. First, an individual or individuals encountering or reporting the crime are interviewed as to the time and circumstances surrounding the event. Second, the "crime scene" is protected against any tampering with the physical evidence until it can be analyzed. Next, witnesses are located and interviewed as to any relevant facts they might possess. Finally, a list of potential suspects is developed and eliminated against the evidence until it is narrowed to the perpetrator.

The whole process might be examined in a different way, however, since all the interviews of the witnesses and sifting of the evidence has several related purposes. First, the object of the crime or the *target* must be established. Was the target an individual (as in the crimes of rape, murder, and assault)? Property (as in burglary, embezzlement, larceny, and arson)? Or both (as in robbery, extortion, and crimes where both people and property are the objects of the criminal act)? It is interesting to note in this connection that a two and a half year study by Apt Associates (Cambridge, Mass.) of the FBI Uniform Crime Reports (UCR) revealed weaknesses in the data being collected from 16,000 state and local law enforcement agencies. The collected data is used by law enforcement agencies, researchers, government policy makers, and the media. Principle among the recommendations was to identify targets or objects of the crime by distinguishing crimes among business, crimes against individuals or households, and crimes against other entities. At common law the target identification is an essential element of any case: it is the *corpus delicti*, or body of the crime.

The second purpose is identifying those who might have had a *motive* for the crime. The motive might be hate/revenge or special needs arising from situational stresses (marital or personal problems, living beyond one's means, special financial needs for medical or gambling debts, and the like). This essential element needs to be established in court cases. The third purpose is focusing the investigation on individuals with personal habits or history which suggest a possible predisposition for antisocial behavior (such as having a criminal record, being an alcohol or drug abuser, possessing a past history of petty theft, mischievous behavior, having a poor work record, and the like). The fourth item is determining who could be placed at the scene of the crime—that is, who had *access* to the target at the time the crime was committed. Fifth, the investigator is called upon to identify the weakness that gave rise to the *opportunity* for the crime and those who had knowledge to be able to take advantage of it.

Thus, the whole investigative process could be described as working towards the *nexus* of the crime. Here, this term means nothing more than trying to establish relationships, connections, and links between individuals and events. This whole book revolves around this concept. It demonstrates how one can understand the relationships of the targets, motives, access, and opportunities to wrongdoing. Once the relationships are understood—along with the consequences of what occur when they come together—then preventative measures can be taken to make sure that a wrongful act does not occur.

Simply stated, for a wrongdoing to occur all of these elements are needed. The equation or formula may be described as follows:

$$\text{Target} + \text{Motive} + \text{Access} + \text{Opportunity} =$$
$$\text{A Successful Criminal Attack}$$

We will examine each of these elements in detail, along with ways in which management of an environment can reduce their overall vulnerability by reducing the risk associated with each element.

SETTING THE STAGE

The problem of crime is difficult to understand because it involves the basic human personality and its interaction with society. Astute organizational managers, concerned about the possibility of criminal activity within their workplace, will find little help in current literature on dealing with the causes of

crime, or limiting its effect. Such books that are available tend
to be either too technical or (in the other extreme) too general to
be of much real use.

We shall focus on wrongdoing by breaking down all its
elements and keeping the recommendations simple and clear.

EXAMINING SOCIETY'S CRIMINAL PROCLIVITY

Where in our society does the criminal element originate?
Sociologists and criminologists generally agree that if we were
to array all mankind in a vast spectrum there would be at one
end of the dispersion a tiny portion of the population who, given
almost any opportunity, would find a way to commit a wrong!
Similarly, at the other end of the spectrum, one would find an
equally small group that would avoid committing a serious
wrong even under strongest inducements. In between are the
vast majority who, given sufficient pressure and with the right

FIGURE 1.1.   Constellation of various vector of forces that result in wrongful
acts. When targets, accessibility, motivation, and opportunity converge, there
is a "Vector of Forces" present—conducive to wrongful acts.

circumstances, are quite capable of wrongful behavior.

It is in this context that this book is written. Many books on the subject of crime tend to be written by academics with little or no practical experience. This book, drawing on our combined experiences as auditors and investigators, is intended to be down to earth and pragmatic.

THE EVOLUTION OF CRIME AND PUNISHMENT

For thousands of years man has lived in communal settings. To live in close quarters, it was necessary to establish certain rules for behavior. Violent behavior had to be restrained for common peace, tranquility, and security. Thus, all societies evolved certain basic laws that are remarkably similar. Laws were developed over the years to deter wrongdoers from and punish them for crimes of murder, rape, pillage, mayhem, arson, mutilation, and the like. In those societies that developed the notion of private property, laws also appeared against taking without permission that which belonged to another. The foregoing have been called *malum in se*, that is, crimes in themselves.

There were, however, no specified crimes against cheating one's neighbor. It was not deemed necessary. Preindustrial society had other effective means to ensure that this type of behavior would be restrained. First, there was social pressure—which was powerful and closely applied. The vast majority of the population lived in small communities or hamlets of less than a hundred families. If individuals cheated their neighbor, they would be subjected to ostracism, heavy peer pressure, and swift personal justice. It was virtually impossible for that individual to get along in society after the exposure of such behavior. It was, for one thing, extremely difficult, if not impossible, to relocate from one community to another. People were tied to their local community by feudal law. To leave without official permission put one outside the

law and in essence made one an "outlaw." Strangers wandering
into a community were looked upon with great suspicion and
hostility. These circumstances in themselves often kept that
type of antisocial activity under reasonable constraint.

A second major force that helped keep in check the cheating of
a neighbor in Europe was the Universal (Catholic) Church.
Medieval man feared the loss of his immortal soul far more than
the loss of his life. Thus, for someone to lie, misrepresent, or
otherwise cheat his neighbor was to risk excommunication and
eternal damnation!

Changing Mores

Two new social forces then came into play that weakened these
constraints dramatically. The first was Protestant Reformation,
which broke down the power of the Universal Church. Rival
religious groups routinely castigated, persecuted, and excom-
municated one another. This materially altered attitudes and
fears about excommunication. Thus the full force and effect of
excommunication began to greatly diminish in the minds of the
populace. It waned significantly as a deterrent to wrongful
conduct.

The second profound change to the social structure and mores
was the rise of commercialism and the emergence of the
Industrial Revolution. At an ever-increasing rate, people began
to move from rural hamlets, where everyone knew one another,
into depersonalized, crowded industrialized towns and cities.
No longer were individuals trading with neighbors who were
personally known to them. Merchants now began to routinely
deal with strangers and, with growing frequency, foreigners. In
fact, the entire merchant class often considered the ability to
cheat a customer as a commendable mark of a clever or sharp
businessman. The open and acceptable practice of bearing gifts
to the nobility for personal advantage made bribing public
officials commonplace.

Increased Accessibility
to Targets of Value

One highlight of the Industrial Revolution was the gradual
withdrawal of the owner of the business from the individual
workers. The advent of major decentralized industry and
business brought scores of people working for—not with—an
owner. There has been nothing yet to substitute for the sharp
eye and continued presence of an owner to assure employee
honesty! One of the more recent problems has been the
acceleration of the dehumanizing process caused by turning
"John Doe, Clerk" into Employee 98760. The alienation of the
employee from the employer, less day to day direct supervision
and control, and easier access to more and more targets all add
up to greater vulnerability to wrongdoing.

TRACING OUR
COMMON LAW HERITAGE

The American system of criminal justice is rooted deeply in
English common law. English common law predates the time of
William the Conqueror, Duke of Normandy, who, with a small
army, crossed the English Channel in 1066 and defeated the
Saxon army under Harold. William established the Plantagenet
line of kings. Much of their success in effectively occupying a
large land lies in the fact that they incorporated the existing
common law of England into their own system of jurisprudence.
This English Common Law, as incorporated by William,
remains virtually unchanged and is being enforced even today
by our local police agencies. It covers all of the major felonies,
that is, robbery, murder, rape, arson, larceny, assault and
battery, and so forth. Evidencing a real flair for administration,
the Plantagenets superimposed their own technique of close-in
control over this preexisting system of law.

The Normans established a King's Officer in each of the shires (counties) called the "shire reeve" (Sheriff) to maintain the king's peace. Today we still interchange the terms "peace officer" and "police officer." The Sheriff continues to be the principle country police officer. Each Norman baron had a local manor court. The principal enforcement officer for this court was the chief of the mounted knights called "count of the stable" (Constable). The Normans also created circuit judges who would move from shire to shire, enforcing the king's peace. These became the circuit courts—a term still used to identify principal criminal courts in the various jurisdictions of the United States.

Continuing the history, we can see nearly 1000 years of unbroken legal tradition associated with common law crimes. The terminology is familiar and our citizenry generally understand the nature of felonies. The elements of these crimes are well known. The role of law enforcement is similarly straightforward. After a citizen reports the commission of a crime, the law enforcement officer has the twofold mission of (1) identifying the wrongdoer and (2) bringing him to the bar of justice.

A common law felony is one in which there is a *corpus delicti* (body of the crime). This establishes proof that a crime has been committed. In the case of a murder there is a corpse, usually evidencing violence. In a robbery there is missing property, as described by the victim, who also attempts to describe the assailant. With burglary, evidence of forced entry and the stolen property, or loot, becomes proof of the crime. As for arson, there is a fire and property destruction. Evidence that the fire was started intentionally establishes the crime. The procedure of obtaining evidence and seeking the wrongdoer is a relatively uncomplicated process.

As mentioned earlier, all these crimes in common law are referred to as being crimes that are *malum in se*—crimes in themselves. These are offenses against human law because they have *always* been considered to be offensive and repugnant. All citizens agree on this. However, there is another body of laws, getting larger every day, which can be characterized as being *malum prohibitum* or prohibited crimes.

THE EVOLUTION OF PROHIBITED CRIMES

Prohibited crimes are crimes that are not derivative of the Common Law of England. They are crimes because they have been deemed to be crimes by socially conscious legislatures who desired additional protections for society. Without the statutory prohibition, they would not be crimes. The term "prohibition" itself is interesting in that it brings to mind a law that was supported by a full amendment to the United States Constitution. It made the manufacture and sale of most alcoholic beverages a crime. This was not a crime before enactment of the amendment, nor was it a crime after the amendment was repealed. But while it was in force, it was prohibited conduct, or *malum prohibitum. All White Collar Crimes are malum prohibitum crimes.*

One may recall from high school history classes major slogans of 19th century American business "laissez faire" (let business be) and "caveat emptor" (let the buyer beware). Times were quite different in the nineteenth century—and social customs then were not what we currently accept. For example, many nineteenth century American statesmen were noted for their ability to raise large sums of money by literally selling their votes in the halls of Congress. One of our most notable Congressmen, Daniel Webster, commanded a high price for his support because he was capable of influencing other legislators as a gifted orator. This practice was not a crime then, and, what's more, it was socially acceptable.

However, other things began happening that caused legislatures to pass the kind of laws which would protect consumers and citizens against what we now consider fraudulent conduct. One of the more notable instances, which in itself acted as a great force to limit shady business practices, came as a result of the Crimean War. When it became known that more British and French soldiers died from tainted British-processed meat than from Russian bullets, a public outcry arose for legislation action governing the quality of products being sold consumers. Similar outcries developed in the United States.

Pre-World War I was characterized by a period of social

reform sparked by the writings of such well-known "muckrakers" as Ida Tarbell, Edwin Markham, Lincoln Steffens, and Upton Sinclair. They were critical of political and financial rings, and problems in such areas as housing, transportation, industry, insurance, and canning. These exposés of political, corporate, and business irresponsibilities led to many pieces of new legislation designed to protect the public such as antitrust laws, beef inspection and pure food acts and child labor laws. Individuals trying to understand the nature of white collar crime must remember that the entire body of law deeming it to be criminal is relatively new. Additionally, it has both created new problems for the public and gone far to protect them. Common law crimes have the *corpus delicti*, the proof of crime manifest. The unknown elements are the identity of the wrongdoers and their whereabouts. In white collar crime, the wrongdoers are not hiding behind the robber's mask, they are known in the community. They may be your doctors, lawyers, politicians, businesspeople. It is their crimes that are unknown. Although the definitions of common law crimes are well known and generally understood by the citizenry, the definition of white collar crimes is still murky, unclear, and generally little understood by most Americans. The "Abscam" investigation by the FBI certainly underscores this point. In that investigation there were video tapes aired extensively on network news which showed a Congressman stuffing money into his pocket in exchange for a promise to return the favor (by votes of influence). Yet many had to stop and reflect: Was this, in itself, a crime that warranted imprisonment? The issue would have been much clearer if the film had shown someone with a gun demanding money. Remember, 100 years ago the activities involved here were quite acceptable—or at least not illegal.

Another odd, but important, aspect of White Collar Crime is that the victim may frequently be unaware that he has been "taken." For example, in the case of both faulty building construction passed on by bribed inspectors and faulty and misrepresented products the victim—the public—is unaware of the criminality. This presents a special problem because the investigator cannot always look to the victim to help sort out and provide all the necessary evidence of the crime. The investigator is often in the odd position of explaining the crime to the victim, rather than the other way around. (How easy it was in the good old "felony" days when a crime was clearly a crime!)

On the other side of the coin, many wrongdoers will go to some extent to convince both the victim and the investigator that his enterprise was a *legitimate* one. Often the wrongdoer is involved in acceptable endeavors along with illegal activities. All this obviously tends to cloud the situation. The wrongdoers frequently go to great effort to rationalize that their acts are not illegal or criminal—in nature. Furthermore, the wrongdoer may be well known and have a valued reputation in his own community.

It is easy to see how absolutely vital it is for the wrongdoer to see that the crime is disguised or concealed. When criminal involvement is uncovered, the wrongdoer is strongly compelled to deny the wrongdoing and fight the case with all of his energies and resources. To capitulate by plea agreement would be devastating to their reputation and community standing. One can almost always expect a trial before any conviction takes place.

Another concern is the wrongdoer's efforts to conceal the crime. The subject may, under pressure from the investigation, commit new crimes—such as perjury, obstruction of justice, and bribery of grand jurors. The motivation to do so (a key factor) is great because "reputation" is so important. It is not uncommon for subjects of investigations to destroy records after they have been ordered by the court to produce them—thus compounding their crimes by adding new charges of obstruction of justice.

In the past, law enforcement authorities often have been reluctant to undertake or even get involved in white collar crime investigations or prosecutions. Some of the reasons are (1) these wrongful acts do not always fall into familiar categories of crime, (2) it is sometimes difficult to decide whether they constitute a crime that is prosecutable without further and frequently extensive investigation; materiality is often at question, and (3) any investigation probably will be relatively complex and time consuming. Thus, white collar crimes are a far cry from the simple ones committed in the confined hamlets of yore.

Investigators can anticipate difficulties in persuading prosecutors to make a commitment. Victims are not always readily identifiable or willing to cooperate, and may not, in all honesty, have sufficient information to really be of much assistance. What's more, the legal system often views white collar criminals as less threatening to society than perpetrators of common law crimes. Punishment and treatment are more lenient and the offender may be allowed to "go free." Finally, white collar crime is perceived as being complicated, dull, academic, and tedious, just not worth the trouble to prosecute!

THE COST OF WHITE COLLAR CRIME

While each individual white collar crime may be a relatively small offense, the sum total is far from small. Individual and business victims should be made aware of the enormous overall cost to the society they live in. For one thing, honest businessmen are becoming less and less able to compete with most white collar criminals. Economic losses are staggering. Huge sums are at stake, all the clues tell us that. But is hard to determine the exact amount, as the following estimates show.[1]

The Bureau of Domestic Commerce estimated the cost of ordinary crime to the business world at $30 billion to $40 billion annually, excluding most white collar crimes, such as major fraud, embezzlement, or even organized crime.

The Attorney General estimated the cost of organized crime within the U.S. at over $50 billion a year but did not determine what percentage related to white collar crime.

[1]Data based on projections shown in "A Handbook on White Collar Crime," Chamber of Commerce of the U.S. 1974.

The U.S. Department of Commerce has estimated white collar crime at $30 billion dollars a year.

The U.S. Chamber of Commerce estimate is $40 billion a year.

The U.S. Senate placed it at over $100 billion annually. It is likely that all of these figures are much too conservative.

We believe that a more realistic figure would be more than $200 billion!

Nearly 6 million firms do business in the United States. Those in retailing alone lose over $6 billion in "shrinkage" (unexplained inventory losses) each year—or about 2% of their retail sales. Most large retailers can sustain this continued loss by passing the cost on to their customers. Many marginal operators who failed could have possibly survived, if they had been able to better safeguard their inventories. (It is interesting to note that many aggressive supermarket and retailing chains, as a matter of policy, flatly inform their store managers just how much shrinkage they will tolerate". It is up to the creativity of each manager as to how this negative difference can be recovered from the store's customers. What happens can be easily predicted—deliberate mismarkings mostly in favor of the store . . . markdowns from artificially inflated prices . . . manufacturers' closeouts treated as first-run merchandise . . . and so forth.

Small businesses are the hardest hit by shrinkage, since established management practices that can effectively combat crime are notably lacking among such smaller firms. Thus, it should come as no surprise that the Small Business Administration has attributed as much as 30 to 40 percent of small business failures to theft. This obviously represents a significant problem.

Another way of looking at the awesome impact of white collar crime is to contrast data on criminal losses associated with our federally insured banking institutions to data on white collar crime. There are over 6000 violations of the National Bank Robbery Statute (i.e., robberies, burglaries, larcenies) each year, with losses of about $40 million. Compare this with a like number (6000) of violations of the Bank Fraud Statute (embezzlement) reported in 1980—involving about $160 million—four times as much. At least five banking institutions a year face bankruptcy as a direct result of fraud. This figure is even more striking when one considers that the embezzlements were only those discovered and reported. In reality these represent only a fraction of the actual occurrences.

Even those statistics are dwarfed by fraud against the federal government—estimated in one candid report by the Federal Budget Office at $25 billion a year, more than 125 times the combined reported losses for all crimes against banking institutions. This sum does not, of course, include such losses by state and local governments.

To continue, it is "known" that annually (1) over $5 billion goes for bribes, kickbacks, and payoffs to buyers, contractors, inspectors, auditors, insurance adjustors, union and management officials, and so forth and (2) over $5 billion of securities are being stolen.

These figures threaten one's confidence in our freewheeling security and commodities exchange systems. Putting aside the monetary highlights, who can measure the impact of our society due to tainted products, health and safety violations, environmental pollutors, and serious misconduct by doctors, lawyers, laboratory technicians, accountants, and others?

PART TWO

THE TARGETS

CHAPTER TWO

PROTECTING
YOUR TARGETS

Throughout life we strive to protect that which is ours—our loved ones, possessions, reputation, health, financial security, and the like. This protective sense carries forth into the world of work. Our buildings and plants all have some form of protective security. We carefully select our employees trusting that those we hire will show a marked degree of concern about the financial health and integrity of our organization.

Major problems are faced when you set out to protect things of value from criminal attack. Each target can present a different problem in terms of restricting or negating opportunity and access. The dock worker or trucker working with the shipments in the dock is in a better position to steal them than someone walking outside the barbed wire perimeter. The individual with a computer room pass and access codes also has the greater ability to engage in wrongful behavior with the computer than does someone on the outside. Each employee has different values, needs, purposes, impulses and drives behind his or her behavior. Motive, access, opportunity: all are factors that must be considered in assessing the vulnerability of your environment to criminal attack.

Up until the Industrial Revolution, the owner/manager of a business was probably able to do a good job of protecting those parts of his enterprise vulnerable to theft, waste, and the like. He knew where the problems were and what was vulnerable. Over the years, as small businesses have given way to massive, decentralized, and rather impersonalized operations, various management disciplines have sprung into place that have been designed to "get a handle" on what is actually taking place in the organization. Systems experts, such as management analysts work towards making sure that management's policies are carried out in a well-organized check, double-check fashion. Auditors, both external and internal, are continuously testing our business operations to see whether they are well run—that our assets are safeguarded and controlled and that the organization is running smoothly. Security staffs oversee the physical side of limiting our vulnerabilities. Other disciplines, such as budget and accounting staffs to one extent or another, concern themselves with protecting the company's or organization's targets from attack. As good as they are, these approaches to target identification and protection (1) are not organization wide in scope, resulting in detailed analyses of some functions and processes and snapshot reviews of others, and (2) are not dedicated solely toward target identification and protection.

This chapter discusses methods by which we can defend and protect our environments from wrongdoers. The first part of the chapter describes a new approach to this task. The second part of this chapter, together with several illustrative applications, discusses the traditional methods for doing vulnerability assessments and a risk analyses.

A New Type of Target Analysis

At this point, though, the focus turns to quite a different approach of analyzing one's environment for motivation factors for wrongdoing—that is (1) the absence of barriers making for easy access to target areas and (2) the degree to which there are opportunities for wrongdoing. Using this approach, you will have the ability to "score" your own environment—and determine the degree of its overall vulnerability to criminal wrongdoing. This approach can be used as a diagnostic tool to identify particular areas of weaknesses.

What follows is a rate-your-target vulnerabilities questionnaire, developed from the succeeding sections of this book.

Before you can reduce the vulnerability of your environment, it is necessary to evaluate what are those vulnerabilities. To do this, complete the following questionnaire. Record your answers on the answer sheet that immediately follows it. Decide on the answer to each question to the best of your knowledge. Score by assigning the value as to how accurately the statement describes the way things are in your organization.

1 = Does not accurately describe
2 = Partially correct
3 = Generally correct
4 = Mostly correct
5 = Accurately describes

If you really cannot choose or it is inappropriate, then leave that question unanswered and go on to the next. However, it should be recognized that the more questions that are skipped the less reliable the results will be. A way of scoring the questionnaire is given immediately following the answer sheet. *This is not intended as an extremely precise measurement, but only as a rough guide to your target vulnerabilities.* The results of this questionnaire can be used in conjunction with the insights shown in this book to alter the vector of forces conducive to criminality, and lessen your chances of being attacked. The area of manifested weaknesses may influence which parts of the book should receive the most attention.

Rate Your Target Vulnerabilities to Criminal Attack

  1. Wage and salary planning services are offered to assist those having financial problems.

2. There are defined limits on the degrees of employee access to information on data considered sensitive.

3. Periodic reviews of internal control systems are made by internal auditors.

4. Employees are counseled whenever debt collection inquiries or garnishment notices are received.

5. Clear rules define who should have access to sensitive data and information either by individual name or position title.

6. Senior officials take an active interest in seeing that identified deficiencies from internal reviews and audits are corrected.

7. Employees are assisted in finding sources of low-cost loans to aid them in financial crises.

8. Sensitive data and information are assigned to designated custodians.

9. There is segregation of duties for all sensitive transactions in that no single individual may complete a transaction.

10. Employee counseling services are available to assist with alcohol and drug related problems that may be interfering with work.

11. Instructions on information storage and/or shipment requirements are clearly defined and identified.

12. There is a system of authorization on use of all resources and assets in accordance with laws, regulations, rules, and ordinances.

13. The special needs and concerns of minorities and women are addressed, not ignored by management.

14. Requirements over data retention, copy restrictions, inventory, and disposal requirements are defined in writing.

15. Employees are aware of and comply with rules that transactions are to be executed in accordance with management directions.

16. Standard written confirmation forms are not used to verify references in applications; it is done in person or by telephone.

17. Well-defined safeguards are in place in the access and use of data designated as sensitive to the operations of the entity.

18. Multipurpose audits are used by management to gauge the efficiency and effectiveness of operations.

19. Applicants for employment are screened for criminal records.

20. Contingency plans for use governing a wide range of possible emergencies have been developed and are kept current.

21. Full personal accountability is maintained over all inventory assets and resources.

22. Preemployment screening checks include personal contacts to verify references.

23. There is an individual appointed as being responsible for executive security matters.

24. All business transactions involving cash, sales, purchases, inventory property, personnel, and so forth, are fully and properly recorded for later review.

25. Employee compensation is comparable to other employees with similar organizations.

27. Appropriate action plans have been developed to anticipate emergency situations that can arise from fire, accidents, and disturbances or criminal attacks.

28. Career opportunities for internal auditors are sufficiently attractive to invite good recruitment and retention.

29. There is a requirement for employees in positions of trust to submit financial disclosure statements on a recurring basis.

30. The application for employment forms have been carefully designed to capture all of the information needed to match the right person with the right job.

31. Internal control reviews are the responsibility of general management, and not the internal audit staff.

32. Supervisory and executive staff offers advice, guidance, and assistance to the troubled employee undergoing financial or other personal crises.

33. Prospective employees are cautioned that their responses to the questions raised on the form must be valid and will be verified.

34. The system of internal controls is deemed to be cost beneficial and cohesive to the organization.

35. Employees who gamble on the stock market excessively or with a "bookmaker" are not ignored but are dealt with as problems to be solved by management.

36. Interviews with prospective job applicants are carefully structured to impress them with the fact that the work environment is hostile to illicit behavior.

37. There are clear and written prohibitions against purchasing agents accepting favors or items of value from suppliers under any condition.

38. Management does not ignore or condone employees with unsatisfactory employment record (performance or conduct).

39. Psychological "honesty tests" are used in the applicant screening process when filling sensitive positions.

40. Accounting policies and procedures are clearly set down and kept current.

41. Standards for employee conduct and performance are high, well monitored, and measured.

42. Employees have identification or badges in order to gain access to work areas.

43. The system of internal controls include "intangible" assets such as trade or process secrets, insider information, goodwill and so on.

44. Personnel guidelines over performance and conduct are fairly and rigorously enforced.

45. There is an ongoing program to assess what information and data maintained are of a sensitive nature warranting special attention.

46. Large balances are kept in non-interest or low interest bearing bank accounts.

47. The executive level environment is characterized as being open, affirmative, honest, and ethical.

48. Sensitive data or information are stored in a specially designated controlled area.

49. Forms, slips, and receipts are serially numbered.

50. Executives and employees in positions of trust are required to take annual vacations of at least two weeks' duration.

51. Sensitive data and information are safeguarded through specially designated custodians.

52. The auditor's responsibility is to test controls, not to maintain them.

53. The overall organization is undergoing stress from external competition, new leadership, reorganization, and so forth.

54. Access to secured information is limited only to the employees who have been designated through a clearance process.

55. Payroll checks are frequently mailed to post office boxes.

56. There is an ongoing awareness program to educate employees in the pitfalls of criminal conduct.

57. Visitors are screened prior to entry to the workplace.

58. Cashier checks are used in the conduct of business.

59. Management is committed to intervene on behalf of employees involved in financial, health, personal, or family crises.

60. Everyone who enters a secured area (data processing room, cashier, vault, etc.) is recorded and checked for proper authorization.

61. Financial transactions are well documented with necessary authorizations.

62. Antisocial, mischievous behavior is not tolerated in the workplace.

63. Prior to hiring employees, statements on their job applications forms are verified.

64. Low turnover among key professionals and managers exists.

65. A profile folder is maintained on all key employees and executives, including photographs, biographical data, names of family members and physicians, lists of clubs and other places frequented, and so forth.

66. Applications for employment provide for written authorization to verify all information on the form.

67. Large overtime payments or commissions are uncommon.

68. Explicit, uniform, and reasonable rules, firmly enforced, govern the workplace.

69. Employees are issued controlled identification cards that are not easily reproducible, which include photographs.

70. There is a staff of internal auditors who operate by constantly testing and appraising the effectiveness of controls.

71. Employees are treated with courtesy, consideration, and respect by management.

72. Verification of references are made in person or by phone, not by form letters.

73. Checks payable to companies do not always get deposited to the same banks or accounts.

74. Swift, affirmative action is taken against those found violating the laws and policies governing the operation of the organization.

75. Interviewers of job applicants verbally review all the information in the application with the applicant to remove ambiguities and clarify statements.

76. Cashed checks to companies are returned block stamped, not handwritten; or with multiple endorsements.

77. Working conditions have been deteriorating with negative impact on employee morale.

78. Job applications require a signed attestation as to accuracy of information provided, and note that omissions or misrepresentations of material facts are grounds for denial of employment or dismissal after employment.

79. Large checks (other than routine compensation) are payable to executives.

80. No key employee has exclusive custody or control over documents, records, or processes.

81. Applications for employment contain full biographical information, including references (personal, business), residences, education, entire work history, service history, medical history, arrest record, and credit information.

82. In sensitive areas such as payroll or procurement, duties and assignments are rotated periodically.

83. Well monitored and measured performance plans that have realistic, achievable objectives are in effect for all employees.

84. Guards or other designated employees restrict access to sensitive areas, and after hours.

85. Each manager is held directly accountable for the functions, performance and operations they oversee (including maintaining the systems of internal controls).

86. The overall work environment can be characterized as being honest, ethical, fair, and free of double standards.

87. The premises and particularly sensitive areas are secured from unauthorized intrusions, fires, and flood by alarm systems.

88. When weaknesses are found in the controls, prompt corrective measures are taken by management.

89. Superior performance is recognized and rewarded in a fair, objective manner.

90. Rules are clear on the conditions of the use of property, materials and equipment of the organization.

91. Management has an ongoing program of testing internal controls not just regularly scheduled reviews within predetermined periods of time.

92. Legitimate means are available by which employees can have their grievances heard and acted upon by management.

93. Security and traffic control measures extend to and include unattended periods.

94. Periodic internal control reviews, vulnerability assessments, or risk analyses are performed by all levels of management.

95. Employees are well matched by skills and experiences to their jobs.

96. There is an ongoing program of briefing and training managers and executives on how to handle various kinds of emergencies (fire, accidents, criminal attacks, etc.)

97. There are "audit trails" to document all authorizations and to track all financial transactions from inception to completion.

98. There has been a deterioration of actual quality of organizational performance.

99. All employees who remain late after work are noted in some official record.

100. There is a system of organized follow up after audits, reviews and studies of operations to ensure corrections of deficiencies.

101. Senior audit and general counsel executives and staff remain stable with little turnover.

102. Expensive equipment (typewriters, data processors, computers) are locked to the work stations with the designated people using them held accountable.

103. Measurable operations have a system of ongoing quality control and testing of error rates.

104. Rules of conduct and table of penalties for infractions are published, disseminated, and uniformly applied.

105. There is a published, strict policy restricting employees from "borrowing" tools, equipment, and supplies for personal use.

106. The quality control system has been set up to pinpoint people who made errors so as to insure proper accountability.

107. Contingency plans provide for all the difficult decisions made in advance of any actual crisis, such as who to notify in case of a bomb threat, whether to evacuate the premises, and so on.

108. Employees follow carefully conceived check acceptance practices.

109. Whenever possible, controls are placed on the "front-end" of the system (prior to entry, payments, hiring, etc.).

110. The individual designated for responsibility over security matters is a high-level executive who has the authority for not only formulating security plans but for executing them as well.

111. Access to cash and negotiable instruments is strictly limited by policies and procedures.

112. All expensive equipment, furniture, tools, etc., are marked, numbered, and assigned to specified employees for accountability and inventory control.

113. Employees on vacation are not allowed on the work premises.

114. Physical security systems are tested for adequacy on a recurring basis.

115. All cash transactions (receipts, deposits of checks, cash, money orders) are recorded under independent verification by another party.

116. Morale has been deteriorating because of recent changes in management, policies, or procedures.

117. Formal security awareness programs are often provided employees and staff.

118. The interval since the most recent independent audit review was about one year or less.

RATING YOUR ENVIRONMENT QUESTIONNAIRE

M = Motivation	A = Access	O = Opportunity
M Pt. Value	A Pt. Value	O Pt. Value
1_____	2_____	3_____
4_____	5_____	6_____
7_____	8_____	9_____
10_____	11_____	12_____
13_____	14_____	15_____
16_____	17_____	18_____
19_____	20_____	21_____
22_____	23_____	24_____
25_____	26_____	27_____
28_____	29_____	30_____
31_____	32_____	33_____
34_____	35_____	36_____
37_____	38_____	39_____
40_____	41_____	42_____
43_____	44_____	45_____
46_____	47_____	48_____
49_____	50_____	51_____
52_____	53_____	54_____
55_____	56_____	57_____
58_____	59_____	60_____
61_____	62_____	63_____
64_____	65_____	66_____
67_____	68_____	69_____
70_____	71_____	72_____
73_____	74_____	75_____

RATING YOUR ENVIRONMENT—Continued

76_____	77_____	78_____
79_____	80_____	81_____
82_____	83_____	84_____
85_____	86_____	87_____
88_____	89_____	90_____
91_____	92_____	93_____
94_____	95_____	96_____
97_____	98_____	99_____
100_____	101_____	102_____
103_____	104_____	105_____
106_____	107_____	108_____
109_____	110_____	111_____
112_____	113_____	114_____
115_____	116_____	117_____
118_____		

Instructions for Scoring

1. Add down the total number points in each column.
2. Total the number of questions answered in each column.
3. Divide the total number of points in each column by the number of questions answered in the corresponding column.
4. Evaluate the scores in each factor as follows:
   - 4.1 to 5 = Indicates environmental factor has low vulnerability to criminal attack
   - 3.1 to 4 = Indicates moderate vulnerability to criminal attack
   - 3 or lower = Indicates high vulnerability to criminal attack
5. For evaluation of overall environment, total the points of all three columns and divide that sum by the total number of questions answered.

Traditional-Type Vulnerability Assessments

In the chapters on motive, access, and opportunity, we will discuss in some detail things that can be done to alter your environment to make it less conducive to those factors inviting criminality. The end result of this exercise will be to alter the vector of forces to strengthen your environment and protect your targets. Moving from this approach, we will now discuss what could be called the "traditional" approach to assessing one's vulnerabilities.

Such analyses require a virtual dissection of the business environment so as to see how effective the internal controls are throughout the organization. While these assessments are similar to audits and reviews of an entity's operations by its own internal auditors they do differ in that these assessments:

1.   Are intended only to establish an inventory, so to speak, of what one has to protect, and a ranking of its predicted vulnerability to attack.

2.   Are organization-wide in scope, while internal audits generally cover one particular segment of an organization.

The first step in developing a target protection plan is giving someone in each major organizational segment the responsibility for the work—including the authority to issue any necessary guidance in the internal control area, and the responsibility and clout needed to adequately evaluate the internal controls within their respective organization. This is, of course, in addition to designating overall responsibility to one officer. Any organization, regardless of size, can be broken down into separate units for this purpose.

Through an inventory analysis process, discussed in Chapter 12, each organizational segment can begin to identify significant internal control function tasks. Once this detailed inventory has been completed, the next step requires determining how each major asset is controlled and protected. This entails developing a flow chart describing the essentials of each procedure involved. At this point, it would be quite helpful to assume the role of a wrongdoer:

Try to figure out the type of crimes that might be committed.

Work your way through the flow charts and focus on weak in the controls.

Where are the weaknesses? When is the best time to attack? How does one gain access?

Ultimately, a decision needs to be made as to the limits of the *cost effectiveness of adding protection and controls.* When does the cost and inconvenience of adding this new protection outweigh the benefits that are derived from item? See Figure 2.1 following for an illustration of the various types of concerns addressed by vulnerability assessments. Figure 2.2 is a sample model of such assessments.

Note: These actions in no way detract from the responsibilities of individuals to establish and maintain appropriate systems of internal controls.

The Trail Signs of Criminal Activity

Once your vulnerability assessment has been completed and the weaknesses identified, the next step is to recognize what it is that might provide trail signs of someone attacking the target and/or targets that are seen to be vulnerable.

By whatever form, wrongdoing leaves trail signs, that is, some deviation from normal patterns, which should arouse suspicions for the manager on watch for them. Failure to be sensitive to these signs and insufficient reaction to them are the major reasons for successful criminality in our midst. Throughout this book we will identify differing types of trail signs to assist in these kinds of evaluation.

This type of "sensitivity" can pay off handsomely. In fact, many of the witnesses we interviewed in cases of wrongdoing (fraud, larceny, burglary, and the like) remembered circumstances—occurring before the fact—that related to the crime.

Extensive and differing concerns can appear on an inventory developed for vulnerability assessment purposes. These important management concerns will probably include the areas of:

General policy direction—Covers (1) the manner in which management communicates its goals, plans, and responsibilities and (2) the manner in which the organization is structured to carry out such actions.

Cash transactions—All actions such as receipt, safe-guarding, and depositing of cash, checks, money orders, and negotiable securities. Includes petty cash.

Receivables, Loans and Advances—Policies controlling, monitoring, collecting, and accounting for such matters.

Inventories—Controlling and managing materials, supplies, work-in-process, and finished goods. Includes taking physical inventories, physical security over stores and supplies, and maintenance of appropriate accounting records.

Property Plant and Equipment—Acquisition, maintenance, storage, disposition, and physical security. Maintenance of the appropriate accounting records.

Payables—Includes vendor billings, voucher packages, purchase orders, receiving reports, and so forth.

Budget Planning, Execution, Fund Control and Equity—As applicable.

Sales—All aspects including accounting treatment.

Procurement and Purchasing—Acquiring goods and services. Entire cycle from the point of initial request for goods or services until the final actions.

Automatic Data Processing—Includes physical controls over computer hardware and software, as well as all policies and procedures for operating Automatic Data Processing (ADP) systems. Also includes systems documentation, operating logs and controls, file protection and retention, input controls, output controls and program controls.

Personnel—Personnel administration, personnel management, time and attendance, and payroll functions as performed within the organization.

Travel—All travel policies and procedures of an organization and all travel performed by members of an organization.

At the federal level, other areas affected include such matters as:

Grants (discretionary and formula)—Includes the entire grants process, from the development of policies and procedures to all operational aspects of grantee selection, award, administration, management, evaluation, and the processes associated with grant closure and/or accountability.

Subsidies, Entitlements and Benefits Payments—This includes the entire process from the time an applicant applies for benefits until the time that payment to the applicant is initiated or other final disposition of the application.

Records Systems—This area includes all record systems where information is queried to determine applicant eligibility for program assistance or of a nature restricted by the Privacy Act, which covers access to information held by the Federal Government. (The Privacy Act, 5USC 552-A, was enacted in 1974 and became effective in 1975.)

FIGURE 2.1 Typical broad concerns covered by vulnerability assessments.

Internal Control Function: _____

_____

Organizational Component:
   Organizational Level _____   Organizational Code _____
   Organizational Name _____

	RANKING FACTORS	*POINT VALUE*

    A. *Results of Audits*
       1. Favorable
       2. Advisory
       3. Negative   _____

    B. *Interval Since Most Recent*
       Audit
       1. Less than 1 year
       2. One to Three Years
       3. More than Three Years   _____

    C. *Impact of Recent Errors or*
       Irregularities
       1. None
       2. Personal Harm/Embarrassment
       3. Monetary Loss/Policy Change   _____

    D. *Access to Cash/Negotiable*
       Instruments
       1. No Access
       2. Limited Access
       3. Extensive Access   _____

    E. *Existence of Internal Control*
       Procedures
       1. Extensive
       2. Moderate
       3. None   _____

    F. *Physical Security*
       1. None Required
       2. Required by Program
       3. Required by Regulation/Law   _____

    G. *Risks From Internal*
       Influences
       1. No Potential Risk
       2. Moderate Potential Risk
       3. Extensive Potential Risk   _____

FIGURE 2.2 Vulnerability assessment model.

RANKING FACTORS	*POINT VALUE*

H. *Risks from External Influences*
   1. No Potential Risk
   2. Moderate Potential Risk
   3. Extensive Potential Risk   _____

I. *Policy Direction*
   1. Usually Written
   2. Occasionally Written
   3. Rarely Written   _____

J. *Recent Changes in Program*
   Control or Resource Level
   1. Less than 10% increase or decrease
   2. 10 to 25% increase or decrease
   3. More than 25% increase or decrease
      (Include new program or phase out) _____

K. *Other*

                                          _____

            TOTAL POINT VALUE   ════════════════

Total Point Value __ ÷ Number of Rating Factors Used __ = Point Value
Average _____

Vulnerability Assessment Rating

Point Value Average Scale	*Degree of Vulnerability*
2.4–3.0	Highly Vulnerable
1.7–2.3	Moderately Vulnerable
1.0–1.6	Low Vulnerability
Override	Highly Vulnerable

PREPARED BY:	APPROVED BY:
NAME: _____	NAME: _____
TITLE: _____	DATE: _____
PHONE: _____	
DATE: _____	

FIGURE 2.2 Vulnerability assessment model (*Continued*)

Witnesses are interviewed for that exact purpose. If managers could condition themselves to recognize these trail signs, most criminality within their areas of responsibility would be prevented.

Executives as Targets

No business or government executive is oblivious to the fact that they are potential targets of terrorist activities. This concern may become quite acute when operating outside the U.S. Attacks most commonly take two forms, (1) the kidnap ransom of officials and their families, and (2) the extortion of money based on threats to either employees or the property belonging to the government or corporations in question.

The odyssey of the highjacked TWA flight 847 reminded the world there is no reason to believe these threats will abate in the near future. What is evident is that small groups of individuals employing terrorist tactics can compel corporations—and even countries—to submit to their demands by acts of sabotage, assassination, extortion, kidnapping, and/or air hijacking. It is important to remember that not all these acts take place in foreign countries.

Enhancing Executive Security Through Advance Planning

One answer to this kind of threat is to develop an executive protection program designed to simultaneously restrict access to our executives and opportunity by would-be terrorists. Any executive protection program can be developed using as its basis the formula on which this book is predicated: motive + opportunity + access + target = the criminal equation. In this instance, of course, the target is the executive.

1. *Engage in target vulnerability analysis:* Develop a list of individuals who might provide an attractive target for terrorists.

2. *Develop a briefing package for these individuals deemed to be possible targets:* Alert them on how to avoid providing access and opportunities to terrorists, what to do if they are under a kidnap-extortion situation, and so on.

3. *Develop a crisis team:* Activate this team immediately in case of an attack; give them the authority to negotiate, make decisions, and so forth.

4. *Create access to specialized and liaison arrangements with proper police agencies:* (for example, local police, FBI, Interpol, or with overseas problems, the Department of State).

The most important first step in any plan is the appointment of a high-level executive as security director with responsibility and authority for formulating plans, supervising their execution, and periodically updating and revising them. Such plans should be ratified at the highest level (for example, the Board of Directors, or the Executive Committee). Tough decisions should be made in advance of any crisis, such as under what circumstances (if any) will a ransom be paid, how it should be generated, or whether there will be negotiations at all.

Measures that can be taken before an attack takes place include:

1. Developing and maintaining a biographical profile folder on each executive. This file should contain all personal information on the executive and his family, including up-to-date photographs. It should be updated every six months.

2. Having executives maintain itineraries and calendars that are in the hands of a trusted party, such as a secretary.

3. Considering some sort of duress signal at their office, residence, and car.

The one thing victims consistently have said on release was that they wished they could have alerted someone. The easiest method is a hidden alarm system, not unlike that to which bank tellers have access. Such a system can set off a silent alarm to a central station. Digital dialers that send emergency messages are also quite common and effective. Remote, hidden switches can be placed in a number of locations at the office and/or residence. Sites can be chosen as result of careful examination of premises. Remote wireless activators are also available for car or person.

Additional discussion on executive protective measures can be found in Chapter 7, Part IV. Also see Part IV, Chapter 9 for a discussion of physical security measures. An example of a biographical profile is Figure 2.3.

Name _____
(show full name)   (Last)   (First)   (Middle)
Permanent residence _____ Phone _____
Secondary residence _____ Phone _____
Description: Ht. _____ Wt. _____ Hair _____ Eyes _____ Date of Birth _____
    Scars/Marks _____
    Physician _____
    Hobbies _____
_____ Clubs _____
    Other _____

Spouse's full name _____ Maiden_____
    Ht. _____ Wt. _____ Hair _____ Eyes_____
    DOB _____ Scars/marks _____ Physician _____
    Hobbies _____ Clubs _____
    Employer _____ Position _____
    Address _____ Phone _____

Children and/or other persons in household:
1. _____ Age _____ Ht. _____ Wt. _____ Eyes _____
        (Name)
2. _____ _____ _____ _____ _____
3. _____ _____ _____ _____ _____
4. _____ _____ _____ _____ _____

Family cars:
1. Driver____ Make _____ Year _____ Model _____ Color _____ Lic. _____
2. Driver____ Make _____ Year _____ Model _____ Color _____ Lic. _____
3. Driver____ Make _____ Year _____ Model _____ Color _____ Lic. _____

FIGURE 2.3. Executive personal profile.

Phone numbers of neighbors or other reliable contacts who generally have knowledge of family members' locations:

1. Name _____ Phone _____
   Address _____
2. Name _____ Phone _____
   Address _____

FINGERPRINTS AVAILABLE ON
FILE?   PHOTOS AVAILABLE?
Yours _____   Yours _____
Spouse's _____   Spouse's _____
Children _____   Children _____
Other _____   Other _____
Additional Information:

_____
Signature   Date   Position
   (Please request and submit new profile when significant changes occur)

_____
Name   Position
Location _____

Full name, including middle and nickname:

Physical description—height-weight-coloring (including eye-
             glasses, hearing aids, etc.):

FIGURE 2.3 *(Continued)*

Scars or special identifying marks:

Date and place of birth:

MD/DDS/Pharmacy (Names/addresses/phones)

Special medication requirements including allergies:

Telephone numbers and schedules of regular events, including yours, your spouses, and your children's schools, teachers' names:

Address (Principal residence/vacation home)

Floor plan (Principal residence/vacation home)

Any additional information deemed useful, such as handwriting samples.

FIGURE 2.3 (Continued)

Children as Targets

People as targets are not limited to government officials, business executives and the wealthy. Even your children can be subjected to criminal attacks. The whole subject of child abuse has been kept behind closed doors. Society has not been able to find a means to deal with it. It has been until recently a taboo subject. It is a concealed crime by necessity and one in which there has been little public discussion.

Formal crime reports of such abuse are tracked by the American Humane Association (AHA) which indicate 77 percent of child abusers are parents (fathers, step-fathers, foster fathers), 16 percent are other relatives (grandfathers, uncles, cousins, brothers) and 1 to 6 percent are others. It further notes that although males are the primary perpetrators, as much as 20 to 30 percent of abusers are women (a higher figure than commonly thought).

A recent study on this subject by the Department of Health

and Human Service's Office of Inspector General addresses the problem. It not only sheds light on how one may analyze a crime vulnerability, but it also describes methods for addressing the problem. The November 1984 study, titled "Preventing Sexual Abuse in Day Care Programs," deals with the twin phenomena of (1) the rising need for child day care service due to the increased number of women entering the workforce, and (2) the increased awareness of sexual abuse in such settings.[1] Its purpose was to find ways to prevent sexual abuse in federally funded day care centers. The major findings included the following information.

1. Most sexual abuse occurs in the home and is committed by abusers who were abused as children. Mothers oftentimes allow their children to be sexually abused because they were so abused by their fathers.

2. Pedophiles who can be attracted to day care centers can abuse hundreds of children without being caught. If caught, they are often not convicted. Thus, they may have no criminal record even if they plead guilty. Experts estimate that only 1–15 percent have any criminal records, and not necessarily for sex crimes.

The extent to which child sexual abuse occurs is not known but most experts estimate that 1 in 4 or 5 girls and 1 in 9 or 10 boys are sexually abused before the age of 18. Research also indicates that offenders can abuse an enormously large number of children before being caught—literally hundreds.

These findings paint a dark picture. Authorities are frustrated by the problems of identifying abusers and/or prevent child sexual abuse when:

1. The vast majority of such abusers do not have criminal records.

[1]This study was conducted by HHS Regional Inspector General Norman Zimlich and his staff from the Office of Program Inspections in Seattle (November 1984). Full text in Appendix 3.

2. The victim population—usually small children—doesn't report the crime or, in most cases, understand it. Children frequently do not tell when they are sexually abused because they are afraid that (a) they or someone they love will be punished or killed, (b) no one will believe them, or (c) they are responsible in some way for the abuse. Also, children may not be able to tell someone directly, either lacking the language skills or being too young to verbalize.

3. The perpetrators are in the home and not the community.

4. Most of the traditional means of prevention are negated. How do you deny access when most such crimes are perpetrated in the home by the people with the most access—relatives—and where the targets are literally millions of children?

The answers lie in great measure on examining (1) the "motive character" and behavior of pedophiles and (2) behavioral patterns among the victim population. By examining these factors we might be able to anticipate the likelihood of child sexual abuse in any particular environment.

The Pedophile

Dr. A. Nicholas Groth (See Appendix III), describes two types of pedophilic behavior: "fixated" and "regressed."

Among the fixated pedophiles he cites the following characteristics:

1. Primary sexual orientation is to children;

2. Pedophilic interest begins during adolescence;

3. No precipitating stress/no subjective distress prior to the assault;

4. Persistent interest—compulsive behavior;

5. Preplanned, premeditated offense;

6. The offender identifies closely with the victim, and

equalizes his behavior to the level of the child; the offender thereby becomes a pseudo-peer to the victim;

7. Male victims are the primary targets;
8. The offender has little or no sexual contact with age mate and is usually single;
9. There is usually no history of alcohol or drug abuse;
10. Characterological immaturity/poor sociosexual peer relationships exist; and
11. The offense becomes a bad resolution of social misadjustment.

Among the regressed pedophiles, the following characteristics are noted:

1. Primary sexual orientation is to age mates.
2. The pedophilic interest emerges in adulthood.
3. Precipitating stress is usually evident.
4. Involvements may be more episodic.
5. The initial offense may be impulsive, not premeditated.
6. The offender replaces conflictual relationships with involvement with the child; the victim becomes a "pseudo-adult substitute".
7. Female victims are primary targets.
8. Sexual contacts with child co-exists with sexual contact with age mates; offender is usually married or in a common-law marriage situation.
9. The offender may be an alcohol abuser.
10. More traditional lifestyle but peer relationships are underdeveloped.
11. The offense is a bad attempt at trying to cope with specific life stresses.

These generalizations can alert authorities and concerned relatives to sources of dangers. Other red flag indicators come from the victim children themselves:

1. Inappropriate sexual knowledge or behavior;
2. Sudden unexplained withdrawal, passivity, or depression;
3. Sudden unexplained active or violent behavior;
4. Fantasy or infantile behavior;
5. Poor peer relationships;
6. Self-mutilation;
7. Suicidal discussions or actions;
8. Reluctance to go to certain places, for example, to neighbor's or relative's house;
9. Changes in eating habits or gagging around food;
10. Multiple personalities;
11. Psychosomatic disorders;
12. Nightmares, fear of the dark, or sudden bedwetting;
13. New fears;
14. Dislike or avoidance of someone previously liked, including a parent;
15. Bodily bruises;
16. Irritation or pain in genital or rectal areas;
17. Venereal disease;
18. Difficulty in walking or sitting;
19. Torn, bloody underwear;
20. Early pregnancy;
21. Truancy or runaway behavior.

Telling children (and adults) about "good touch/bad touch," that it's o.k. to tell, whom to tell and how to avoid the abuse will prevent and deter the crime. It is ironic, but many child abusers have deluded themselves into believing that what they are doing is not wrong. Therefore, this kind of education program has the secondary benefit of deterring wrongdoers from the commission of such criminal actions.

In this example, we cited many indicators or trail signs. We also focused on the analytical approach of examining the who, how what, where, when, and why of child sexual abuse. One cannot successfully devise preventive strategies without similar kinds of analysis. Thus, after each element of the criminal equation we will provide indicators, trail signs, and warning signals to alert responsible people to possible dangers warranting systemic correction. We shall turn to the people who would attack the targets you wish to protect. These are the individuals who are motivated to wrongdoing.

PART THREE

MOTIVATION

CHAPTER THREE

MOTIVE:
EXAMINING THE
WHY FACTOR BEHIND
WRONGFUL ACTS

MOTIVE DEFINED

In the popular mind intent and "motive" are not infrequently regarded as one and the same thing. In law there is a clear distinction between them. "Motive" is the moving power which impels to action for a definite result. Intent is the purpose to use a particular means to effect such result. "Motive" is that which incites or stimulates a person to an act.
BLACK'S LAW DICTIONARY, Fourth Edition as defined in the case of People v. Weiss, 252 App. Div. 463 (1951).

The mere definition of motive, however, is not enough. If we understand *why* people commit crimes, then it would be a relatively simple process to take away those negative motivators and eliminate crime. But, alas, this quest has eluded mankind just as the all-curing panacea or a Utopian society have. Human behavior and motivation is still very much a mystery. However, we have learned some things, as this part of this book will show, which provide clues to man's unsociable behavior. This chapter explores some of the forces which affect behavior patterns. It also identifies some of the indicators and warning signals individuals project which can place us on guard. Lastly, this chapter discusses strategies that either (1) alter forces or circumstances nudging individuals toward wrongful acts or (2) allow us to diminish individual access to the targets we are securing.

Motive as a Factor

For someone to intentionally engage in a wrongful act, there must be a desire or motivation to do so. Without that desire there could be no translation into wrongful action. In the absence of desire, the only wrongful acts would not be of malice of aforethought but as a result of accident, happenstance, or unreasoning emotion. Therefore, interdiction of either the formation of the desire for the wrongful act or the act itself would have a significant effect on whether the crime would be committed (See Appendix 2 *Convicted Providers in Medicare and Medicaid* for a discussion of this point.)

Traditionally this element was attacked through the philosophy of deterrence, that is, aggressive law enforcement with speedy and just courts. It continues to be the prevailing philosophy as to how crime and abuse may be controlled. Yet, relying on deterrence alone would be a mistake. The problem is far more complicated (see Appendix 5).

At first blush, the question of motive in a white collar crime case would seem to be one of life's simpler questions to answer: Everyone wants something for nothing. Advertising experts well know the most eye catching term they can use is the appealing word "free." But the true answer is much more complicated and much harder to understand.

Why, after all, would someone of good character and

reputation, a pillar of the community, suddenly start committing crime? We are all aware of: the military officer or businessman who tries to sell national secrets; well-paid physicians who double bill for services or bill for services not performed, and the trusted employee or bank official who embezzles funds or steal inventory or property. Through the use of a fictional example, let's examine an all too common set of conditions that together can lead to a criminal act.

Our subject is Alex J., age 44, married, with two children, ages 10 and 12, a loyal employee of one company for 21 years. During this time he has earned the trust and respect of management and staff.

Things are going reasonably well for Alex and his family. His wages aren't all that high, but sufficient for the family's day-to-day needs with a small amount faithfully saved in a local bank. Alex has always lived an exemplary life, and has never engaged in any kind of antisocial behavior except for some typical teenage high jinks.

Alex is beginning to have nagging doubts about his life, though. It just isn't working out as he thought it would. No world travel; no big job. In fact, he is beginning to feel threatened by several of the younger people employed at his firm. They are much better educated than he, and seem to be pushing for his job! His mother and his dad, now deceased, were well liked in their community and had instilled a strong work ethic in their only son. He worked hard, but this competition from younger, more educated people is worrisome. He begins to wonder about lost dreams. He used to hope that maybe there would be more advancement here, but now, he can barely hold on to what he's got.

As a boy, Alex had always believed that things would be better for him when he reached middle age, as it was for his parents—a nice home, a couple of stylish cars, and so forth. But whenever he looked at his young children lately, he would think, "They'll be going the same way as me. Nowhere. Some pleasures. Sure! But a lot of hard work, too. But I guess the kids are lucky," he mused. "At least we're WASPS. Minorities always have to fight for even the smallest of gains." His spirits remained low, and he began to drink just a bit more. Those who knew him well thought he would soon pull out of this midlife crisis.

But trouble began to strike his family. One financial reversal after another. More trouble with the car was followed almost immediately by unexpected, steep dental bills for the kids. The roof on the family's 15-year old house began leaking badly after a heavy rain storm. The family's small savings account became quickly depleted. Credit sources began drying up once Alex's meager credit limits were reached. Nothing seemed to be going right.

Though desperate for money, Alex was too proud to explain his situation to the firm's management and ask for a loan. "How would it look," he reasoned, "I'm supposed to be one of the wheels in this 'crummy' place." Resentment over his plight began to reach a boiling point, particularly when he thought of all the money he was making for the company. "Look at what they pay me! It's just $50 a week over what that new creep is being paid, and he doesn't know anything."

In an alcoholic state one night, previously unthinkable thoughts began shaping in his mind about ways to get the money he needed—from the company. "The daily receipts. That's it. I've got full responsibility over them. Why, I could borrow what I need and pay it back before it's ever missed."

Reality set in the next day when, cold sober, he began weighing all of the ramifications of this act. If they ever found out, could he take being branded a thief? What would his family and friends think?

As far as we know, Alex's personal qualities are excellent. He comes from a law-abiding background. His employment record is spotless. He's a good family man. In essence, he is not predisposed toward criminal behavior. However, Alex is functioning under a lot of financially-motivated stress plus an assortment of midlife crisis assaults to his sensibilities. He feels that his work is mediocre in substance, he's underpaid, his future at the company is bleak, and, lastly, that his children seem to be heading along the same boring path that he followed.

What will happen now in Alex's life? It depends. It is accepted that an individual with a predisposition toward criminal behavior will need but a nudge of situational stress to do a criminal act. Alex appears not to be disposed towards criminality. Thus, it may well take quite a bit of situational stress before he takes a step towards criminality. If one of Alex's managers knowingly or unknowingly did something to relieve one or more of the situational pressures (for example, arranging for a low-interest loan, rewarding his performance with promotion, or giving Alex a company car), then these pressures would be relieved somewhat—possibly even to an extent that they would not be of importance.

SITUATIONAL STRESSES AND THE INDIVIDUAL

This hypothetical situation may be overdrawn somewhat but it is not far from the situation in which many find themselves. The question is whether Alex will "rip off" his employer or commit some other kind of wrongdoing. How might the manager of an entity deal with this kind of situation? Can anything be done to reduce an organization's risk to these kinds of situations?

There are two strong forces affecting people on the brink of committing a crime: internal and external. The *internal ones*, which are the sum of the experiences and values built into a person over a lifetime, with respect to the family, home, school, peers, church, and community. All of these develop into tendencies towards social or antisocial behavior. Alex had had many stabilizing influences in his life: a nuclear family as a child, marriage and family, continuous gainful employment, and so on. We can probably assume that he has had good role models.

Too many individuals have far less. Consider the negative impact of backgrounds replete with such traumas as broken homes, grinding poverty, bad companions, and the like. A person can become the product of his own environment. An individual's psychological makeup becomes all important, too, with respect to the positive impact of such deterrents to crime as respect for the law, fear of public disclosure, peer pressures to excel, and the like. The *external forces* are the second factor impacting on the conscious or unconscious decision of whether or not to commit a crime. They are definable as being the situational stresses or pressures of the moment—extraordinary financial stress, anger, the need to fight perceived inequities, and the like.

The subject of our case, Alex, presents many of the conditions prevalent in criminality. Alex is being battered by strong *external pressures* (financial and job related among others) to get some "easy" money to remedy his situation. He has Access, Target, and Opportunity—three of the four factors in the criminal equation. Motive is all that is lacking. But the external pressures motivating Alex towards criminality may well be offset by the internal factors always present in such cases: the individual's personal characteristics and attitudes formed through lifetime coping with the basic physical and emotional drives. As a result of these experiences, certain personal characteristics and attitudes emerge. Many will act as a deterrent to the formation of a desire for wrongful behavior; others may result in a predilection to engage in wrongful conduct when confronted with an appropriate set of circumstances.

Given the information that we have about Alex, will he commit the crime? No one can give an answer here. There are just no absolutes. Consider the infamous bank robber-murderer of the 1930s, John Dillinger, who was a study in violence. The environment which produced him was also the same one that nurtured a sibling who became a member of a well-known peace loving religious denomination, the Society of Friends (Quakers). What accounted for the difference?

Will a person's background and associates influence them away or towards criminality? There have been many theories about this. Sociologists, psychologists, and criminologists have been totally unsuccessful in predicting human behavior by environment. But they do use it to explain why a person came out this way or that—after the fact. As a manager or businessperson, there isn't much you can do to influence your employees' internal factors or characteristics. You cannot change these characteristics, but you can appreciate their impact.

MOTIVATION AND THE SPY

All throughout 1985, the country was rocked by a series of spy cases involving U.S. citizens. By the year's end there were over a dozen individual's under espionage charges awaiting trial. *The Washington Post's* July 12, 1985 edition noted that only a few persons were indicted for espionage related crimes by the Department of Justice from 1966 to 1975, whereas it has obtained indictments for 38 persons from 1976 to the present. Who are these people who commit such heinous crimes against their country, and what was their motive? As part of a series of articles on the subject the *Washington Post* cited in its July 21, 1985 edition a number of cases including the following:

1. No case has become as well known as that of Christopher Boyce and Andrew Daulton Lee, the subject of a recent book, later made into the movie *The Falcon and the Snowman.* Over a two year period they sold documents about extremely sensitive U.S. satellites and communications to the Soviet Union. They are seen as symbols of the alienated 1960's generation.

2. James Harper, a defense contractor employee, sold secrets to the Polish Intelligence Service that dealt with U.S. defenses, against ballistic missile attack.

3. William Holden Bell, an aerospace engineer, also sold out to Polish Intelligence. He was recruited after his son died in an accident and after experiencing a break-up of his 29 year marriage. To further aggravate matters, Harper had been downgraded at his job. Among the documents and information he sold for around $500,000 were NATO air defense systems.

4. Other cases included a Navy ensign who tried to sell

national secrets because he needed to buy a car. A former CIA watch officer sold a top secret manual on a super sensitive KH-11 "Spy in the Sky" satellite to the Soviets, not for money but for "kicks." In yet another case, a retired CIA employee was found guilty of attempting to sell documents to the Soviets and was sentenced to 15 years in prison. This person, Edwin G. Moore, had pleaded not guilty by reason of insanity.

The motives of these people are the same as those given by other criminals and described in this book: love, money, thrills and the like.

It should go without saying that the more sensitive the position you wish to fill, be it a cashier or an accountant, the more careful the screening. Job applicants cannot be judged solely by outward appearances. While appearance, experience, and personality may be points in the applicant's favor, he or she may still be a high security risk—a thief, an alcoholic, or a drug user. Even when additional staff is urgently needed, screening practices should not be loosened. One mistake could well be devastating. No security measure is more important than running a conscientious reference check on every new person you want to hire, as discussed in Chapter 8, Part Four.

The following two chapters examine some of the forces at work in individuals which can largely determine whether they are likely or not to engage in criminality. Chapter 4 examines some of the internal factors associated with the personality makeup and how manifested characteristics from a flawed individual may be identified in the working environment. Chapter 5 looks at the external factors—those pressures and forces that may be operating at the moment the decisions are made as to whether an individual chooses to engage in wrongdoing or not.

CHAPTER FOUR

MOTIVE: THE INTERNAL FORCES

What are these "internal forces"? They are the sociopsychological forces hidden within each of us that may eventually result in a criminal act—if target, opportunity, and access present themselves. Another good term for such factors is "predisposition"—how a person is inclined (see Figure 4.1). Internal forces consist of:

Ingrained attitudes: Ranging from strong to negative. They include a sense or lack of feelings of responsibility; ethical standards and mores derived from family, community, and friends; and religious and legal standards.

Emotions: Often most carefully masked. These include fear, love, hate, revenge, and greed.

In this era, there is a belief that all things can be explained by scientific laws. The scientists ask themselves, "What particular

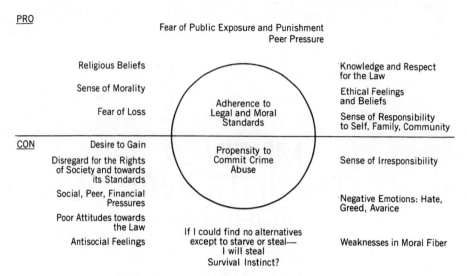

FIGURE 4.1.   Vector of forces affecting behavior.

aspect of a particular kind of crime is capable of explanation in terms of a sharply defined facet of human behavior or nature?" The problem with this approach is that it has not been successful. All that we can say for sure is that crime represents a special form of social deviance and that form of deviance is defined as such by law. To understand the criminal mind, at least in part, would require some knowledge of the social structure of our society. This requires some understanding of its values. The problem is that as society has evolved, changed, and grown more complex, so have the mores and expectations of individuals. This, in turn, has created additional stresses on all of us, which makes normative behavior harder to define and more difficult to adhere to with consistency. We seem to have some duality in our nature when it comes to crime in that we seem to be simultaneously attracted and repulsed by it. The tabloids, crime novels, television, motion pictures, and the like cater to our attraction while we continue to deplore the consequences of criminality.

PROBLEMS IN DEFINING NORMATIVE BEHAVIOR

There is little agreement on the definition of crime other than that it represents violations of the law. Criminology attempts to extract meaningful patterns from masses of social data and to relate these patterns to coherent and integrated theories. From these efforts, it is hoped that scientific laws leading towards predicting criminal behavior can be formed. Thus, the whole field of criminology has become a study of individual behavior in relation to social systems. The primary interest of criminologists has rested upon those who have deviated from normative patterns which have their origin in law. The problem arises, however, in the fact that no one has been able to clearly define normative behavior outside of the criminal code definitions. There has been no way that criminal conduct can be clearly defined and distinguished from acts in violation of ethical codes.

This discussion is limited to that behavior which Blackstone defines as "an act committed, or omitted, in violation of a public law forebidding or commanding it." We leave the rest to the criminologists, sociologists, psychologists, and so on. We will linger a little longer, though, with those who would try to describe and understand one set of subspecies of crimes that we have come to call white collar crimes. By and large these are crimes of guile, deceit, and misrepresentation. These are the crimes causing the greatest grief for modern business and government.

THEORIES ON CRIMINALITY

Society has long researched the causes of crime. There have been countless theories developed to explain it, as well as how to eliminate it from our society. In the last century, it was commonly believed that people were born criminals. Much of this approach fits nicely with the emerging theories on evolution pioneered by Charles Darwin.

Criminals were thought by many to be some kind of throwbacks in the evolutionary development. Some believed that criminality manifested itself in physical differences. Considerable energies were expended in unsuccessful efforts to identify those physical criminal features. Heredity theories continued for some time as a major explanation for human behavior. Today, there are some who still look to this as a possible explanation for criminal behavior. Others, though, offer explanations for such actions in terms of physical disability resulting from brain injuries, tumors, epilepsy, glandular abnormalities, and so on. But all of these physiologically and hereditary-based theories have not been able to hold up to tests and were not reliable in predicting behavior.

More recently, sociological theories on criminality have become dominant. This school of thought believes that behavior is learned and not the result of biological or physiological factors. They suggest it is the environment that creates the criminal: poverty, materialism, the broken home, racism, unemployment, peer pressure, pornography, television, and so on.

Criminology Studies

The following reflect the views of some of the giants in the study of criminology. What is illustrated by their views is that there is little agreement on the causes of criminal behavior. The differences in our judgment are as significant as the areas of agreement.

Professor Edwin H. Sutherland[1]

One of the foremost criminologists of this century was Professor Edwin H. Sutherland of Indiana University, the author of the

[1]Edwin H. Sutherland, *Principles of Criminology*, 5th ed. (Revised by Donald R. Cressey. (New York: J. B. Lippincott Company, 1955), pp. 74-81.

so-called theories of differential association. He saw two types of scientific explanation of criminal behavior: the first being stated in terms of the processes which are operating at the moment, and the second being the processes operating in the earlier history of the criminal.

Sutherland attempted to address the causes of criminal behavior by formulating his now famous theory, which focused upon certain socio-psychological phases of the problem of criminology. He believed that criminal attitudes are transmitted by a preponderance of associations with individuals and values hostile to authority, instead of with those representing conformity to and respect for the law; or, in other words, that all criminal behavior is learned from associations with criminals.

Some of the significant elements of his theory follow (more details can be found in the appendices):

1. Criminal behavior is learned, not inherited and the person who is not already trained in crime does not invent criminal behavior.

2. Criminal behavior is learned through interaction with other people, through the processes of verbal communications and example.

3. Occurs with intimate personal groups.

4. The learning of crime includes learning the techniques of committing the crime and the motives, drives, rationalizing and attitudes that accompany it.

5. A person becomes delinquent because of an excess of definitions for personal reactions favorable to the violation of the law over definitions unfavorable to the violation of the law. (Expressed differently: One finds more reasons to commit than not to commit a crime.)

Differential association has been subjected to a considerable amount of adverse criticism by Sutherland's colleagues and defended with equal strength by those partial to this approach. The views of several opposing authorities follow.

Sheldon and Eleanor Glueck[2]

Sheldon and Eleanor Glueck have been considered giants in the field of criminological studies, especially with regard to juvenile delinquency. Their approach to the study of crime has been almost exclusively oriented to case studies. They became among the harshest critics of differential association as the explanation of the causation of crime. They have expressed deep concern over the volume of material written about bad companions and membership in gangs as causes of delinquency. The Gluecks point out that it has been taken for granted by many that boys living in slum areas would be "infected" by bad companions who play the roles, as they put it, of the "proverbial rotten apple in the barrel." They, on the other hand, "do not see boys as apples."

Their findings show boys tend to be attracted to, or to choose companions who are congenial to them. Also, by and large, they found that the troublesome kids were maladjusted and delinquent long prior to gang membership. Gang membership may have increased their antisocial activities, but the Gluecks found that it rarely originated persistent delinquency.

They further found that delinquents (almost without exception) associated largely with other delinquents. Nondelinquents, though, despite the fact that they also lived in the slums, had few intimates among delinquents. Thus, they conclude the evidence strongly suggests that tendency to develop companionship selectively is a much more fundamental fact in the analysis of the explanation and origination of criminal behavior than the psychologically naive theory of differential association. They do not believe that any mending of the logic or language of the theory can make it acceptable to them.

In his book, "Theory and Fact in Criminology," Sheldon Glueck summed up their argument by asking whether anyone has actually counted the number of definitives favorable to violation of law—and definitives unfavorable to violation of

[2]Sheldon Glueck and Eleanor Glueck, *Delinquents in the Making.* (Harper and Bros., New York: 1952), pp. 88–90.

law—and was thus able to demonstrate that (in the predelinquency experience of the vast majority of delinquents and criminals) the former exceeds the latter.

Marshall B. Clinard[3]

Professor Marshall B. Clinard of Vanderbilt University, in a paper read before the Criminology Section of the American Sociological Meeting in 1946, attacked the limitations of Sutherland's theory in his study of violations of wartime regulations, especially the Office of Price Administration (OPA). Professor Clinard stated that this theory did not allow sufficiently either for an independent invention of a complex technique for violations which are extraordinarily simple. He noted that many OPA violations involving similar techniques had appeared in widely scattered and isolated places. In many violations, he states, only a single person appeared to have been involved.

Professor Clinard further noted that there appeared to be ample evidence of rather complex evasions and violations of rent regulations in relatively isolated areas, and they, too, appeared to have been independently devised. He also remarked that he did not believe violations arose to any degree out of contacts with criminal conduct norms or resulted from negative attitudes towards OPA. Differential association, in his view, only explains some cases, nor does it explain why some with extensive differential association engage in such activity while others do not.

Clinard summed up his position by asking: Why is it some businessmen with numerous opportunities to violate do not do so, while others with only limited opportunity have readily violated? He then partially answered his own question by speculating that an answer must lie in the individual

[3]Marshall B. Clinard, "Criminological Theories of Violations of Wartime Regulations." *American Sociological Review*, XI, 3, June 1946, pp. 258–270, and *Sociology of Deviant Behavior* (New York: Holt, Rinehart & Winston, 1963), p. 55.

personality pattern. There may be, he felt, psychogenic characteristics (general reaction patterns such as disregard for the rights of society in general, or basic attitudes toward law) which were developed in earlier years. In other research he offered that one environmental force causing delinquency and crime is substandard housing. He quoted a 1939 U.S. Housing Authority report that stated the elimination of substandard housing would result in a crimeless world.

Daniel Glaser[4]

Daniel Glaser, a leading criminologist, believed that on the whole Sutherland is correct in his approach to the sociology of crime. He found, however, that the theory of differential association is weakened by its ambiguity of terms. He suggests the substitution of "identification" for "association" would greatly reduce the ambiguous nature of the theory. Furthermore, Glaser states that some critics point out that Sutherland neglects the accidental and transitory situational causes of crime. (This problem, too, would be eliminated, according to Glaser, if Sutherland's theory were reconceptualized in terms of differential identification.)

Glaser describes identification as "the choice of another from whose perspective we view our own behavior (self-image)." The theory of differential identification, in essence, is that "a person pursues criminal behavior to the extent that he identifies himself with real or imaginary persons from whose perspective his criminal behavior seems acceptable." Thus Glaser's amended theory focuses attention on the interaction in which the individual reacts with himself in rationalizing his conduct.

Glaser is quick to note, however, that his contribution to Sutherland's theory does not solve all of the weaknesses it has. For example, he notes that other theories can more easily explain lone or unusual crimes, the source of which is not readily apparent.

[4]Daniel Glaser, "Criminality Theory and Behavioral Images," *American Journal of Sociology* (1956) 433–445.

An even greater problem which is not solved by differential association is that it does not account for accidental crimes. It still assumes that all crimes are a form of voluntary behavior, rather than an accident. All in all, though, Glaser sums up by stating that even with its drawbacks and weaknesses differential association is the most all-encompassing and sound theory on the sociology of crime.

Gilbert Geis[5]

Gilbert Geis, of Los Angeles State College, is another person of considerable stature in the field of criminology. His criticism of differential association is summarized into four categories:

1. The theory is not predictive.
2. It does not deal with measurable quantities. Therefore, it can neither be verified nor rejected by means of empirical demonstration.
3. It is skewed in its emphasis. By concentrating on the effect of experiences in learning, it tends to ignore the significant fact that some experiences have different meaning to different individuals.
4. Sutherland's theory has actually been shown in field studies to be inaccurate. In many cases, criminal behavior was shown as not having been learned by differential association, but merely by utilization of prior knowledge of potentially illegal methods. (See for example the above discussion on Clinard and the OPA).

Donald Cressey[6]

Perhaps the foremost supporter of Sutherland's theory of differential association is Donald Cressey of UCLA. After

[5]Gilbert Geis, "Sociology and Crime." In *Sociology of Crime*. Edited by Joseph S. Roucek. (New York: Philosophical Library, 1961), pp. 7–33.

[6]Donald Cressey, "The Theory of Differential Association," *Social Problems* 8:1 (Summer 1960): 2.

Sutherland's death, Cressey brought out the amended editions of his *Principles of Criminology*. Cressey has since assumed the role of the champion of differential association.

Even this stoutest supporter, though, found problems with the theory, stating that it is neither precise nor clear, even after considerable amendings. Sutherland presented nine propositions, Cressey noted, to explain criminal and delinquent behavior, and the distribution of crime and delinquency rates in just two pages. Thus, it is not surprising, in Cressey's view, that the words do not always convey the meaning intended. Problems in ambiguity (for example, see discussion on Glaser), make for confusion on the reader's part.

In his work on trust violations Cressey notes that he was unable to get embezzlers to identify specific persons or agencies from whom they had learned behavior patterns favorable to such violations. Cressey's general conclusion on the point is that it is doubtful that differential association can be shown empirically to apply to any kind of criminal behavior.

Edwin H. Sutherland[7]

Perhaps the best known critical analysis of differential association, though, has been made by its author, Professor Sutherland, in his essay "The Swan Song of Differential Association," circulated privately among his associates and later published after his death.

Sutherland recognized the crucial questions and criticisms centered around the sufficiency of differential association as a cause of criminal behavior. He further stated that merely one exception is needed to disprove the hypothesis.

Professor Sutherland cites that opportunities to commit a crime are often due to physical factors which are neutral to crime. Thus (1) criminal behavior is not caused solely by

[7]Edwin H. Sutherland, "Critique of the Theory." In *The Sutherland Papers*. Edited by Albert Cohen, Alfred Lindenmuth, and Karl Schuessler. (Bloomington: Indiana University Press, 1956), pp. 30–41.

association with criminal and anticriminal patterns and, therefore, (2) differential association is not a sufficient cause of criminal behavior.

As an example of this, Sutherland points to the fact that Blacks are seldom convicted of embezzlement. But, he states, this is due to racial prejudice which has prevented Blacks from obtaining positions of financial trust—and, consequently, from having the opportunity to embezzle.

Another weakness of his hypothesis is that there is evidence that crime varies with intensity of need, independently of differential association. (For example, survivors on a life boat who engage in cannibalism to avoid starvation.) Sometimes alternative behaviors give no choice in the individual's mind except crime, although he may be against it all the while he is committing his crime. Consider also the often-quoted statement made by respectable persons: "If I could find no alternatives except starvation or theft, I would steal."

Professor Sutherland finalizes his critique with a look at his methodology. He suggests that perhaps looking for the single answer is wrong, and that taking the multiple factor approach might prove more fruitful in studying all the variables—and further case studying. This critique was not meant to destroy his differential association. On the contrary, it was merely intended to show his colleagues that he was aware of its weaknesses. Today, in spite of the considerable criticism, Sutherland's approach remains a widely accepted theory for the explanation of criminal behavior.

Stanton E. Samenow[8]

More recently there have been other voices questioning the whole notion of criminality being learned behavior. Dr. Stanton Samenow, a clinical psychologist, began his work believing that criminal behavior was a symptom of buried conflict resulting

[8]Stanton E. Samenow, *Inside the Criminal Mind* (New York: Times Books, 1984).

from early traumas and deprivation of one sort or another. He further believed that people who turned to crime were victims of psychological disorder, an oppressive social environment, or both. With this as a premise, he saw crime as being almost a normal, if not excusable, reaction to poverty, instability, and despair. Criminals from more advantaged backgrounds were said to have been scarred by bad parenting and led astray by peer pressure.

After many years of working with criminal behavior at St. Elizabeth's Hospital for the Mentally Ill in Washington, D.C. Samenow believed a new approach for explaining criminality was in order. His new research and evidence suggested that criminals choose to commit crimes. That is, crime resides within the person and is "caused" by the way he thinks, not by his environment. In support of his thesis he notes that most poor, disadvantaged, and unemployed people are not criminals. Neither are most members of minority groups. The crux of this approach is that "criminals think differently from responsible people."

Samenow points out that a criminal's unresponsibility occurs as a pattern throughout his life. Their deviousness and exploitation of people is manifested as small children and continues to develop as they grow into adulthood. A selfish, manipulative nature is a tip-off to possible criminality. Even crimes of passion can be explained as part of the individual's predisposition to criminality.

Although a matter of great debate, Samenow's thesis is shared by a growing number of people in law enforcement—including investigators, prosecutors, judges and corrections officers. A December 1984 news report in *The Washington Post* reports this very point.

After discussing the facts of a slaying of a junior high school student by a 15-year-old boy from Alexandria, Virginia, who was first sent to juvenile court and then ordered to stand trial as an adult, the news item discussed how such transfers are becoming increasingly common. They are said to result from society's general get-tough attitude on crime. Opinions differ on whether this attitude is justified.

An offender in the juvenile system can be eligible for counseling, educational training, and a number of supervised programs designed to foster responsibility. An offender in such systems cannot be imprisoned past his or her twenty-first birthday. As an adult, this offender may receive none of these services and could spend life in prison.

About 21 states in the last five years have toughened their laws against juveniles. The FBI's Uniform Crime Report indicate that violent crime among juveniles has fallen by 13.6 percent since 1978. As of June 30, 1984 over 6000 juveniles were in adult facilities nationwide. This total is not complete, as certain jurisdictions either did not respond to a survey on this point or listed juveniles as adults if they had been tried as adults.

These facts say that juvenile crime has dropped, but that society has taken a stronger approach toward punishing the individuals involved in such actions.

LOOKING FOR PEOPLE PREDISPOSED TO WRONGFUL BEHAVIOR

There is no shortage of varied and confusing theories to explain criminal behavior. For the layman, the result could be resignation to the fact that no one can demonstrate a cause and effect relationship in any of the theories. But there is something useful in each. Regardless of the theory's approach (biological, heredity, sociological, psychological, and so on) each begins with trying to explain the cause—the why. They agree that regardless of its origin, criminality is manifested in behavioral patterns. These patterns, in turn, are often evidenced as far back in an individual's development as childhood. The "trick" is to look for these signs *before* the crime is committed. This is especially true for those with ongoing contact with the target areas, such as *those* responsible for disbursing cash, or safeguarding valuable inventories.

In many cases, it is a fine line that separates criminals from socially responsible citizens. No one factor or indicator provides a litmus test for someone who is going to turn to a life of crime; however, some behavioral patterns do exist which indicate the likelihood of someone engaging in wrongful conduct. After-the-fact criminal investigations search for clues to identify the culprit. They follow the same kind of process that a manager of a target area can do before a criminal act occurs. To illustrate, among the things that investigators search for are people with a motive for the crime. They focus on individuals who have a history of antisocial or deviant behavior. Thus, individuals with a record of excessive spending, gambling, drinking and/or drug abuse, extramarital or deviant sexual patterns, history of violent behavior, or any other unusual patterns of activities are high on the suspect list. The investigator makes background inquiries on possible suspects, focusing similarly on evidence of previous behavior suggestive of wrongful or irresponsible actions. This includes checking arrest, work, military, and school records, among others.

In an extremely high proportion of cases where the wrongdoer is not known but where there are suspects, this process narrows the focus down to a list which includes the criminal. It is very difficult for someone to suddenly commit a crime without giving any clue to his nature or predisposition sometime during the course of his life. Investigators have learned this fact from trial, error, and experience.

Knowing this to be the case, it is a small step to assume that similar kinds of behavioral patterns might suggest a vulnerability to wrongful activity within the system *before* a crime occurs. While this may seem farfetched, it is very common for the manager of an entity where an embezzlement, pilferage, or some other kind of theft has occurred to provide his own list of suspects on just that kind of information. The question is why must a manager wait for the crime to take place before addressing the problem? Does it make sense to not hire someone with a history suggestive of antisocial or irresponsible behavior? Conversely, such individuals who are already employed can be placed under closer surveillance and/or limited in access to vulnerable targets in the company. Managers who ignore the warning signals mentioned are inviting trouble later.

The following are among the personality traits most commonly present in individuals found to have engaged in white collar crime. However, these traits are not totally reliable in predicting wrongdoing. Many highly successful, honest employees may exhibit some of these characteristics. It is often a matter of degrees. They merely represent added vulnerabilities on which to be on guard.

1. *Low self-esteem.* A lack of self-respect or belief in self can more easily lead to decisions to take short cuts to otherwise avoid inevitable failure.

2. *Psycopaths/Sociopaths.* A mental disorder, particularly one that is aggressively antisocial, is by nature one that often leads to criminality.

3. *Arrogance and egocentricity.* An overbearing pride or exhibited sense of exaggerated self-importance has its limits before it becomes antisocial. When an individual becomes so self-centered as to view everything in relation to one's self, it becomes dangerous. That individual becomes quite able to commit crimes if it is deemed of value to himself. The consequences to others gets submerged in his consciousness.

4. *Poorly developed code of ethics.* This is a built-in system for susceptability to criminal opportunities. It means the individual does not fully subscribe to the organization's, community's, or society's standards of conduct. A low sense of value in moral honesty leads an individual only one way when confronted with an attractive target, open access, and an opportunity.

5. *Emotional instability.* This category includes neurotic, manic-depressive, and paranoid behavior. We all generally have elements of neuroses. It seems to be a product of our modern society. It manifests itself in many forms, such as anxiety, compulsions/obsessions, phobias, and depression. A manic-depressive behavior is characterized by alternating periods of exaggerated feelings of well being (excessive activity) or mental depression. The paranoid behavior is characterized by systematized

delusions of grandeur or persecution. In all the above cases the individual can behave quite normally much of the time but can be more easily susceptible to engage in antisocial behavior under stress.

6. *Exhibited desire to beat the system.* This is a character flaw that should be watched closely, especially if the system is the job environment in which the individual is working.

7. *Taking pleasure in manipulating others.* This is a character flaw worth watching.

The best rule of thumb in trying to resolve the degree of vulnerability associated with the above traits is to remember that the negative consequences of them, in all likelihood, will have previously manifested themselves in some way. Therefore, any individual possessing these characteristics (or personality flaws) should have left a record of any predisposition to criminality. It is for this reason that an employer should carefully screen for (1) a prior criminal record, (2) a history of undesirable job or social performance/conduct, or (3) association with individuals whose records are undesirable. (See Chapter 8 for further discussion on how this can be handled.)

CHAPTER FIVE

THE EXTERNAL FORCES

SITUATIONAL STRESSES

External forces are those pressures/stresses operating at the moment of decision affecting an individual's judgment on whether he should commit or not commit a crime. While it wouldn't be possible to compile an all-inclusive list of red-flag stress signs that can alert an organization to the likelihood of an impending crime by one of its own people, it is known that such stress signs relate to expectations that simply cannot be met. Whenever you have rising expectations (in others or in yourself) and these expectations cannot be met, a sense of frustration takes place. This in turn leads to resentment, which leads to the kind of stress that can lead to criminality (see Appendix 5 discussing "Computer Related Fraud in Government: Perpetrator Interviews.")

Consider the classic problem of a person "trying to keep up with the Joneses," and the resulting pressures that can lead to disaster. Consider an individual receiving journeyman's wages who is living in a pleasant, but not exclusive neighborhood. Despite severe misgivings, but urged on by his wife, he agrees to move to an expensive area. Once there, the family is faced with the further expenses of blending into the neighborhood scene (say, clubs, parties, and the like). This individual simply cannot afford to maintain the lifestyle in which he has thrust himself. The pressures resulting from this need for increased income can be conducive to wrongful behavior. The pressures may make such people try to make quick gains by gambling, speculating in the stock market, or using other risky means. Cash needs can become so acute that some sort of criminality would be a near foregone conclusion.

We know that in retrospect people who commit crime seldom do so in spontaneity without having given clues to their predisposition. In almost every case the would-be criminal gives off signals that might precede a criminal act. It is important to recognize some of these signals, recognizing that only sometimes do they precede wrongful behavior. In the aforementioned case, the warning signal was the family's drastic and expensive life style change.

The external factors are those personal pressures generating at the moment of the decision to engage or not engage in wrongdoing. The situational stresses, pressures, or problems are most often associated with decisions to commit crimes, especially with regards to employee-employer relationships are discussed later. The existence of any of these factors should warn management of the vulnerability to wrongdoing, if not its actual presence. There is nothing extraordinary about these factors except their tight correlation to wrongdoers.

Peer Pressure

The peer pressures of the work environment dictate informal rules of behavior that are oftentimes quite different from the official ones. It is important for management to learn about and understand this informal system and move to have it modified if it is contrary to management's interests. This can be done through a policy of aggressive enforcement of the official rules, that is, transgressors are prosecuted to the full extent. In the case of criminal behavior this would include bringing formal charges and following through until conviction.

The employee's perception of the quality of the work environment is a significant factor affecting the decision to become involved in theft and/or counterproductive activity. Dissatisfaction with the job is a major reason for performing deviant acts in the work place. Suffice it to say that disgruntled employees are a great risk for management. Employees seem to take their behavioral clues from management's response to all types of rule-breaking activity. Much can be done to influence the behavior of employees and it is worth investing time and energy in this effort.

Financial Stresses

Living Beyond Means/Expensive Life Style

It is common for the investigator to encounter the presence of this factor after a major embezzlement or crime. For example, a few years ago one of the largest bank embezzlement cases in the history of the country was committed by a vice president and loan officer whose salary was about half the national average. Although he was poorly paid and had no expense allowance, he was expected—by the owners of the bank, as well as by his family, friends, and community—to live up to the image of his office. He was a diligent, dedicated, conscientious employee who never took leave. What no one questioned was that he was able to live up to this image. He wore the appropriate attire, joined the proper clubs, and ate at the proper restaurants. He did so at the generosity of the bank's largest customer, a major discount chain. They were showing their appreciation for his courtesy in holding overdrafts until they could be covered. This type of "courtesy" is illegal but unfortunately not uncommon.

In the beginning the discount chain covered the check the same day, then within a couple of days, and so on. Eventually, the company was so far behind that the bank officer was left holding millions of dollars in worthless checks and a term in federal prison alongside his benefactors. When the case broke, the bank expressed shock, surprise, and dismay that "their" man could possibly have done that to them. This story illustrates other factors that are discussed below.

High Debt/Financial Losses

The number of employees who find rationale in their personal financial straits to steal is surprising. It is even more surprising that management doesn't make efforts to not only become aware of these situations but to attempt to assist with loans or loan guarantees to relieve the pressures. In the absence of management intervention into the problem area, they could at least move to reassign the individual to a less stressful (i.e., vulnerable) job activity during the period of financial crisis.

Illness

Prolonged, severe, and costly illnesses in the family can be one of the most stressful situations any individual might encounter. Not only does it represent potential financial crisis but it can also be emotionally disturbing.

This type of stress provides one of the easiest rationales for wrongful behavior. More people who would not otherwise consider a criminal activity will commit crimes in order to protect the vital interests of the family. Any organization that ignores an employee's emotional and financial needs in this kind of situation is begging for trouble. After all, who would blame or convict a man for stealing medicine for his sick spouse or child or for stealing money to pay for medicine or surgery? Consider the case of 60-year-old Paul Crafton reported widely by the media:

> Crafton used 33 aliases between 1977 and 1983 to get college teaching jobs throughout the Northeast. In every instance where he obtained employment under phony credentials and aliases, there was virtually no background inquiries or verification

made. He was sentenced to six to nine months in prison on four counts of forgery for impersonating professors at Shippensburg State College and Millersville State College in Pennsylvania. Crafton, who was a qualified part time engineering professor at George Washington University in Washington, D.C., while he held the other two jobs, said he needed the money for his daughter, a victim of cerebral palsy.

Unemployment

Periods of unemployment, layoff, or underemployment could mean that an individual is financially "stretched out." Once again, if this problem exists, management should take pains to find out and assist, lest other means or short cuts are devised at the employer's detriment.

An example comes to mind from the recent recession where an executive was laid off during cutbacks by his company. He had difficulty surrendering all of the trappings of a lifestyle developed to indicate his "proper status." He had no experience in dealing with poverty. In addition, he had not provided for emergencies. The living standard he had chosen had him living from pay check to pay check.

The lay off was a rude awakening. He dropped into immediate arrears on his car, house, and charge payments. Although the layoff was for only a few months, by the time he regained employment he was desperate for funds. His renewed salary could not recoup his position. The result was an almost immediate selling out to competition of all the inside information he could find. Apparently the situational stresses triggered his decision to engage in this illicit behavior.

Personal Habits

It has been said that employees fall into four categories:

1. Those who have no personal problems and who are nearly always productive.

2. Those who have personal problems and are still nearly always productive.
3. Those who have personal problems and whose productivity is adversely affected.
4. Those who don't have any personal problems (at least by their own perceptions) but are not productive.

While people in any of the four categories could engage in criminality, evidence strongly suggests that it occurs far more frequently among those with acute personal problems, especially when it goes so far as to affect performance. Most people fall into category 2 or 3. Perhaps all of us are potential candidates for category 3 at some time in our life.

It is almost impossible for a manager not to be aware of the telltale signs, if he would only look. Unfortunately, most supervisors prefer to ignore the problem rather than deal with it. It is the manager's duty to (1) remain aware of stresses affecting performance and conducive to crime and (2) address the problems or at least remove the individual from sensitive target areas during the period of high personal stress. See Figure 5-1.

Types of Personal Problems

What are some of the more severe, common problems that adversely affect work performance and honesty, and how prevalent are these problems in the workforce? While firm data is difficult to obtain, studies of various work populations have shown that in the average workforce:

10 percent suffer from alcohol abuse,
2 to 3 percent suffer from drug abuse, and
6 to 7 percent suffer from other emotional problems.

Considering that some employees have overlapping problems, it is estimated that approximately 18 percent of the workforce

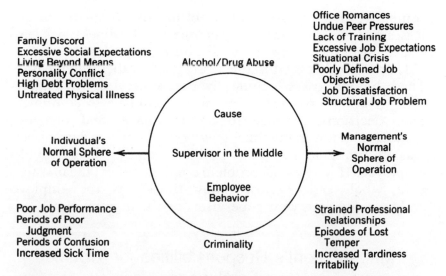

FIGURE 5.1. Stresses operating in the work place. Source: Office of the Assistant Secretary for Personnel, HHS (Graph has been modified).

at any given time has an alcohol, drug abuse, or emotional problem adversely affecting work performance.

Overindulgence in alcohol, use of illicit drugs, and misuse of prescription drugs can all cause a volatile situation, especially if there is a predisposition towards criminal behavior. Such abuses could tip the scales and make a previously trustworthy employee irresponsible. Alcoholism simply does not lead to responsible behavior—it leads to an abandonment of ethical and moral standards.

Dollar Costs Due to Troubled Employees

What do these troubled employees cost? In the U.S. Department of Health and Human Services, which has 140,000 employees, annual losses are estimated at more than $136 million in terms of lost productivity and other costs due to absenteeism, tardiness, sick leave abuse, insurance claims, disability payments, and overtime pay for other employees to do the work. The costs are paid by the taxpayer. In a privately-owned company, the costs are paid out of profits. Other measurable losses include: absenteeism, overtime pay, tardiness, sick leave abuse, insurance claims, and disability payments.*

There are other identifiable losses more difficult to measure: These hidden losses include diverted supervisory/managerial time, friction among workers, waste, damage to equipment, poor decisions, damage to public image, and personnel turnover.** How many times have you felt a whole day has been wasted trying to resolve a problem relating to a troubled employee? How does the problem employee affect the morale of your whole office? How many times has the employee embarrassed you, your supervisor, or the organization?

Management's Responsibilities for Troubled Employees

A manager cannot take the position that the personal problems of a troubled employee are none of his business. If he does, what generally happens is that the problem situation continues until it reaches a point where it can no longer be tolerated. Then, more drastic measures are called for, such as transferring the employee to another office or terminating his employment. But these approaches are of limited value to the employee, manager, or organization. Supervisors often go through the following stages in dealing with problem employees.***

1. You ignored the employee as long as you could. This is the "praying for a miracle" stage.
2. When you could no longer ignore the situation you had a few good "heart-to-heart" talks. This is the "reason will prevail" stage.
3. Then you randomly begged, cajoled, and threatened. This is the "pleading" stage.

*Source: Office of the Assistant Secretary for Personnel, HHS.
**Ibid.
***Ibid.

4. And finally you disciplined, fired, forced to resign, transferred, or retired the employee. This is the "bleeding" stage (probably both yours and the employee's).

Well, then, what can be done? While managers may not be able to resolve many of their employees' personal or emotional problems, they can play the most important role in early identification of the troubled employee and serve as a catalyst in motivating the employee to seek professional assistance. Thus, most enlightened organizations have employee counseling groups for those with emotional, alcohol, and/or drug abuse problems. The troubled employee may ask for assistance, or be referred for treatment of such problems by their supervisor. Programs that help troubled employees to understand their problems pay off dramatically by increasing productivity, reducing lost time, and perhaps even deterring criminal wrongdoing.

One of the best and simplest ways to ensure proper employer-employee relationships is to enter into a "work contract" situation wherein the terms and specifications of the employment are adequately spelled out. A full disclosure up front of each party's responsibilities and expectations helps to negate an employee's feelings of frustration and anger at some later date—thus eliminating a very strong negative motivating factor. Benefits also accrue to the employer who monitors work performance against standards with which the employee has agreed. If the work contract fails to bring about satisfactory performance, unsatisfactory employees can be removed.

The Troubled Employee: Alcohol and Drug Abuse or Other Emotional or Personal Health Problems.

These related factors can be considered together. The authors found, from the cumulative experience of many decades and thousands of encounters in audits and investigations, that these factors tend to go hand in hand.

Other, perhaps less apparent problems such as the following

must be considered and their potential adverse impact appreciated.

Illicit Sexual Involvements

This can represent a difficult set of problems for management. Whether the involvement is with the opposite or same gender, its the general concensus that this is commonly found to be in existence when otherwise deemed honest people commit crimes. When there are indications that this kind of problem exists, it should raise concerns for various reasons.

First, it is most often associated with some sort of deception (of self, spouse, family, friends, community, etc.) which is not a desirable quality to be cultivated. After all, white collar crime is defined as a crime of guile and deceit. Therefore, any evidence of deceit warrants attention.

Second, it is worth observing that this kind of behavior is also associated with a general degeneration of moral values and ethics, thus increasing susceptibility to other wrongful behavior.

Third, maintaining complicated social relationships can be not only emotionally demanding or distracting (and thus diminishing the employee's capacity of productive labor) but expensive as well (thus creating new financial needs).

Marital and/or Family Discord

Generally, this type of problem is related to any number of other factors, such as alcohol or drug abuse, health problems, financial pressures, peer pressures, frustrations, illicit affairs and so forth. It has often been observed that nothing triggers wrongful behavior faster than the trauma of a deteriorating home situation. Discord with spouse or offspring can result in severe damage to one's sense of self-worth and self-esteem. This, in turn, can transform itself into a sense of extreme frustration and anger that can result in striking out against someone or thing. Child and spouse abuse are frequent outcomes. Other times the employee "transfers" his anger to the workplace and a crime against the employer may result. Employers should recognize this as a problem.

Routine Borrowing

Another sign of a potential problem is the employee who routinely borrows small sums of money from fellow employees. Not only does this represent a possible irritant to the working environment, but it could be indicative of other problems. The employer should question why this person is always so "short." Is the employee living beyond his means or does he just have careless spending habits? Whatever the reason, the practice should not be permitted and the employee should be confronted. In the Federal Government, for example, employees are forbidden to make loans from fellow employees. Their supervisors once aware of such situations are expected to step in and stop the practice.

Excessive Speculation/Gambling

Any employee who gambles excessively—whether on the stock market or with a bookmaker—should be of concern to any manager since such situations can lead to embezzlements or violations of fiduciary trust. There is a whole range of obvious reasons why a manager should have these concerns: Is there any inside tracking going on? Is the employee losing money through these activities, and, if so, how much? Does the employee owe money? Are there pressures to collect on debts owed to bookmakers? Is the employee in a position of trust that could be violated in return for money?

Many people who are frustrated by their lot in life seek to gamble their way out. The greater the dissatisfaction, the more the attraction to gambling; hence the success of numbers games, lotteries or horse betting among the poor. One particularly memorable first hand experience of the author comes to mind. About 10 years ago a bank teller was waiting at the local FBI office one Monday morning in Chicago to report himself for embezzling $15,000 the previous Friday. He had been a model in his community but his financial situation had been deteriorating and his frustration growing for several years. He decided in desperation on a single bet that would bail him out of his mess or bring it to a head. He was not a gambler but he began making inquiries about the race track. After studying the matter he picked "his" horse one Friday, stole the money, and placed it on a single race. If he won, it would return three to one and he would be in the clear. It was a photo finish but his horse lost and he was unable to return the money as he hoped. He, therefore, turned himself in to the authorities to pay his just "due."

The employer-bank, when told of what had happened refused to believe it until they had an audit which verified the story. It leads one to wonder how many cases never see the light of day because the horse won and the money was returned.

Unsatisfactory Employment Records
Warrant Close Watching

Excessive sick leaves, unauthorized absences, poor job performance, and the like, are warning signals. At best, such signals represent an employee who is irresponsible and uncaring about employment. It could, however, represent much more. A careless, uncaring, irresponsible employee fits the kind of profile of the individual most often found stealing from his employer. Abusing the rules makes it easier to violate the law. It is a relatively small step from stealing one's salary (taking it under false pretenses) to falsifying time attendance and/or travel claims.

The example from the author's personal experiences that comes most readily to mind that illustrates this common occurrence was a cartage case in Pittsburgh. A local truck terminal was having a terrible time with warehouse and dock thefts. They had done everything to restrict outside access to the area. Fences were built, guards employed, lighting throughout the area installed, and a wide variety of other security measures were taken. Yet, the thefts continued unabated. The company had done everything but when the thefts were compared against the time and leave records of all the employees, one employee stood out. That employee, who had a terrible work record, matched beautifully with the dates and places of the thefts. He had a record of having a bad attitude, poor attendance, and poor performance. He had not been fired because the employer thought it was better to tolerate him than deal with the union. When the employee was arrested at his home, over $100,000 in merchandise was stacked throughout the house. The employee had taken courage and rationalized ever-increasing steps to rip off his employer, encouraged all the way on management's lack of resolve to deal with his behavior.

The Overzealous Employee Can Be the Biggest Danger of All

It is hard to imagine the workaholic as a vulnerability but, employers have learned many hard lessons on this subject. Suffice it to say that any employee who puts in extensive overtime, compulsively protects exclusive dominion over certain records or processes, and who declines vacation periods represents a great threat to the organization. First, it is not psychologically healthy for an employee to put so much energy (and self) into the job. Second, compulsive behavior can be unhealthy in itself if an individual possessing those characteristics is disturbed by changes in his environment. Third, it is difficult to know what reasons, other than dedication to the job, motivate that kind of behavior. There are many examples to illustrate this vulnerability. Banks are especially susceptible. In fact, banks today operate under strict segregation of duty controls. No single individual should be able to complete a transaction. All employees are also required to take two weeks' continuous leave and are not allowed to enter the bank during that period so that any embezzlement schemes can surface during their absence.

In another case investigated by the author, a woman employee of a midwest bank was involuntarily retired after 40 years of dedicated, single-minded service to her bank. She had taken virtually no vacations in all that time. She was a legend in her community. One of the largest retirement parties in the community's history was planned—but it had to be called off because she was not available for the festivities. No sooner had she retired than she left town. The reason soon became apparent: For most of her 40 years at the bank she had been embezzling money and covering the transactions with a compounding series of other transactions of near infinite complexity. Even bank examiners had failed to detect her complicated scheme. She had never taken much time off because she had to work nearly full-time just keeping the embezzlements from surfacing. It is not known whether she was ever caught. What has come out, however, was a sense of her enormous frustration and hostility to being underpaid and overlooked for promotion year after year, while people she trained passed her by. She got her $1 million revenge when the bank went under because of her embezzlements.

Personal Feelings

Perceived Negatives in the Organization

There are many reasons why employees may feel they are unappreciated, underpaid, poorly assigned and managed, ill used, and working under improper conditions. Some of these perceptions are legitimate and some are not. If these perceptions truly exist, there is a problem. The problem may be the improper conditions or it may only be the misperception. In the case of the 40-year bank employee discussed above, it is fairly obvious that the revenge motive arises out of her perceived inequities.

The ability of individuals to rationalize wrongful behavior by finding their own formula for compensation of the inequities is legendary. People can convince themselves that no one cares about them and no one cares about what they do. The example of the cartage thief also illustrated this point. Few people do not know the difference between right and wrong. However, human beings are prone to rationalize events to fit a situation in a manner they can be most happy with. This can become dangerous when individuals develop a rationale as to why they do not have to conform to society. They may believe they are not being treated fairly and that society owes them something. This point is further illustrated in a study by the federal department of Health and Human Services' (HHS) Office of Inspector General of convicted health care providers. The study determined to find "why" and "how" these professionals defrauded the Medicare program. (See Appendix 2 for full text). Essentially, the purpose of the study was to identify:

1. *Vulnerabilities* in Medicare's provider reimbursement system by finding those things for which medical providers had been caught and penalized

2. *Deterrence methods* that would have prevented convicted providers from committing these crimes or deterred others from engaging in fraudulent actions

3. *Detection devices* in the system that worked in that they identified those who were caught and/or would better identify others who were attempting to defraud Medicare.

The methodology employed included discussing these issues with individual convicted practitioner-providers, as well as by reviewing the case files that had been established on them. Some interesting results came from the study.

For example, these convicted providers expressed considerable dissatisfaction with the amounts they were paid for their services (i.e., level of reimbursement) under Medicaid-Medicare programs. This dissatisfaction led them to seek various ways of "presenting" their claims to maximize income—and thereby right what they perceived to be an inequity. In doing this a number of the providers became a little too creative and wound up being arrested, tried, and convicted for fraud.

These providers said they had little or no "preventative contact" with the carrier who processed their claims. This further led them to believe no one cared. They had never been warned of the consequences of falsifying billings—an action which might have deterred many of them. They were also almost totally unaware of how the carrier processing their claims focused on aberrant billing practices. Had they known such detection procedures were in place, they might also have thought twice about trying to beat the system. One provider—who freely admitted to submitting numerous false claims and to systematically milking Medicaid for large sums—stated it was so easy for so long, that he thought no one was ever reviewing anything. This encouraged him to cheat in ever-increasing amounts.

These providers stressed the need for early intervention by the carrier or the government to change the environment they found conducive to criminal conduct. They felt an affirmative program of education and indoctrination (i.e., establishing a "sense of presence" on the part of the authorities) would be more effective in preventing fraud and abuse than relying on penalties and sanctions to frighten people away from committing fraud.

None of those interviewed for the study believed they would ever pay a penalty for their actions, except for a routine financial adjustment or repayment. None considered that they might be convicted of a crime or go to jail. Fear of lesser sanctioning did not even enter their minds, except for possible loss of license to practice (which they believed could only come about for bad medical practice, not for financial manipulation). For many, the lack of concern about their behavior was due to the self-deception that they were not doing anything really wrong (rationalization) or that they could always evade detection or that they could work their way out of anything if caught. Recommendations arising from this study could have wide applicability in many other situations:

1. Early or frequent reminder, so that everyone fully understands the process or the responsibilities of all parties concerned. (Affect motive.)
2. Consistency and controls so that there can be no expectation of slack or leniency for wrongdoing. (Reduce opportunity.)

3. Increased highly visible administrative oversight, including routine audits with quick response to identify problems so that they are dealt with immediately. (Reduce opportunity, increase deterrence to improper motivation.)

4. Increased use of management's testing of the system to minimize the "profit-out-of-opportunities" for wrongdoing. (Reduce opportunity.)

5. Use of peer groups to educate about the problems or pitfalls of fraud and abuse, including using selected individuals who have been caught or punished to spread the message of what can happen to someone who goes astray. (Affect motivation.)

6. More effective prosecutions and the publicizing of the investigations for deterrent purposes. (Deterrence of improper motivation.)

Peer Pressures and Social Expectations

Peer group pressure is another powerful motivator. It can result in beneficial as well as detrimental effects. The good effects relate to expectations placed on the individual to relate to societal norms. Detrimental pressures include employees who are told by a "friend" that they are not getting a fair deal at work. In many cases, such a remark can lead or allow an individual so predisposed an excuse or rationale to engage in criminal conduct. However, an employee who is brought into an organization that will not tolerate and has not tolerated wrongdoing, is far less apt to indulge in it than an employee who is part of an outfit where "everybody does it."

Some years back, the U.S. Department of Agriculture (U.S.D.A.) ordered certain of its employees to attend special training about resisting bribes and other illegalities. One of the Department of Agriculture's major functions is inspecting and grading agricultural commodities such as meat and grain. When dealing in large volumes, the difference in value in beef graded prime and choice, for example, can add up to huge sums of money. ("Prime" has fine veins of fat throughout and is more tender and expensive than "choice.") The same is true for grading corn. To illustrate, Number 2 yellow corn is worth several cents more per bushel than Number 3 yellow corn. The difference in U.S.D.A. grade assigned a single shipload of a million bushels can total the annual salary of more than one grain inspector.

The temptation was great—too great it seems for many grain inspectors in 1975. At that time, the grain inspection program was in the midst of a national scandal. The FBI was investigating bribed officials in every major port handling the great grain sales to the Soviet Union. As a result, inspectors were indoctrinated as to the rules on the consequences of violating the rules. In addition, the Department added an Office of Inspector General. This office is responsible for carrying out the ongoing investigations and audits that help insure proper controls.

Ambition is yet another two-pronged motivator. It is positive in impact when it leads a person to strive to improve himself and his position in an organization. But overly ambitious people will take shortcuts to reach their goals with probable negative consequences. These are the organizational "throat cutters"!

Personal, Family, Community Expectations That Cannot Be Met Lead to Frustration

All organizations should be alert to this phenomenon. It is seldom the case where expectations rise that there is an ability to meet those new expectations. When a child is raised to believe they should "rise to the top" and they don't, there is potential danger. When families expect too much from the breadwinners, there is potential danger. Church and community expectations may similarly strain and stress individuals.

Psychologically one of the toughest burdens for children is a parent who expects too much from them. In our daily lives we can see signs of the visible anxieties, frustrations, and neuroses that arise when too much is expected from people. The impact on some people might turn them into slovenly performers, unwilling to keep up the pace that is unfairly demanded. In turn, others may become bitter and unresponsive in rebuke to the perceived harsh demands they face.

There is an enormous set of expectations that press against all of us. We have parental expectations that are inculcated from childhood. The degree to which they foist their hopes and aspirations on us places great burdens on us to succeed. There are also work role expectations from the job as to the kinds of psychic rewards it may offer; social expectations from fellow workers, neighbors and friends; economic expectations to maintain a certain lifestyle; cultural expectations that we somehow must be better off and improve over the previous generation; and espousal/family expectations to support and defend hearth and home.

Many times our best employees get more work heaped on them as rewards for getting other assignments completed well. We tend to burn out our best people by expecting more and more. All this leads to potentially harmful stress.

Enlightened management should recognize this problem. Work loads should be shared more equitably. High performers should be recognized for good work with positive rewards, not more demands and higher expectations. A balance needs to be struck to guard against frustrating people.

ON BEING A GOOD MANAGER

In considering situational pressures in the workplace, one ought always look for those things that will provide a rationale for an individual predisposed to engage in some wrongful behavior. There are many positive steps that can be taken to nullify or temper an employee's predisposition to commit a criminal act. The following should be considered a partial list of "Rules for Enlightened Management":

1. Striving for excellence of conduct and performance. People respect high standards and well monitored and

well measured performance and tend to copy the good habits of individuals who set such standards and enforce them.

2. Remaining alert in seeking ways to remove the temptation to steal. Providing work uniforms without pockets is becoming a classic method. Simple, direct.

3. Exercising good interpersonal skills and treating employees with courtesy, consideration, and respect. Preserving their dignity can help erase any feelings of alienation, or of simply not caring about the work. While such actions will not reform a hardcore criminal, they will help others to keep from straying.

4. Properly motivating employees by setting realistic goals. Moderate expectations to realistic, achievable levels. People obviously cannot do the impossible. If they feel pressure to achieve the impossible, then you will be repaid for your carelessness by some form of cheating or retaliation.

5. Matching each person to his or her job. Mismatching can easily result in lying or cheating about performance and become a strong negative factor.

6. Having explicit, uniform and reasonable rules, firmly enforced. It must become your benchmark as a manager. Loosely administered rules are more harmful, in fact, than no rules at all.

7. Having affirmative leadership from the top down and letting all know what is expected by setting clear lines of authority and responsibility.

8. Awarding superior performance in a fair manner; otherwise, contempt and frustration will result.

9. Having an honest, ethical environment and shying away from setting double standards of moral ethical conduct.

10. Maintaining adequate employee feedback and grievance procedures and watching for unusually high turnover of employees. Without such systems management cannot learn sufficiently of the nature of problems in the environment or find ways to release some of the

anger and frustration that might be building in the organization.

11. Making clear to employees that fraud, theft, cheating and the like will not be tolerated.

12. Taking swift, affirmative action against those caught violating the laws and rules governing the operation of the entity.

13. Paying attention to details of policies and procedures of operations.

14. Proper screening of all new employees, including (a) checking all references and (b) conducting background inquiries.

15. Documenting all infractions of discipline or dishonesty so as to leave a trail for future actions should patterns or problems develop.

16. Requiring all executives and employees in trust positions to take annual vacations of at least two weeks duration (for their rest and recuperation, as well as to permit wrongful schemes to surface).

17. Rotating and transferring key employees periodically.

18. Avoiding domineering or autocratic top management.

19. Avoiding the "management by constant crisis syndrome" which keeps employees in a constant state of stress.

20. Not permitting executives or key employees exclusive custody or control over documents, records or processes.

21. Having a policy of trying to assist troubled employees through employee counseling services (for example, for alcohol, drug, or mental health problems).

22. Intervening to assist employees who are in financial need as result of some unusual legitimate circumstance, such as injuries, accidents, prolonged illnesses in family, and so forth.

23. Paying and rewarding people adequately for proper performance. Underpaying leads to job dissatisfaction, low morale and a rationale for theft.

CHAPTER SIX

THE CORPORATE MIND

THE TROUBLED ORGANIZATION

Is your company's attitude conducive to wrongdoing? It is a well-documented psychological fact that people within a group can rationalize antisocial behavior far better than they can acting alone. This can be a dangerous mentality: think back for a moment to Nazi Germany where many pillars of the community suddenly were engaging in atrocities. What about reported massacres by American troops or lynch mobs? The individuals with these groups allowed themselves to be swept up into a frenzy—something they would not in all likelihood have done as individuals acting alone.

This same type of antisocial behavior exists in companies. People will do things as part of a company that they would never do as individuals. They surrender their individualities to the corporate gods they serve. Businessmen may engage in commercial bribery or commercial espionage. Such actions may be considered acceptable by these businessmen although they would not even consider trying to bribe a police officer to, say, forget a traffic ticket.

True pillars of the community, the ones who are civic group members, deacons of the church, and the like, have committed great crimes on behalf of their organizations. In one case investigated by the author a minister burned down his church for the insurance money so he could build a new one. This man was able to rationalize his criminal behavior on the fact that he was working for the greater good of the church.

One thing we have learned about situational pressures is they are amplified in a group setting. Corporate or organizational esprit de corps can be very strong. It may be the most powerful and least understood of all positive motivators. Look at our armed forces, for example: What keeps them from breaking under some of the extreme situations they face? Most analysts agree that it's a combination of esprit de corps and the fear of looking weak, inept, or unworthy to one's peers.

But there can be negative consequences, too. It should always be understood that people acting together are capable of more easily engaging in criminal behavior than people acting alone. This is true in corporate life, within a military unit, and in a crowd of teenagers. Pressures exist at all levels of corporate organizations to promote activities and behaviors conducive to corporate good—regardless of means. "You are a real company man" is, perhaps, the ultimate compliment one can pay a loyal corporate employee. Such loyalty can become perverted particularly if the individual(s) believe that their company is in trouble from any of the myriad problems that can plague an organization, for example, complications caused by cash flow or credit problems, rough competitors, inventory problems, and the like.

Under the law, corporations are defined as individuals, can enter into contracts, are required to pay income taxes, are subject to criminal prosecution when warranted, and, like real people, can develop predispositions for and against criminal behavior. Thus, corporations can and do respond to situational stresses. A late 1977 news article discussed how U.S. and foreign shipping firms were paying millions in illegal rebates. It went on to say that large shipping firms, both foreign and domestic, had been paying tens of millions of dollars in illegal kickbacks to attract customers who ship goods to and from the United States. The kickbacks, or rebates on rates that must be charged by law, were apparently being paid by "every liner carrier in the American foreign trade." According to one source quoted, "we hear of false booking, off-balance sheet accounts, bagman payoffs, use of third-party conduits, all unreachable through audits or other investigations."

At about the same time the December 12, 1977 edition of the *Wall Street Journal* released a story of yet another type of corporate misdeed. An official of a large U.S. company was found guilty of giving illegal gratuities to an Internal Revenue Service supervisor. This official, the company's vice president for tax administration was found guilty by a federal jury of giving illegal gratuities to an IRS supervisor, the supervisor in charge of audits of the company's tax returns.

A different type of situation was reported in the news media in the fall of 1984. TRW, Inc. said that it had discovered irregularities in its cost-estimating process for certain government contracts. These discrepancies resulted from the actions of a few of its employees. These irregularities could result in several millions of dollars in overcharges. TRW planned to discipline those involved and to make refunds as required.

Evidence strongly suggests that an organization tolerant to criminality in its midst is inviting its own employees to engage in similar behavior. An organization concerned about being ripped off by its own employees should engage in a little self-analysis to determine if its environment is conducive to wrongdoing and whether there are stresses existent which might also nudge someone into criminality. To illustrate from the personal experience of the author:

A few years ago, there seemed to be a rash of small thefts being reported by one major bank in Chicago. All of these thefts were unrelated and each resulted in termination and prosecution of the embezzler. There seemed to be no apparent explanation for this situation. Comparable banks in the area were reporting only isolated instances.

It was only after the entire institution was looked at that the answer manifested itself. It seems the whole bank's environment from the top down was to "cut corners" and make "sharp deals." From the president on down through the loan officer, there were special deals. Questionable loans and conflicts of interest pervaded the entire system. The impact of this negative workplace environment ended up affecting some of this bank's lower level employees and making them feel as though it was all right to cheat and steal.

The public sector, of course, is not immune. Consider the following case. About five years ago, a fire chief in New England was sentenced to one to three years in prison after pleading guilty to extortion and bribery charges involving the selling of jobs and promotions. Although the defendant claimed to be deeply ashamed, he added that "we" never skulked or sneaked: these illegal practices were just the way it was in New Britain. The assistant state's attorney confirmed that this had gone on "for years and years"—long before the defendant became a willing participant. Note that the abusive situation had been longstanding, long tolerated, and long fostered by management.

The following is a partial listing of some of the situational stresses confronting business. Like individuals, companies can bend and break under sufficient stress. The degree of predisposition to engage in wrongdoing is also largely dependent on the moral and ethical fiber of the company's history and environment. Most pressures that influence business behavior are financial.

Warning Signals of the Possible Existence of Fraud[1]

1. Highly domineering senior management and one or more of the following, or similar, conditions are present:

    An ineffective board of directors and/or audit committee.

    Indications of management override of significant internal accounting controls.

    Compensation or significant stock options tied to reported performance or to a specific transaction over

[1]Reprinted from March 12, 1979 CPA Letter. American Institute of Certified Public Accountants, Inc.

which senior management has actual or implied control.

Indications of personal financial difficulties of senior management.

Proxy contests involving control of the company or senior management's continuance, compensation or status.

2. Deterioration of quality of earnings evidenced by:

    Decline in the volume or quality of sales (for example, increased credit risk or sales at or below cost).

    Significant changes in business practices.

    Excessive interest by senior management in the earnings per share effect of accounting alternatives.

3. Business conditions that may create unusual pressures:

    Inadequate working capital.

    Little flexibility in debt restrictions such as working capital ratios and limitations on additional borrowings.

    Rapid expansion of a product or business line markedly in excess of industry averages.

    A major investment of the company's resources in an industry noted for rapid change, such as a high technology industry.

4. A complex corporate structure where the complexity does not appear to be warranted by the company's operations or size.

5. Widely dispersed business locations accompanied by highly decentralized management with inadequate responsibility reporting system.

6. Understaffing which appears to require certain employees to work unusual hours, to forego vacations and/or to put in substantial overtime.

7. High turnover rate in key financial positions such as treasurer or controller.

8. Frequent change of auditors or legal counsel.

9. Known material weaknesses in internal control which could practically be corrected but remain uncorrected, such as:

    Access to computer equipment or electronic data entry devices is not adequately controlled.

    Incompatible duties remain combined.

10. Material transactions with related parties exist or there are transactions that may involve conflicts of interest.

11. Premature announcements of operating results or future (positive) expectations.

12. Analytical review procedures disclosing significant fluctuations which cannot be reasonably explained, for example:

    Material account balances.

    Financial or operational interrelationships.

    Physical inventory variances.

    Inventory turnover rates.

13. Large or unusual transactions, particularly at year-end, with material effect on earnings.

14. Unusually large payments in relation to services provided in the ordinary course of business by lawyers, consultants, agents and others (including employees).

15. Difficulty in obtaining audit evidence with respect to:

    Unusual or unexplained entries.

    Incomplete or missing documentation and/or authorization.

    Alterations in documentation or accounts.

16. In the performance of an examination of financial statements unforeseen problems are encountered, for instance:

    Client pressures to complete audit in an unusually short time or under difficult conditions.

    Sudden delay situations.

    Evasive or unreasonable responses of management to audit inquiries.

    Some additional situational measures that warrant attention would include the following:

    a. Fear of a takeover

    b. Sanctioning or administrative action against the company by the government (e.g., IRS, SEC, Licensing agencies, etc.)

    c. Declining conditions for the national economy or for the industry

   d. Excessive competition

   e. Long-term financial losers

   f. Poor return on investments

   g. Overspecialization, over capacity and obsolescence leading to reduced sales

   h. Urgent need for new capital

   i. High amount of serious litigation

   j. Declining management prestige

   k. High debt that is restrictive or at high interest rates

   l. Inability to collect on billings

   m. Reduction in profits.

The above list is not exhaustive, but it is representative of the kinds of pressures found in cases of corporate fraud and crimes. For a fuller discussion of the consequences of a poor business environment that is undergoing the kinds of stresses discussed here, see Chapter 15 (Indicators of Criminal Activities by Business).

PART FOUR

ACCESS

CHAPTER SEVEN

DENYING ACCESS: PROMOTING SECURITY

Access Defined

1. The act of coming toward or near to; approach. 2. a way or means of approaching, getting, using, etc. 3. the right to enter, approach, or use; admittance.

WEBSTER'S NEW WORLD DICTIONARY OF THE AMERICAN LANGUAGE

"Getting within range to attack a target" is another way to define access. The means by which one establishes barriers to control such access to a target is called "security." There can be no crime without access to that which the owner wants to protect.

CONSIDERATIONS ON DENYING ACCESS

This section of the book deals with how an environment might be altered in a way that makes it more difficult for a wrongdoer to reach the target. By making targets more inaccessible, fewer opportunities are presented and potential wrongdoers are discouraged, deterred, and affected in their motivation. Most of the data presented in this part have been gleaned and compiled from nonclassified government documents as well as from personal experiences and study. This material should provide a good overview of what is available and the considerations affecting its use. See Appendix 5.

If a particular target is inconsequential, or less attractive than others, there is less concern about denying access to potential wrongdoers. If any target is only of material value to the owner or user, or cannot be readily moved or used by outsiders, then providing elaborate means of access through denial mechanisms or techniques is obviously nonproductive and noncost-effective. For example, heavy, ponderous equipment located within a plant needs but minimum security. The techniques and trade secrets employed in its use, though, may need careful guarding against unauthorized access.

On the other hand, if the target is attractive, useful, valuable, and portable, then denying access becomes a priority issue. Sometimes very basic protective measures are needed; and other times more sophisticated state-of-the-art measures should be used. A desirable target becomes less appealing to a potential wrongdoer when access to it is restricted by utilizing one of several broad categories of security measures.

Some employers may think that the "access" portion of the criminal equation isn't a problem they face. Perhaps their jobs don't deal with things that have a ready market value. But consider the following "facts of life": you lock your car upon leaving it; you heed the medical advice of your family physician assuming that his professional credentials (that is, access to the practice of medicine) are immaculate; your daughter driving her car is pulled over to the curb by a car with a flashing red light. She assumes (rightly?) that it is driven by an authorized law official. The point being here is that problems of access face us on a daily basis. We deny (through use of a locked car door) unauthorized access to our automobile. We allow access to our person by physicians who we assume are properly credentialed for such access.

Consider a recent item reported in the *Washington Post* about a woman bilking poor people in a housing scam. Perhaps 50 poor people were reportedly cheated of $200 to $600 each by a con artist preying on those seeking low-rent apartments in housing projects, according to New York Housing Authority police. A housing police detective said there were probably many more victims. This con artist would find out from neighbors or superintendents of run-down tenements the names of residents who had applied for city housing. She then visited prospective victims, pretending to be a housing employee. All the victims were made to think that they were paying a fee or rent in advance.

This story can be analyzed in terms of the criminal equation. This con artist found ready targets among the poor seeking housing with subsidy. To gain access to the intended target, the wrongdoer gathered the names of people from neighbors or superintendents of run-down tenements who had applied for city housing. This gave credibility among her intended victims who opened their doors and wallets to her. The *opportunity* was in the fact that these people needed housing assistance, and had applied for it, or let it be known to their neighbors and building superintendents.

ACCESS IMPLICATIONS IN THE BUSINESS ENVIRONMENT

The business world is always seeking to improve its security measures:

1. Companies go to great lengths to avoid industrial espionage resulting in the theft of their trade secrets. Consider the secure Coca-Cola formula. Knowledge of its composition is restricted to a very few.

2. Employee/executive honesty can make or break an organization. We can recall for a moment how Prime Minister Tanaka of Japan fell from power and was successfully

prosecuted when he was personally involved in a scandal whereby Lockheed had bribed officials in order to gain access to that market.

3. Once established, security measures against wrongful access must always be tested again and again for weaknesses. (There was penetration of a plant dealing in atomic energy related matters a few years back. Access problems were experienced with guards.)

4. Constant diligence is required. Consider commercial banks with decades of experience in impeding access to unauthorized individuals (physical partitioning, strict rules about which employee is allowed where, daily cash checks and the like).

5. Health care administrators in hospitals and nursing homes know the importance of remaining alert to employees with access to medical supplies, drugs, and/or patient valuables.

The whole multifaceted field of security can be defined as providing security to an environment through denying access to those who would disturb that environment from its intended purpose. There is much to secure: information, people, inventory, equipment, and other assets.

SECURING INFORMATION

Security is big business. There are more than one million people involved in the security industry in the United States. The private security industry is a multibillion-dollar-a-year business that grows at a rate of 10 to 12 percent per year. It is a major employer in this country. In fact, the number of security personnel is considerably greater than the number of police and law enforcement personnel. Of those individuals involved in private security, some are uniformed, some are not; some carry guns, some are unarmed; some guard nuclear energy installations, some guard golf courses; some are trained, some are not;

some have college degrees, some are virtually uneducated. Even our nation's capitol, which lacks most major industrial activity, has an extremely large body of uniformed security services. In fact, there is the rather odd fact that more uniformed guards protect federal buildings in Washington, D.C., than the Kremlin in Moscow.

The field of security can be divided into three function areas:

1. *Information security* to protect the confidentiality of information owned or held,
2. *Personnel security* designed to protect the employees of a facility from hostile influences including theft,
3. *Physical security* to protect the facility against the effects of unauthorized access, theft, fire, and so on.

We have also certainly been reminded recently that espionage is not limited to agents of various governments trying to steal vital secrets from one another. In late December 1984, a Northrop Corporation engineer was arrested by the FBI. This "debt ridden" person was charged with allegedly tring to sell billion-dollar "Stealth" technology to undercover FBI men posing as Soviet buyers. But industrial espionage between competing companies can certainly rival that which goes on among governments, both in scope and scale.

During the spring of 1985 spy scandals rocked the U.S. with the revelations that John Anthony Walker, a retired Navy Warrant Officer, along with his son and brother may have engaged in espionage for the Soviet Union over decades. Among other things all of this may have imperiled our ability to keep our submarine fleet from being tracked in peace and destroyed in case of war. All of the Walkers arrested had security clearances. One of the outcomes of this episode was the House of Representatives (at the time of this writing) voting approval of the death penalty to be applied to those individuals engaged in espionage during a period of undeclared war. In addition approval was granted for polygraphs to be used by the Department of Defense on employees and agents of the government in matters relating to national security. Weeks later another spy case surfaced when a CIA employee returning from Ghana took a routine polygraph exam. The test showed discrepancies and led to questioning the truthfulness of the answers. Another significant turn of events related to the whole question of document security and the "need to know." Approximately 4 million Americans have security clearances.

We are beginning to find that there is no way secrets can remain secure with so many people having knowledge of them. The foreseeable trend will be to limit the number of people granted clearances and to further restrict classified information on a "need to know" basis, that is, if there is no valid reason why an individual *must* have knowledge of a secret then regardless of the level of clearance they should not gain *access* to them.

Each company or agency that is attempting to protect insider information, patent information, trade, or process secrets and the like should promote some sort of security awareness. The importance of protecting such information must be stressed on a continuing basis. This can be accomplished through formal briefings by the security office or through the management of each organizational component. In any event, it should be clear that when it comes to sensitive information, *access* should always be on a "need to know" basis.

The foregoing examples reinforces the basic tenet that only management can determine (1) what information needs protection, (2) the extent of access limitations on employees, and (3) the degree of compartmentalization and controls necessary to limit opportunities to a manageable level. Strict rules need to be established as to (1) who should have access to the information, (2) the circumstances of such access, (3) who should have custody over the information, (4) storage and/or shipment requirements for the information, (5) the types of access controls to be used, (6) acceptable reproduction equipment and procedures, (7) information (data) checkout procedures, (8) logs and audit trails to be in place to monitor/control access, (9) inventory maintenance and control procedures, (10) methods of destroying or disposing of information; and (11) steps to take (termination? prosecution?) when the rules are violated.

Information Security

In varying degrees, much information generated in both the private or public sector can be considered sensitive in nature and thus worthy of protection. There are also many kinds of information not generated for public consumption. This information, too, is worthy of protection.

1. Information of a national security nature, maintained by the U.S. government, its agents, and contractors;

2. Predecisional information at all levels of government and business which would injure the system were there unauthorized disclosure;

3. Information protected under various privacy acts (federal and state), such as financial, medical, personal records, or other information of a personal or private nature;

4. Proprietary information relating to research of products, processes, and design; and

5. Certain personnel, medical, investigative, commercial, and financial records. Such information and material should be appropriately marked (e.g., for "Office Use Only") and afforded the physical protection required to safeguard it from unauthorized, inappropriate disclosure.

While many of the points discussed below may apply only to units of government or specialized business enterprises, they are indicative of the considerations applicable to information and data security for anyone. As with other matters of importance, the first step in carrying out a program of information security is to assess and grade data according to its sensitivity. The next step is providing appropriate physical security through using such devices as restricted access and passwords (particularly for automated data).

Secured information should be stored under conditions that provide adequate protection and prevent access by unauthorized persons. For example, such information could be stored in a specially designated area or in an area where entry is restricted or controlled. Whenever controlled or classified information is not under the personal control and observation of an employee who has authorized access to information on a need-to-know basis, it must be kept secure in a locked container such as a locked file or safe. The more sensitive the information is, the tighter the security should be.

In one case a few years ago, employees of a major U.S. company decided to go into business for themselves and build a state-of-the-art plant without having to undergo the research and development costs. For many months they systematically purloined or copied every design and specification associated with the plant. It was a monumental effort since many thousands of documents were needed. All went unnoticed by the company. The documents were available because there was no segregation of duties or compartmentalization—even though many of the processes were secret. In the end, the well-laid plans were betrayed by one of the greedy insiders who turned his friend in to the company for a cash award. The general casual attitude displayed by this company would have spelled disaster were it not for plain luck.

Employees should be considered eligible for access to classified information only when that employee has been determined to be trustworthy by background and clearance checks and access is essential. A need for access ought to be demonstrated perhaps by a written request from a superior official, before a request for security clearance is begun. The number of employees cleared and granted access to controlled or classified information should be kept to a minimum, something that we seem to have to be reminded of over and over again. Any employee who has possession of, or is charged with the responsibility for controlled or classified information is responsible for its protection.

Following are several well-established concepts on how to tighten up access to the documents an organization wants to protect:

1. While in use, controlled and classified documents must be kept under the observation of an authorized person.

2. An office that receives a controlled or classified document and has no authorized storage equipment available should either return the document or arrange with another office that does have authorized storage equipment to store the document. It may even be necessary under appropriate circumstances for example, if the document's security classification has expired to destroy the document by an approved method.

3. Each employee who has been granted a security clearance should have:

    a. Initial security briefings on the inherent responsibilities and proper procedures for handling classified information.

    b. Attend refresher briefings (at least annually). These briefings should (i) remind these employees of their continuing responsibility for safeguarding classified information and (ii) brief them on any new security regulations or procedures.

4. Certain information as to the reason a document is considered controlled or classified ought to be shown on its face:

    a. The extent to which it is to be controlled or restricted

    b. Information on the source of the data, particularly if the "classified" information was derived from more than one source document

    c. The date (or event) on which the material can be "declassified," that is, made available upon appropriate request; and

    d. Any necessary instructions regarding special dissemination and reproduction limitations.

Security Matters, a Manager's Responsibility

While certain employees may be assigned specific security responsibilities, it is nevertheless the basic responsibility of the office manager and supervisor to insure that all controlled and classified information entrusted to their offices is handled and safeguarded according to the organization's policies and procedures. See Figure 7.1 Any office manager or supervisor who handles or stores such information should also establish a system of security checks at the close of each working day to ensure that:

1. All such information has been returned for safekeeping (that is, removed from desks and file trays) and stored in an appropriate security container.

2. All typewriter ribbons, floppy disks, extra copies, classified waste, and working papers that may contain classified information are stored, until destruction, in an appropriate security container.

3. Wastebaskets do not contain any controlled or classified information.

4. Security containers are checked to be sure they are locked.

5. All windows and doors, where appropriate, are locked.

Finally, it has been a practice in government to give security debriefings to all employees upon termination of their security clearance, either by separation, transfer, or change in duties. Employees are advised on their continuing responsibility for protecting the classified information to which they had access as well as the consequences of any breach of security measures.

PERSONNEL SECURITY: EXECUTIVE PROTECTION

An organization's executives may also become targets. The odyssey of TWA flight 847 brought back vivid memories of a nation held hostage by terrorists attacking American business and citizens. Once again Americans were seized by terrorists in the Middle East and held for the ransom of 734 Shiite prisoners in Israel. Subsequent to the release of the last 39 American hostages, terrorists bombed TWA offices in Spain and another

General
1. Is a copy of the last internal review of procedures and inventory report on hand?
2. Have discrepancies which were noted during the last review or audit been corrected?

Area and Personnel Access Controls
3. Are proper visitor control procedures in effect?
4. Do personnel of the facility wear the prescribed identification badges?
5. Is the data storage area located in a SECURE AREA?
6. Is the area correctly marked?
7. Is a list posted within the secured area which contains the names of persons authorized entry and the names of persons who have authority to authorize entry?
8. Is a visitor register maintained within the secure area?
9. Are clearances verified and need-to-know established for access to restricted information?

Physical Security
10. Are approved secure storage facilities available for safeguarding classified material?
11. Has the lock combination of each safe, vault, or secure area door been changed in accordance with requirements?
12. Are employees who change combinations properly cleared?
13. Has a means been provided for recording the names of persons who open, lock and check vault or storage room doors, and each storage container?
14. Are safe combinations properly recorded and stored?
15. Have procedures been established to assure that all restricted material received at a location is opened only by an authorized person?
16. Is restricted material inventoried as often as required?
17. Is a local destruction file maintained which shows all material destroyed?

FIGURE 7.1   Document Security Checklist.

explosion took place at the Frankfort Airport. All of this reminds us that American entities, enterprises, political officials, and businessmen (as well as their families) have increasingly become targets for terrorist activities. For purposes of discussion terrorist activities include:

1. Hostage taking/kidnapping
2. Blackmail/extortion

3. Assassination/armed assault

4. Air hijacking

5. Arson/bombings

Each can be addressed through an executive protection plan, as discussed in Chapter 2, Part II.

There are two primary *motives* for these terroristic acts—pecuniary gain and political advantage. Individuals singled out to be targets usually have high public visibility, influence and/or money. The odds against such happenings are greatly in favor of any particular individuals possessing these characteristics. However, the number of overall attacks are increasing—and so is the risk. The individual risks also rise proportionate to the amount of public visibility, individual wealth, or degree of control over financially powerful entities. Individuals and companies closely associated with cash handling (such as banking, airlines, marketing, utilities) are subject to greater threats. Enterprises most symbolic of "capitalism" are potential lightning rods for political dissidents.

To successfully deal with the threat of these kinds of acts, certain logical preventative measures are necessary. The most successful countermeasures recognize the basic principles of denying access to the target area and elimination of opportunities to attack them. Attacks against individuals are most likely to occur at the office (or school), at home, or in transit between these locations. Americans divide most of their time in these three activities. A detailed target analysis of each of these areas should be prepared. The vulnerabilities of the office, home and travel environments should also be detailed. Then a contingency plan should be developed.

A vulnerability analysis should be prepared based on this analysis. It should parallel what was suggested in Chapter 2, (Target Analysis). The report should also include a summary of the possible forms the criminal attack might take and what the objectives might be. The following list of preventive measures might assist in analyzing whether the company is protected against burglary, arson, bombings, and kidnap/hostage taking.

1. Since a company's executive offices tend to be located on the same floor, the task of securing this area (that is denying access to unauthorized individuals) is somewhat lightened. Tightened access can be achieved by having a receptionist and/or a guard on duty. (Entry Access cards, pushbutton, readers, and the like). Mechanical access systems are also advisable (see Chapter 10).

2. All persons should be screened before they are admitted—at home as well as in the workplace. Ask for identification from repairmen, meter readers, other service personnel, and even police officers. Don't hestitate to telephone for verification.

3. There should not be any special identifiers in or on a vehicle that provides personal information about the driver (such as vanity plates or stickers).

4. Automobiles should always be locked when not in use, and should be kept in a garage whenever possible. There is no reason to make access to the interior of the car easier than need be. While traveling, the car windows should be rolled up and the doors should be locked.

5. Protecting the premises should be the first rule of denying access to intruders. All exterior doors should have secure deadbolt mortise locks. Sliding doors should be fortified with bolts or bars in the sliding track. Similarly, all windows should have tamper resistant locks.

CHAPTER EIGHT

THE INSIDERS: ALLOWING ACCESS TO EMPLOYEES

The greatest degree of access to our targets of value is enjoyed by one's employees. There are many things that can and should be done to ensure that the people you intend to employ have (1) the qualifications they purport to have and (2) strong traits of socially acceptable behavior. Prospective employees may be active or latent thieves or embezzlers, and their professional credentials can be suspect.

As we have seen in Chapter 4 (Motivation), psychologists, sociologists, and criminologists have been unsuccessful both in predicting how personalities may emerge from their early development (particularly as to issues of honesty) and in modifying introduced antisocietal behavior patterns once they have been exhibited. Social rehabilitation of criminals has been the major emphasis of penal correction systems in the U.S. over the last several decades. By and large, it has been a tremendous disappointment. Recidivism continues to be a major cause of high crime rates. Furthermore, managers trying to protect targets do not have the capability of psychoanalyzing every potential employee, contractor, or individual wishing to do business with him. But the concerned manager can do much to determine whether their prospective employees are trustworthy, capable, and are who they purport.

PREEMPLOYMENT SCREENING

Preemployment screening should include the screening interview, background investigation, honesty tests, and other psychological aptitude testing. These two tests are described in detail later in this Chapter. The vast majority of employable individuals have left adequate indications as to whether they are basically honest, exhibit antisocial behavior, are emotionally stable, are physically fit, and have good work ethics.

Preemployment screening of individuals helps determine their suitability for the job. It can also help to detect characteristics that would prevent or hinder satisfactory job performance and recommend against access to target areas.

Many employers unwisely accept statements made on application forms without verification. Unfortunately, this is true even for fairly sensitive jobs. Whenever this practice is tolerated, the results can be the general endangerment of the safety of individuals and property. Further it invites poor performance, waste, inefficiencies, and costly mistakes.

The breadth and depth to which an advance screening process is dictated is governed by a number of legal and cost-beneficial issues, such as (1) the nature and value of the targets to be protected, (2) screening costs, (3) time consideration, and (4) legal constraints.

THE NATURE OF THE POTENTIAL TARGETS. The target itself dictates the process needs. The target value, its degree of vulnerability to other risk factors, and the amount of risks inherent in the environment all suggest the level of need for advanced screening.

SCREENING COSTS. The overall costs associated with screening—along with the availability or lack of human and dollar resources to run or finance these investigations—are major considerations. Also, with the extremely high turnover rates in some segments of the workplace, such as computer specialists, the costs of in-depth personnel prescreening may not be economically feasible for some employees. The cost impact on limited budgets must be measured against what could be lost without such screening. The size of an operation could also limit the kinds of professional reviews available.

TIME CONSIDERATIONS. Employers often do not have a lot of time to replace needed employees. This is particularly true if the marketplace of the particular type of employee you want to hire is competitive, and the applicant may choose another employer if delays in the hiring process materialize. This was found to be the case in a government-wide study of computer fraud and abuse by Health and Human Services' Inspector General for the President's Council on Integrity and Efficiency (PCIE). Chapter 16 discusses the results of this study. The employing agency's needs were so great for certain types of computer-related skills that employees were hired without detailed checks being made. As many as one-fourth of the computer-related fraud perpetrators discussed by this study were hired even though they had preexisting felonious records relating to larceny and violation of fiduciary responsibilities (see Chapter 16 for more detailed discussion.)

This points out how careful one must be when assigning someone to sensitive areas of responsibility. No matter what the time constraints are, one should not entirely eliminate verifying information for people—be they employee, contractor or visitor—who will gain access to the company's target area. The degree of vulnerability can be enormously reduced by a verifying phone call. Under no circumstances should access to a target be granted without some real efforts being made to validate information given by the individual desiring admission.

Examples of responsible parties who have on occasion failed to adequately guard exposed targets by verifying information has been found in the area of health practitioners. In 1984, the Department of Health and Human Services Office of the Inspector General began encountering a number of medical practitioners with bogus credentials. Thus began a major continuing investigative effort called MEDPHODOC (Medical Phoney Doctorates). The main purpose of this undertaking was to identify all those practitioners who obtained medical credentials fraudulently and then used them to (1) submit bills for medical services rendered beneficiaries of the Medicare and Medicaid programs; and/or (2) obtain employment grants or contracts with the federal government. Both are lucrative targets. It should be added that this project was also intended to ensure proper coordination of all program and investigative agencies dealing with this particular problem (including such organizations as the U.S. Postal Inspection Services, FBI, State Licensing Boards, American Hospital Association, American Medical Association).

A notable example of this situation, widely reported in the news media, involved an Alexandria, Virginia man who prosecutors said collected $1.5 million in a scheme providing bogus medical degrees to at least 97 individuals. He was sentenced recently on charges of mail fraud and conspiracy to three years in federal prison. Before sentencing the defendant, the judge told him that he had made a mockery of the whole medical accreditation system. The defendant had taken sums ranging from $5,225 to $27,000 from 165 U.S. residents seeking medical degrees. Ninety-six people were reported as having received degrees from CETEC University and one from CIF AS University, both in the Dominican Republic.

The problem of phoney certificates, degrees and licenses in the health provider community is not confined to the medical doctorates. Despite constraints (legal, cost and other) it's terribly important to verify that job applicants have the credentials they claim to have. For example, chiropractor certificates under various aliases have been purchased in undercover operations. Similar false credentialing problems have been found in many fields of specialty (pharmacists, social workers, medical laboratory technicians, and so on). One expert states that lying about credentials is reaching epidemic proportions, occurring in 10 to 15 percent of the people who submit resumes.

What makes this type of fraud possible? Pieces of paper are accepted as de facto evidence, identity, and proof of professional competence. Validation of such paper is often lacking. As a result of the failure of the system to screen out false credentials, there has been considerable public interes : in trying to develop better ways to ensure the noncontinuance of the problem. (See Appendix VI for further discussion on this matter.)

Legal Constraints

In an effort to ensure individual rights to privacy, more and more information is denied by laws, regulations, and the courts. For example, many juvenile records have been legally placed off limits by public policy. Criminal records of juveniles are expunged when they attain adulthood. Similarly, school records are difficult to access, particularly those portions relating to conduct. The rationale behind these constraints is that children should not be prevented from straightening out their life at the advent of adulthood by the disclosure of youthful delinquent conduct. Unfortunately, these constraints also conceal what may be extensive criminal behavior from public view and limits managers from being able to detect high risk employees. In this same vein, it might be noted that fear of law suits have greatly limited the type and amount of information that may be found in "official records" of employment.

After detecting and arresting thieving tellers and/or officers at a bank, the FBI would often find the culprits had been previously dismissed or allowed to resign from one or more similar jobs for dishonesty. Being previously suspected or caught for dishonest behavior did not discourage them. In fact, their deviant behavior had been reinforced in that they had not been punished sufficiently for their misdeeds. Their conscious or unconscious response was to steal more because they felt that the risk factor was minimal when compared against returns.

To illustrate, one of the authors tracked a bank teller back through six prior jobs. At each of these places, this person had stolen or embezzled. In every case she was allowed to resign and no charges were filed. In each successive job this person stole a bit more, until it could not be ignored by the employer and she was reported and arrested. It is noteworthy that every employer went through a *perfunctory* clearing of this person's references, using form letters mailed to previous employers. But none of her employers kept an "official record" of her misconduct in her personnel folder; all feared putting anything in writing for which they might later be sued.

OPTIMAL PREEMPLOYMENT SCREENING TECHNIQUES

The pattern of embezzlers and pilferers moving from job to job, until finally being arrested, is very pronounced. In fact it is a standard investigative technique to conduct detailed, face-to-face interviews of previous employers of all potential suspects in theft and/or embezzlement cases. More often than not this technique alone identifies the thief.

Recognizing all of the constraints and limitations there may be in any given situation, every effort should be made to generate a complete and effective preemployment (that is, preaccess) process. Some of the more basic components in such a process include:

1. Application
2. Screening Interview
3. Deception detection techniques
4. Written honesty test
5. Background inquiry

The Application

Proper use of a basic employment application is an important way to ensure that any prospective or new employee has nothing in their "official history" which might indicate predisposition to wrongful, destructive, underproductive, or counterproductive behavior. In many organizations the application may be the only official information document in an individual's employment file. It is the basis for much of the prescreening process (e.g., interviews, background inquiries, and the like). Such an application should contain the following information:

1. Full name and any nicknames (*also known as*—AKAs).
2. Date and place of birth with record (may be supported by birth or hospital certificates, driver's license, statement of citizenship, or work permit number (green card).
3. Social Security Number.
4. Current residence, whether such residence is owned or leased, length of time at that residence, and phone number.
5. Prior residences (for the past 10 to 20 years).
6. Educational and training background (proof of education should be provided with written permission to verify with institutions attended).
7. Entire adult work history, including place and nature of work, rates of pay, names and titles of direct supervisors plus work references, duration of employment, reason for leaving, and written authorization to verify employment history.
8. Medical history (physical and mental) as they relate to job, with written permission to verify.
9. Service record history (including the "Armed Forces of the United States Report of Transfer or Discharge [DD214]").

10. Record of any and all arrests, convictions, and pending charges, including traffic violations.
11. Credit information relevant to the job, with written permission to verify.
12. Personal references.
13. Where appropriate multiple sets of fingerprints.

Be sure to impress upon prospective employees that valid responses must be made to the questions raised on the employment application. On the face of the form there should be a clear statement that any misrepresentation of fact or material omission are grounds for denial of employment or dismissal after employment. This warning should also be given verbally.

Once the form is filled in, an interview should follow discussing the entire form to remove ambiguities, clarify statements, and draw out additional pertinent information. Responsive answers to a well-designed form indicate that the applicant can be presumed to be qualified for the position in question. Adroit questioning can help to draw out more details on the individual's background and their suitability for the job in question may further serve to eliminate questionable applicants. This process will (1) screen out individuals of questionable character and (2) help select the most qualified personnel.

The following cases from a U.S. News and World Report article illustrate the failure importance of making basic inquiries on data supplied by an applicant:

Seagate Technology a firm in Scotts Valley, California, hired a man who claimed to speak 13 languages and possess a degree in electrical engineering from Oxford. After 12 days executives found out that Sidney Friedman was a phony who was on probation for a grand-theft conviction. Friedman was later sentenced to two years in prison for stealing money from Seagate. [Note: How easy it would have been to verify his credentials.)

Recent exposes of military physicians practicing medicine without credentials, or after they were found to be incompetent has the Department of Defense reevaluating the whole military and civilian health administrative processes. In one case an individual was posing as a doctor. He improperly administered anesthesia during surgery to remove a bladder tumor. The patient, a retired Navy chief petty officer, lapsed into a coma and remains "brain dead." The "doctor" had in fact lied about his background in applying to be a staff doctor.

The Screening Interviews

By definition, an interview is a dialogue, during which both parties exchange information, ideas, opinions, concerns, and so forth. It is an opportunity to engage in mutual assessment. One can be sure that wrongdoers looking for additional rip off opportunities are going to use a job interview to asses; the potential in the environment for engaging in such enterprises. Management ought use the same process to convey to these individuals that the work environment is hostile to illicit behaviors. Therefore, interviews should be structured to indicate the organization is well-managed, has good internal controls, and is not lax in its security.

A simple, direct, no nonsense "this is how it is" approach can work. This was brought out in the HHS' Inspector General's report on Sexual Abuse in Day Care Centers (See Chapter 2, and Appendix III). The report noted that prosecutors who were contacted during the study felt that one of the most effective methods of deterring pedophiles from gaining employment in day care centers is to simply tell all applicants the kinds of behavior that will not be tolerated—and that offenders would be sought out and prosecuted. This simple step of making it clear that the environment is not tolerant to wrongdoing, reduces the vulnerability to such acts.

Screening interviews should include such specific questions as why the applicant wants the job, his career objectives, and the factors in the job that interest him. There should also be active discussion about the applicant's previous employment history, including why the applicant left each job. Applicants should also be queried about what they liked and/or disliked about each job, who they reported to, the nature of their relationship with their supervisor, and so on. The responses to these and similar questions provide clues to the applicant's background that are not provided by the employment application.

In addition, the manager should clearly and honestly describe the job requirements, including both the positive and negative aspects of the work, promotion opportunities (or lack thereof), and the salary and fringe benefits being offered. There should be no false expectations raised about the job or its potential which can later lead to frustration (and the consequent forming of a rationale for "striking back" at the entity. (See discussion on situational stresses, Chapter 3, Motivation.)

It is wise to have the applicant interviewed by several different people to allow for multiple assessment of his character. This way, it is simpler to arrive at a reasoned determination on how the applicant will fit into the organization. Admittedly, interviews are a subjective—though important—process. The applicant's demeanor and attitude during the interview phase may be the determinant as to how detailed and complete the background inquiry should be or whether additional testing might be warranted.

Psychological Stress Testing

This is but a fancy way of talking about a lie detector or polygraph test. The use of the lie detector to measure honesty has become widely used. It measures certain responses during questioning. These may include skin resistance (electrogalvanic), blood pressure, respiration (rate as well as depth), and restlessness.

Detractors of the use of this technique look upon it as some sort of "witchcraft," but most law enforcement officials and security officers look upon it as the single most effective tool available to detect wrongdoers. It has been a subject of controversy since the first device was invented about 60 years ago. In the 98th Congress the House of Representatives declined to consider authorizing its use by the Government in matters of national security. However, no sooner had the 99th Congress organized itself in 1985, than the "Walker Spy Case" broke. By June 1985 the House of Representatives voted overwhelmingly to grant the Pentagon broad power to polygraph test more than 4 million military and civilian employees cleared to see classified information. American Polygraph has routinely asserted that polygraph tests are accurate more than 90 percent of the time.

The theory behind the use of a lie detector test is as simple as it is ancient: the emotional stress created by lying manifests certain physiological changes. For many years, prior to the popular re-emergence of lie detection methods, there was a general scoffing and belittling of the lie detection methods employed during the Middle Ages. A variety of different tests of truthfulness were in use throughout the world. In some parts of the Medieval world the authorities would test the accused by various "trials by ordeal." Among the more common ordeals was to have the accused touch his tongue to a fire heated stove or metal. After three days the tongue was checked and if it were scarred, God was deemed to have marked his guilt. Also, in the ecclesiastical (church) courts, accused clerics were made to read a selected passage from the Bible. If he faltered at any point, God was also revealing his guilt.

We have subsequently begun to appreciate these trials as crude but possibly effective "lie detector tests." What may have been occurring in a time of deep belief in the power of God and church was that the innocent's autonomic responses were likely to be quite different from those of the guilty. In other words, today we know that the emotional stresses of someone lying tends to dry his mouth and tongue. Therefore, a "trial by ordeal" such as that described above might very well have scarred the tongue of a wrongdoer as his mouth and tongue would be relatively dry. An innocent person, though, believing in the divine justice of God, would not experience the stress of lying and probably would have the protecting saliva to reduce or negate any effects caused by the trial.

Similarly, the tension created by the stress of lying frequently manifests itself in the constriction of the throat, resulting in some impairment in speech. Thus, the lying cleric's faltering in the reading of the Scriptures may have been as the result of his own internal tensions and fears, rather than God's sending judgment on his sins. In fact, today very sensitive "voice printing" instruments have been developed that perform almost an identical (albeit by a more scientific method) type of lie test performed by these ancient clerics.

The present theory on the use of polygraphs rests on the same premises. The emotional stress created by lying manifests itself in a number of significant autonomic changes which can be measured with a certain amount of precision. Among changes that most people exhibit during lying are accelerated pulse, elevated blood pressure, and shallow respiration.

There is no single universally accepted polygraph technique. While there are many methods for administering and interpreting test results, the positive correlation among examiners of test results is high. However, polygraph examinations are still considered more of an "art" than a "science." There has been only very limited acceptance of polygraph examination results in the courts. It is still the general rule that a polygraph examination is inadmissible as evidence in a court of law. There are even restrictions on the use of polygraph examination in investigations as well as preemployment screening or in making personnel decisions.

Nevertheless, the acceptance and respectability of this tool as a means of measuring personal honesty is rising. Recently, there has been considerable controversy generated over the use of this tool to find national security "leaks." The most current facet of this has been the recent White House directive that all government employees with Secret and Top Secret Clearance should submit to polygraph examinations upon demand.

Many employers consider certain jobs to be of such a sensitive nature a polygraph test is warranted as part of the screening process, *prior* to hiring or assignment. In addition, polygraph tests have proven useful in the routine updating of a person's clearance. The cost of employing these kinds of techniques is generally minimal when measured against the potential loss to a target judged to be sensitive enough to need extra protection.

The Written Honesty Test

In recent years there have been a flurry of psychological tests designed to measure attitudes on honesty, general trustworthiness, and proclivity towards theft. This is a relatively new approach to the detection and prevention of crime. Its rudiments require the development of in-depth profiles of perpetuation which could be used to design tests to identify individuals with characteristics typical of wrongdoing, that is, those prone to wrongful behavior.

One of the early advocates of this approach was John E. Reid and Associates in Chicago, one of the top polygraph firms in the country. Their Reid Report[1] is a written test designed to predict employee theft by using specific questions, the answers to which clearly alert the examiner to the fact that this undesirable proclivity is present in a measurable form. This particular instrument focuses on two dimensions, attitudes toward punishment for stealing and the individual's own attitude and behavior relating to stealing. This particular test, which was developed as a preemployment screen, claims high reliability and validity with a positive correlation to polygraph test scores. In fact, this type of screen is often used in conjunction with lie detector tests to further increase its reliability.

As a cautionary note, it should be mentioned that members of the community asked to submit to such examination may find such a written honesty test to be insulting, demeaning, and an infringement on their rights. Nevertheless, today one can find in almost any university someone who is prepared to market this kind of instrument.

Once an employee is hired, the security considerations for the employee does not end. One of the gravest errors a manager can make is to not place a limit upon the employee based upon the specific need that exists for his access to something and on the level of trust that is warranted for him based on his personal history.

[1] J. E. Reid, *The Reid Report* (Chicago: John E. Reid and Associates, 1967).

Background Investigation

No applicant should be hired or assigned prior to verification and validation as to qualifications and personal conduct and performance history. Background investigations will help ensure that employees are reliable, trustworthy, and of good conduct and character. They will also help ensure that the applicant's employment and retention is clearly consistent with the best interests of their employer. This is a tall order, but of supreme importance to a well-run organization regardless of size.

Many employers use the background data and fingerprints to make checks with the FBI Identification Division records and/or local as a routine part of screening. This is particularly true of the banking industry and state licensing agencies. Fingerprints are unique identifiers of an individual, regardless of how they might disguise other characteristics. All applicants for federal and many state jobs go through such checks. Many individuals with concealed prior criminal records are found as a result of this exercise. Although prior records do not necessarily preclude employment, it alerts the employers to the issue and may affect the kinds of assignments they may consider the employee for, depending on the nature of the record and the nexus to the assignment. In a study made of perpetrators of computer fraud in federal programs (Appendix V) it was found that 22 percent of offenders had a prior criminal record to the offense on which they were caught. Congress occasionally mandates into law screening of individuals by use of fingerprints, as was the case of Public Law 98-473. This required states, as a condition of receiving certain Title XX social services grant, to have procedures and regulations for providing employment history and background checks, for all current and prospective operators, staff and employees of child care facilities and juvenile detention, treatment, or correction facilities. It will necessitate the fingerprinting of literally millions of Americans (for fuller discussion of the rationale, scope and impact of this effort see Appendix III).

In determining whether or not an individual should be

occupying a "sensitive" position, managers must pay considerable attention to the possible existence of such detrimental characteristics as:

1. Any behavior, activities, or associations which tend to show that the individual is not reliable or trustworthy;

2. Any deliberate misrepresentations, falsifications, or omissions of material facts;

3. Any known criminal, infamous, dishonest, immoral, or notoriously disgraceful conduct, habitual use of intoxicants to excess, drug addiction, or sexual perversion;

4. Any illness, including any mental condition, of a nature which in the opinion of competent medical authority may cause significant defect in the judgment or reliability of the employee, with due regard to the transient or continuing effect of the illness and the medical findings in such case;

5. Any facts which furnish reason to believe that the individual may be subjected to coercion, influence, or pressure which may cause the person to act contrary to the best interests of the employer;

6. Any evidence of acts of a reckless, irresponsible, or wanton nature which indicate such poor judgment and instability as to suggest that the individual might disclose classified information to unauthorized persons, or otherwise assist such persons, whether deliberately or inadvertently, in activities harmful to the employer.

You may also wish to consider a "reinvestigation program" designed to assure the continued eligibility of selected individuals for occupancy of a sensitive position. See Appendix 5.

CHAPTER NINE

PHYSICAL SECURITY

Physical security encompasses those measures necessary to protect the facility against the effects of unauthorized access, theft, fire, sabotage, loss, or other intentional crime or damage. Some of these measures include:

1. Preventing unauthorized access by means of security officers, barriers, fences, lighting, and alarms;
2. Controlling authorized entry by personnel identification;
3. Preventing employee crime and pilferage;
4. Implementing fire prevention and control measures;
5. Implementing security surveys; and
6. Implementing adequate procedures of control for such purposes.

Figure 9.1 gives you an idea of what the security dollar is being spent for.

The business of providing physical security for property is a multi-billion-dollar industry. In fact, it is one of the fastest growing industries in America today. It represents the lion's

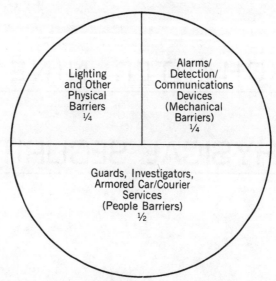

FIGURE 9.1. Expenditures on physical security and services.

share of all revenue devoted to commercial security—some 85 to 90 percent. The remainder of security services are for investigative and consultative services.

Some of the giants in providing physical security services on a contract basis in alphabetical order are:

Advance Industrial Security
Allied
Burns
Globe
Guardsmark
Guard Services, National
Pinkerton
Wackenhut
Wells Fargo

Each of these companies provide a wide range of services, such as security guards, armored car transport, and alarm systems. In addition are a host of firms specializing in one or more services.

Developing an Environment for Security

Through the centuries people have learned to employ architectural design as an element of protecting their environment. From the great medieval castles with their parapets and moats, to the simplest dwelling of today, the physical security of the structure's inhabitants is always a consideration.

Employers contemplating new construction should always keep security considerations in mind and involve themselves in every phase of the development from the initial planning and design to the final stages of construction. They should consult with experts to ensure the new facility would be secure in whatever targets might exist there worthy of protection. A target analysis should be made to focus the site selection, design, and construction to insure against easy access by unauthorized individuals.

By preparing your *own* target analysis, (discussed in Chapter 2, Part II) proper decisions can be made as to the vulnerabilities that may exist in the locale you are considering construction and the levels (and resultant costs) of access reconstruction necessary for adequate security. Following this procedure only reduces the likelihood of successful attacks on the company's targets: it is not a guarantee that none will occur.

Alarm Systems

Substantiated figures show that alarm systems do hinder criminal acts. In communities where such systems are used extensively, the burglary rate has been significantly reduced. Further, most insurance companies offer lower premiums to businesses that are protected by alarm systems. Federally insured institutions such as banks are required by law to install such systems.

Alarm systems, whether manually or automatically activated, are a means of communicating a warning of potential or present danger. There are systems available to protect against vandalism, burglary, fire and smoke, and to control entry and exit. However, these systems are designed to detect—not prevent. They must be used where there is police, fire, or contract guard response.

The three fundamental parts of modern instrusion detection systems are:

SENSORS. That function of the intrusion detection system that detects or senses a condition which exists or changes, be it authorized or unauthorized. This definition can be related directly to the animal senses of touch, hearing, sight, smell, and taste. This definition includes all actions that occur since sensors have no means of distinguishing authorized or unauthorized actions.

This is easily pointed out in one of the most common and simplest sensory devices—the magnetic contact on a door. This device is activated each time the door is operated. There is no means of determining whether the operation of the door is authorized.

Sensors, though, have many problems that may occur with their use. They are far more complex in makeup than simple contacts and switches, and a higher degree of skill is required for proper installation of such equipment. Thus, they are more susceptible to a false alarm.

CONTROL. That function of the intrusion detection system that provides the power, receives the information from the sensors, evaluates the information, and transmits the required information to the annunciation function.

The control function can be thought of as relating to the physiological functions of the human brain, nervous system, and circulatory system. The nervous system collects and evaluates information from the various senses and transmits signals to the muscles for appropriate action. The circulatory system provides the power source (i.e., nutrients and oxygen from the blood) to maintain the ability of the system to function.

ANNUNCIATION. That function of the intrusion detection system that alerts someone to initiate a response that will result in an investigation of the sensor environment. This could be done by a bell, buzzer, light flashing, and so forth. This function is analogous to the squawking of geese, barking of dogs, or calling for help.

When these three fundamental parts are combined, they form an alarm system that transmits and articulates a message for help upon detection of an intrusion. Numerous types of alarm systems are available—some simple, some highly complex. A user's choice of systems is limited only by the dollars he has available. In any event, these systems, coupled with a well-trained response force, can afford a measure of protection which has not been available in the past:

1. They permit more economical and efficient use of manpower by substituting a mobile response force for a number of patrol and fixed guard posts.
2. They provide protection where more common physical protection measures, such as locked doors, partitions, and bars cannot be used because of safety regulations, operations requirements, physical layout, and so forth.
3. They provide additional controls at critical points and areas.

Power Sources

All alarm systems terminating at a law enforcement agency should be equipped with a standby power source such as a portable generator. Requirements to ensure the continued operation of law enforcement agency-linked alarm systems in the event of power lapses or failures should be established. Underwriters' Laboratories, Inc., states the following specific requirements for standby battery power in their standard entitled "Police Station Connected Burglar Alarm Units and Systems":[1]

---

[1]"Private Security," report published by the National Advisory Committee on Criminal Justice Standards and Goals, 1976.

If a power supply with standby battery is provided, the battery shall have sufficient capacity to operate the system for periods as follows:

Bank alarms—72 hours,

Mercantile alarms in areas served by power facilities shown by experience to be dependable—4 hours.

Improving Door and Window Security

The majority of all burglary cases entry was gained through doors or windows.

Door and window security is a sound, simple, proven way to make a facility more secure. Yet, builders consistently use low-security hardware and materials; manufacturers continue to make locks that can be easily and quickly opened; and citizens do not voluntarily act to make their facilities more secure.

Target Hardening

Several publications containing helpful information for those considering the establishment of building security codes are available. *Security Planning for HUD-Assisted Multifamily Housing* is published by the U.S. Department of Housing and Urban Development. Chapter 4 of this booklet presents common sense information on target hardening that could be transposed into building (or code) ordinance form.

Adequate Security Lighting

Where appropriate, property should be adequately lighted to discourage criminal activity and enhance public safety. The benefits to be gained from improved lighting are great. Good lighting not only creates an effective physical barrier against criminal acts, but also provides increased surveillance opportunities. Adequate lighting is a form of self-defense. It provides a means of continuing a degree of protection approaching that which is maintained during daylight hours. Adequate lighting for approaches and entrances to building or facility not only discourages attempted unauthorized entry but also reveals persons within the area. Protective lighting also provides the best visibility practical for such duties as identification of badges and people at entrances—and for inspection of vehicles and prevention of illegal entry. Managers should better educate themselves on the crime displacement effect of localized adequate lighting.

Controlling Access

Whenever access must be controlled, employees must be provided with a means of personal identification. As appropriate, controlled access buildings and/or areas can then be established together with admittance and identification procedures for employees, visitors, vendors, and contractors.

A controlled building is definable as a building closed to the general public, so as to provide increased protection for building occupants, and preventing and/or controlling the loss or theft of organization and personal property. Several rules of thumb apply when a building or some part thereof is designated as being controlled:

1. All entrances except those absolutely necessary must be closed.
2. Where necessary, all open entrances should be staffed with security guards or receptionists.
3. Procedures must be in place covering positive identification of employees. One such positive identification of employees is the use of a photograph identification pass. Using a simple entity-wide identification card is not desirable in that access cannot be firmly controlled. Instead, consideration might be given towards separate types of identification (ID) cards for:
    a. Permanent full-time employees,
    b. Special access cards for sensitive or secure locations,

    c. Temporary and/or newly hired employees,

    d. Service and/or other similar nonemployees requiring ready access to certain areas.

4. Care must be taken during designated security hours to ensure that each person shows his ID card when entering and upon leaving controlled buildings. Additionally, ID cards should be worn visibly displayed on outer clothing at all times during prescribed security hours.

5. ID cards issued for access to buildings ought not grant access to specially designated security areas within such buildings. Admittance to such areas should be restricted by requirements prescribed for those areas by responsible officials.

6. It may be considered necessary to also have employees sign in and out when entering or leaving the building after normal duty hours. If the situation warrants, identification passes may be checked during duty hours.

7. Building entry should be restricted to only those persons with valid reasons for entering the building.

8. Consideration should be given to inspecting all packages being brought into the building.

9. Those operations which involve dealing with the general public, if possible, should be grouped and located near the entrance and/or the first floor of the building thereby reducing the need for the general public to wander throughout the building.

10. Careful consideration must be given to controlling access of members of the general public who must conduct business in the building. As a minimum they should be required to sign a register upon entering and leaving the area. In some installations they ought to be allowed to proceed only after a security employee has telephoned the visitors' destination to announce their presence. Other situations may call for them to be escorted by employees to their destination.

11. A good property and equipment control system is an

invaluable aid in helping minimize thefts. It is essential that a positive system be established to control movement of packages, material and property into and out of controlled locations. Any person removing property from a facility should have written permission. A property pass authorized by a designated official, and identifying the property to be removed, should be required. The pass should be given by the bearer to the guard as an individual leaves the facility. Examination of any property should be made when there is reasonable or probable cause to suspect a theft.

Other Considerations

FIRE PROTECTION. Fires occur more frequently when a building is occupied. However, the presence of people results in early detection and low fire losses. Guards should not be relied upon to detect and extinguish fires. A better way to ensure that fires will be limited and contained if they start, is to develop a fire protection plan based on a soundly built structure, adequately protected by fire alarms. Such plans must also consider the types of materials stored within the building and the kind of operations being conducted there. Special considerations for such activities must be built into your plan. A basic fire protection plan is better than leaving your guards with the responsibility of detecting fires and acting on that information.

CRITICAL OR SENSITIVE AREAS. Computer sites, telecommunication facilities, and life support functions (i.e., power, water, gas, ventilation, and so forth) are areas that require special consideration. Thought should be given to restricting entry into these areas to persons whose presence is not absolutely essential to operations. When such areas are not in use or occupied, they should be locked and the keys kept under strict control.

CHAPTER TEN

CONTROLLING ACCESS BY MECHANICAL MEANS

IDENTIFICATION TECHNIQUES[1]

The past decade has witnessed a dramatic increase in both the use of personal identification cards, primarily in access control and commercial transactions, and the use of photographs as the key identifier on those cards. Many businesses and large jurisdictions are turning to photo IDs, and more elaborate alternate delivery systems, as a means of controlling unrestricted access, and cutting back losses from forged and fraudulently cashed checks, credit cards, and the like.[1]

Unfortunately, along with the expanded use of photos, has come a significant increase in the counterfeiting and alteration of the cards. Essentially, any card that is photographed or has a photograph on it, can be rephotographed. Additionally, an individual can change his appearance to resemble a photograph of someone else. Therefore, a picture of an individual, while

[1]See Health and Human Services, *False Identification: The Problem and Technological Options*, Office of Inspector General (April 1983).

clearly the most widely accepted personal identifier, is no guarantee of the identity or the legitimacy of the cardholder. Other identifiers and/or security devices are needed on a card to provide reasonable assurance of identity. A combination of several techniques, discussed later in this chapter, including personal identifiers, secure paper and printing, and coding or electronic devices, provides the most effective deterrent to counterfeiting and tampering.

To repeat the obvious: if the "checker" of the ID is careless or casual about the process, then most techniques and methods will fail by definition. Training and management quality control techniques are important for success in any methodology.

Personal identifiers are needed to establish the connection between access or benefit authorization and the identity of an individual. As Professor Jacques Mathyer stated in a 1980 article for the *International Criminal Police Review*, ". . . a link must exist between the identity document and its bearer."[2] It is the personal identifiers that link the bearer (i.e., the individual) to the document. It is of paramount importance in the development of identity or authorization documents that those documents should be of no use to people other than their legitimate bearers.

Some of the most sophisticated research on identification technology has been conducted or sponsored by the Department of Defense and other Federal agencies. While their concern has been primarily access or entry control rather than personal identification per se, their analysis is equally appropriate to both. Sandia National Labs, in a study conducted for the Department of Energy on entry-control systems, cited three possible methods of identity verification:[3]

1. Something possessed by the individual (a key or credential)

[2]Mathyer, Jacques, "The Problem of Security and Identity and 'Authorization' Documents," *International Criminal Police Review* (March 1980): 66–79 (a publication of Interpol).
[3]Sandia National Laboratories, *Entry-Control Systems Handbook* (September 1980).

2. Something known by the individual; a memorized number or word, a Personal Identification Number (PIN)

3. A personal characteristic of the individual (a fingerprint, speech pattern, and so on).

While the latter method has commonly been considered as "what a person is," the category in reality includes not only innate unchangeable features, such as a fingerprint or the blood vessel pattern on the rear of the eyeball, but also acquired personal characteristics. These characteristics, including handwriting and certain voice patterns, among others, have been called by some "cultivated biometrics." Such characteristics are more vulnerable to imitation than are innate features.

One or another method may be seen in the personal identification techniques outlined later in this chapter, as can a further form of categorization—that of manual, machine-aided, and automatic systems.

As pointed out in the Sandia report, and by numerous specialists in the field, the verification error rates and resistance to counterfeiting of the different methods and techniques vary greatly. Every personal identity verification system, which may include one or more of the methods listed above, has the potential for verification errors that affect its accuracy or validity. These errors are categorized as:

1. Type I—Rejection of a claimed identity when the identity claimed is valid.

2. Type II—Acceptance of a claimed identity when the identity is false.

While Type I errors do not pose a threat to the integrity of the system, they do create an operational problem requiring the availability of an alternative or backup method to assure the acceptance of legitimate persons. Type II errors, on the other hand, demonstrate the vulnerability of the system to the casual imposter gaining access by claiming to be an authorized individual.

Ideally, neither type of error should occur. In practice, of course, they do. Indeed, they tend to act in opposition with one another, with the likelihood of Type II errors increasing as Type I errors are reduced. For a nuclear installation concerned with entry-control, for example, this inverse shift could be critical. For a state welfare department or other government agency concerned about benefits security, the possibility of moderate levels of Type I or II errors must be balanced against client inconvenience and the cost of a backup system. (That is not to say that welfare agencies should not be aware of verification error rates in designing a personal verification system. Rather, more attention should be paid to the susceptibility of the different identification techniques to counterfeiting and tampering.)

The following table lists several of the techniques of personal identification according to their vulnerability to such fraud and abuse. Fingerprint and voiceprint analysis are considered most resistant to counterfeiting because of the amount of information needed to obtain a necessary match. A PIN or memorized number is least resistant, due to the ease of collusion or sharing the number. As could be expected, automated techniques fare much better than manual techniques, which rely on the time and judgment of the viewer; however, they are also much more expensive.

RELATIVE RESISTANCE TO COUNTERFEITING

Identification Technique	Resistance Level
1. Retinal Imagery	High
2. Fingerprint (automated)	
3. Voiceprint Analysis (speech)	
4. Signature Dynamics	High/Medium
5. Hand Geometry	
6. Palm Print (automated)	
7. Handwriting (manual)	Medium
8. Fingerprint (manual)	

9. Video Comparator   Low
10. Photograph (manual)
11. Personal Identification
    Number (PIN)

IDENTIFICATION TECHNIQUES

Retinal Blood Vessel Pattern. Automated system using a fundus camera to obtain and match unique retinal pattern.

Automated Fingerprint Techniques. Digital coding and recognition of minutiae and ridge endings for computer-based storage and retrieval of fingerprint data; Holographic recordings of fingerprints and recognition of same using lasers and optical correlation technology.

Voiceprint Analysis. The recording and analysis of speech segment spectrograms and processes to automate spectrogram analysis.

Signature Dynamics. Automated handwriting verification utilizing velocity, acceleration, and pressure as a function of time.

Automated Hand Geometry Measurements. Optical or mechanical scanning of certain hand dimensions to obtain a unique personal code for automated comparison against a central file or a magnetic stripe.

Automated Palm Print Recognition. Optical scanning and digital encoding of palm prints for automated comparison.

Handwriting Analysis. Manual method of comparing signatures, usually used for retail transactions or check cashing purposes.

Finger or Thumb Prints (Manual). Various techniques for enhancing the practicality of manually obtaining and recognizing fingerprints.

Machine-Aided Photographic Techniques. Video comparator systems, where a securely stored image is used for comparison with a real-time image of the individual who is seeking entry of check cashing privileges; Three-dimensional photo credit card with card printer which transfers photo with embossed number onto back of documents or checks.

Personal Photography Techniques (Manual).   A wide range of procedures and equipment frequently used to produce credit or ID cards bearing a person's photograph, signature, and certain descriptive information (may include a photo insert, a full photo of person and data, or a portrait photo); Various black-and-white and color photographic techniques including wet and dry processing alternatives (including printing on bank note paper); A protected identity system for enhancing personal recognition through the use of three simultaneously taken photographs of an individual (full front, three-quarter, and profile views); Invisible photographs only observable under ultraviolet light source.

Passwords.   Identification by recording in the document information which must be remembered by the bearer, but which is unknown to others. Could include Personal Identification Number (PIN).

DOCUMENT SECURITY: PROTECTING AGAINST COUNTERFEITING

Techniques are needed to assure or improve the odds of cardholder authenticity, card validity, and benefits security (that is, making sure the proper recipient receives the correct benefit) the three remaining critical features of a card. Machine-readable codes and automated access systems, while gaining increased acceptance among high security agencies and industries and large welfare benefit paying organizations, continue to take a back seat to the document or card protection methods to be discussed later. Cost, and the availability of a good number of manufacturers, largely explains why.

Document security techniques relate to print and paper security and document lamination. The related subject of

Automated Data Processing (ADP) security, an issue of utmost concern to all organizations, is treated elsewhere in this book.

Printing and paper techniques, with only a few recent exceptions (discussed later in this chapter) have long been used to protect currency and other documents of value (for example, stock and bond certificates) from attempts at counterfeiting and alteration. While providing little inherent security themselves, with the possible exception of intaglio or steel engraved printing in combination, several features can effectively deter all but the most serious counterfeiter. Their protection is in the intricacy of the designs or artwork, the use of multiple tints, and the backup security of invisible or fluorescent inks or paper planchettes.

The Intaglio Process

The use of multiple or prismatic tints, in lithography or offset printing, largely prevents an accurate reproduction through photocopying. A complex, fine-line design is needed, however, to prevent duplication due to the large number of people or firms capable of doing offset work. Intaglio, on the other hand, is a process limited to only a few private companies and the U.S. Bureau of Engraving and Printing. It is widely used in the manufacture of paper currency. With the appearance of variable ink tones, achievable by controlling the depth of the engravings, and a three-dimensional printed surface, intaglio is both extremely difficult to duplicate and to photograph. Still, the use of an intricate design is highly recommended by all the experts in the field.

Latent Images

The latent image, a relatively new process, uses an elaborate steel engraved design to hide a special image which becomes apparent when the angle of the paper is adjusted. It is being used extensively now in the printing of bonds and other securities. The image would not be clearly visible if the document were laminated. The key to the effectiveness of all these printing and paper techniques, of course, lies in the ability of the viewer to detect the counterfeit or altered card. This involves both training as to the way an authentic card should look, and possible penalties should a bad card be passed.

Added Protection

While printing methods, combined with one or more paper security devices, go far to guarantee card validity, cardholder authentication requires the added protection of micro-line or scrambled indicia printing and a secure laminate or film. The two printing techniques, applied over the data portion of the card and possible part of the photograph, prevent both effective photocopying and alteration of the existing card. That is, neither the date nor the photograph (that is any area covered) can be changed without noticeably breaking the image on the line or scrambled background. When using the indicia printing, it should be kept in mind that the single color print has been successfully photographed while the multi-tint has not. As is the case with all security techniques, the agency or user must determine the level of security needed and the expense that can be borne. Each feature will add to the total cost of the card.

Lamination Techniques and Problems

Lamination, or the process of affixing a thin layer or sheet of material over an insert (for example, a card), further enhances card security while providing increased resistance to moisture, dirt, wear, and aging. Several techniques are currently being used for laminating documents and cards. The most common consists of a polyester film coated with a polyethylene adhesive. Complete encapsulation of the card is achieved by placing the card between two sheets of film slightly larger than the card, and applying heat and pressure to activate the adhesive. Unfortunately, just as heat can aid the adhesion, so can it be used to break it, particularly at the edges of the card. Tampering, therefore, is a possibility.

There is a second type of lamination consisting of a similar thin polyester base that largely ensures against tampering or alteration. This technique utilizes an acrylic thermosetting adhesive which cannot later be separated by applying heat. It is extremely difficult to remove without damaging the photograph or data. The effect can be enhanced by using a nondurable, fibrous paper stock for the insert, or the newly developed "Tyvec," which is itself polyester. For a government agency concerned with benefits security (i.e., getting benefits to the correct person(s)), this protection against tampering is extremely important.

In both types of polyester lamination, several additional features may be incorporated to increase overall card security:

1.   Preprinting the film with an overall pattern of fine lines which would be hard to duplicate or counterfeit

2.   Preprinting emblems or seals in either a regular or random pattern

3.   Preprinting a visible or invisible design on the film which will fluoresce under UV or black light.

Using any of these techniques would result in a design appearing over the card or insert but under the polyester laminate, making it even more difficult to alter or counterfeit.

Other lamination techniques exist, the most notable being that used in credit cards—that is, several layers of polyvinyl chloride (PVC) fused together under pressure and heat. The printing is generally applied directly to the PVC, though a paper insert can be used if soaked with a liquid vinyl coating before fusing. The resultant card can be used with a wide variety of machine-readable codes and magnetic stripes and is quite difficult to alter. It may also be used to house memory chips and recorded infrared data. However, the primary security of these encoded "smart cards" is based on automated technology. Unless additional security is built into the insert, they are fairly easy to duplicate. All codes can be broken.

A further word of caution is in order. An all-PVC card (i.e., one made solely out of PVC) when cooled to room temperature becomes brittle. It is easily cracked or broken which, of course, interferes with card use and machine readability. For that reason, most credit card companies and banks recommend annual or at least biannual reissuance. For an agency concerned with improved durability and cost, an available alternative is mylar. Used strictly for the card's central core, it does the same job as PVC but is not fragile. It can be handled frequently and even bent without breaking.

A final type of lamination material, worth considering because of its effective resistance to both successful alteration or counterfeiting, is a patented retro-reflective transparent film that is laminated to the face of a completed document or card. Tiny glass spheres in the thin film of adhesive material can be positioned to produce a customized overall pattern or random design that becomes visible when seen under a simple light viewer. Any altering, tampering, or counterfeiting appears under the light as a break or change in the continuous pattern, or simply as a lack of pattern. Three levels of security can be added during the development process for agencies particularly concerned with access or benefit protection. While documents using this film initially suffered from a lack of durability in that it could originally be applied only to paper, it can positively identify an individual. In that any type of coded credential can be decoded and duplicated given sufficient time and resources, it is imperative that an agency or facility requiring moderate-to-high security utilize one or more personal identifiers in conjunction with the coding. Agencies with low-to-moderate security needs, and an already secure identification card, may not need coded credentials unless their access system is automated.

Types of Coded Credentials

Considerations for using coded credentials or ID cards and their relative resistance to counterfeiting and decoding should entail the "whole" system. They may be grouped roughly into three categories:

1. *Low Resistance*—Regular (low-energy) magnetic stripe, proximity, and electric circuit coded badges are all easy to decode and duplicate.

2. *Moderate Resistance*—Metallic strip, magnetic spot, and optical coded badges are difficult to decode and duplicate, as is the high-energy (high-coersivity) magnetic stripe.

3. *High Resistance*—Active electronic, capacitance, infrared, coded badges are all difficult to decode and require extremely special equipment to duplicate.

SUMMING UP

There are a number of alternate issuance systems and secure identification cards that can provide the capability of radically reducing the incidence of lost, stolen, forged, and fraudulently cashed checks while, at the same time, improving the integrity of systems as a whole. See Figure 10.1 for manufacturers of identification systems. Technological advances, particularly in

Company	Location	Chief Product
AB ID Kort	Sweden	ID cards
Addressograph Multigraph Corp.	Mountainside, NJ	Printing
Agfa-Gevaert Corp.	Teterboro, NJ	"Agiss" ID card
American Bank Note Co.	Bronx, NJ	Printing and engraving
Appleton Paper Co.	Wisconsin	Papers
Avant, Inc.	Concord, MA	Coded credentials— — Mag. stripe
BAI Corp.	Stamford, CT	ID cards
Battelle Institute	Columbus, Ohio	Consultants, applications analysis

FIGURE 10.1 A partial list of industrial manufacturers of Identification Systems (Note that this field is changing rapidly and this listing may not be all inclusive.)

Company	Location	Chief Product
Bello ID Systems, Inc.	West Haven, CT	Photo credit ID machine
Bogen, Photo Corp.	Englewood, NJ	Photo ID
Burroughs, Corp.	Leonia, NJ	On-line systems
Caid, Inc.	Dover, DE	ID cards
Calumet Photographic, Inc.	Elk Grove, IL	Photo IDs
Cardkey Systems	Chatsworth, CA	Magnetic spot encoding
Carters Ink Company	Crossville, TN	Printing, inks
Cii Honeywell-Bull	France	Smart cards
Clarion Corp.	Bethesda, MD	"Cardinal" infra-red cards
COE Manufacturing Co.	El Toro, CA	Photo IDs
Computer Gesellschaft	Konstanz, Germany	Optical reader
Computer Identification Systems, Inc.	Sacramento, CA	Engraved photo card
Control Data Dorp.	Rockville, MD	On-line systems
Dactech Int., Inc.	Van Nuys, CA	Photo IDs
Data Card Corp.	Minneapolis, MI	ID cards
Datakey	Burnsville, MI	Smart card systems
Datatype Corp.	Greenwich, CT	ID cards
DEK Products	Ft. Wayne, IN	Photo IDs
Del Norte Technology	Euless, TX	Magnetic spot encoding
Digi-Data Corp.	Bladensburg, MD	Coded badges
Morgan Adhesives Co.	Stow, OH	Adhesives/lamination
National Cash Register	Dayton, OH	Readers, terminals
North American Rockwell, Microelectronics Co.	Anaheim, CA	Electronics
Norton Door Controls	Charlotte, NC	Electric circuit badges
Optronics International	Cambridge, MA	Optical readers
Phillips Data Systems	Holland	Smart cards
Plastron Systems, Inc.	Wellesley, MA	Laminates
Polaroid Corp.	Cambridge, MA	Photo ID cards, "Polaproof" film
Potdeven Machine Co.	Teterboro, NJ	Printing machines
Roehlen Engraving Co.	Rochester, NY	Printing and engraving
Royal Copier Products	Englewood, NJ	ID cards
Rusco Electronics	Glendale, CA	Magnetic spot encoding
Saxon Business Products	Miami Lakes, FL	ID cards

FIGURE 10.1 *(Continued)*

Company	Location	Chief Product
Schlage Electronics	Santa Clara, CA	Proximity badge encoding
Scott Graphics, Inc.	Holyoke, MA	Printing
Secom	Culver City, CA	Infrared optical encoding
Sensor Engineering Co.	Hamden, CT	Wiegand-effect badge
Stellar Systems, Inc.	San Jose, CA	Hand geometry
Sweda	Carlstadt, NJ	Readers/terminals
Sycon, Inc.	Santa Clara, CA	Sycon SD-10 (signature verification)
Systematics Incorporated	Piscataway, NJ	Wiegand-effect badge
Texas Instruments	Dallas, TX	On-line systems, voiceprint analysis
Thomas DeLaRue International, Ltd.	Basingstoke, England	Printing and engraving
United States Plasfilm Corp.	New York, NY	Laminates
U.S. Bank Note Co.	Philadelphia, PA	Printing and engraving
U.S Research & Development Corp.	Des Plaines, IL	Consulting
Vernon Plastics Corp.	Haverhill, MA	Laminates
Vikonics, Inc.	New York, NY	Magnetic spot encoding
Western Data Products, Inc.	Los Angeles, CA	ID cards
Western Financial Printing Co.	Los Angeles, CA	Printing
Xerox Corporation	Mountainside, NJ	On-line systems

FIGURE 10.1 *(Continued)*

electronics and automated systems, offer organizations an ever-widening array of techniques for personal identification, document security, controlled access, and benefits security that was not available 10 years ago. Of course, the effectiveness and costs of the individual techniques vary greatly, as the preceding discussion suggests.

No one system is appropriate or cost-effective for all users. Combinations are often advisable. However, no one can legitimately question the nationwide magnitude of the problem of false identification. What can and should be questioned is whether the size or scope of an individual organization's losses or security vulnerabilities warrants the development of a more secure system.

CHAPTER ELEVEN

THE PROBLEM OF FALSE IDENTIFICATION

HISTORY AND BACKGROUND

Our society is very dependent on identification documents in order to conduct business. People no longer live in small hamlets, and businessmen no longer intimately know those they do business with. The 19th century Industrial Revolution changed all that when people began migrating in ever-increasing numbers to larger towns and cities. Now, we deal with strangers whose identity and reputation are unknown to us. Because of this, we now depend on written substitutes (i.e., paper or plastic documentation) to attest to our identities. In lieu of cash, we use checks and credit cards—which in some instances must be supported by "breeder documents" that establish the basic identity—birth certificates, Social Security cards, or driver's license.

Thus, identification cards or other official documents are used by almost all developed and developing countries to both provide the populace with a legal identity and to allow them to participate in a variety of activities and benefits. While the U.S. has been reluctant to establish a national identification system, bank cards, alien identification cards ("green card"), passports, Social Security cards, and two critical state or city issued documents—birth certificates and driver's licenses—are routinely used to establish both a person's identity and eligibility for a wide range of benefits and services. Consider how difficult it is to cash a check at a bank or retail outlet without some form of identification—preferably one that includes visual identifiers such as a photo and a signature.

THE EXTENT OF THE PROBLEM

Today, the criminal use of false identification is big business. False identification is the primary *modus operandi* in such crimes as fraud against business or government, illegal immigration, drug smuggling, terrorism, and flight from justice. In fact, if there is one common denominator between the welfare cheat, illegal alien, smuggler, terrorist, bad check artist, and fugitive from justice, it is probably that they all used some form of false identification.

You will probably recall a shocking news item that illustrates this point: During the summer of 1982, the media reported that during a security test in 1982, seven counterterrorist experts, *using forged credentials,* infiltrated the government's Savannah River nuclear weapons plant, seized hostages, and took over the control room of a large atomic reactor.[1] This demonstrated the vulnerability of our weapons facilities to theft and sabotage. Thus entry-control systems remain a major worry.

The use of false I.D.s is a mode of procedure rather than a separate category of crime. Thus, it is difficult to accurately quantify the losses to the public and private sector because of crimes involving false identification. But it is clear that the

---

[1]This was a widely reported item in the news media. This particular item was excerpted in part from a *Washington Post* article published during the summer of 1982.

public is the ultimate victim. In 1976, the Federal Advisory Committee on False Identification estimated that crimes involving false identification cost the American public and business $15 billion annually.[2] In 1982, the staff of Senator William V. Roth's Permanent Subcommittee on Investigations updated that estimate to $24 billion. Whatever the figure, it is a horrendous price tag. Of all the areas, fraud in Government benefit programs is probably one of the most difficult to quantify. The Federal Advisory Committee on False Identification believed ". . . these losses could easily number in the billions of dollars." In June 1985 a report "Delegate Recommendations to the Fifth Conference on the Judiciary" was released which addressed in part the report of the Task Force on the criminal implications of false identification. As stated in the report ". . . the subject of false identification and its impacts is both vast and complex . . . ." Thus the Task Force "limited its deliberations to the three types of Federal identification documents (Social Security cards, immigration documents, and passports) and the impacts of false identification-related crimes involving these documents on large state and locally administered programs". A copy of the Task Force's report is shown in Appendix VI.

False identification documents and cards can be purchased in virtually any city in the country. Document vendors along our southern borders sell counterfeit U.S. immigration documents and border crossing cards for whatever the traffic will bear. Mail-order businesses supply blank birth certificates and baptismal certificate forms. Individuals cut open laminated driver's licenses, replace photos, alter data, and then relaminate. Driver's licenses and birth certificates are termed "breeder documents," because they are base documents that can be used to generate others. A number of cases illustrating this situation in the world of computer-based payment systems is shown in Appendix V.

[2]FACFI, *The Criminal Use of False Identification*, November 1976, p. xii. Report of the Task Force on Criminal Implications of False Identification Laws at Work, fifth Conference on the Judiciary, Los Angeles, CA May 23–24, 1984.

Using counterfeit or altered breeder documents, a person can obtain almost any other kind of "valid" identification document, cash stolen checks, obtain welfare benefits, or participate in a broader range of criminal activity. It is not surprising, therefore, that the control of document fraud is becoming a major concern of Government and businesses alike, and the focus of intense technological review.

SCOPE OF THE FALSE ID PROBLEM

It is important to examine some of the problems relating to proper documentation and some possible solutions, or at least considerations in accepting one's identity from documentation. In *The Criminal Use of False Identification*[3], the Federal Advisory Committee on False Identification (FACFI) provided the following generally accepted definitions:

Alteration. Abuse of a legitimate document by changing significant elements such as name, photo, age, or physical description of the legitimate bearer.

Counterfeiting. Unauthorized creation of a complete document by an unauthorized source to support a false identity (may include use of genuine blank official forms).

We must add a third category known in the financial community, *"false applications."* In those cases, a seemingly legitimate document is issued and a file established in the system to match it. The document, however, is invalid because the information used to generate it, or to establish eligibility, was false. These cases are probably the most difficult to detect and to eliminate.

The False Identification Crime Control Act of 1982 (Public Law 97-398) was passed in recognition of the growing problem

[3]U.S. Department of Justice. "The Criminal Use of False Identification" *The Report of the Federal Advisory Committee on False Identification* (November 1976).

of false identification and the need for specific legislation to deter crimes involving false identification. The Act has two primary purposes: (1) it allows prosecution and conviction for offenses involving federal identification documents, including counterfeiting and trafficking in counterfeits; and (2) it creates certain federal offenses specifically relating to counterfeiting and trafficking in counterfeit or stolen state, local, or foreign identification documents. The intent of this legislation, however, cannot be fully realized without strong enforcement priorities and innovative and cooperative techniques on the part of federal law enforcement agencies.

Although the bulk of the information that follows relates to federal activities, many of the techniques and practices discussed can be adopted by the private sector in combatting problems they face due to false identification. The federal government has had problems controlling the simplistic Social Security identification card. It has been a giant problem for the Social Security Administration (SSA).

On August 13, 1982, Senator Moynihan (D-N.Y.) announced that the Social Security Administration would begin issuing a new tamperproof card printed on bank note paper in 1983. SSA has been under heavy attack for several years over its handling of Social Security cards and the number issuance process. Fake, or illegally obtained Social Security cards are being used regularly by criminal and illegal aliens to obtain work, cash checks, and apply for welfare and other benefits. The total dollar value of the fraud perpetrated is unknown.

The HHS Inspector General has investigated numerous cases of schemes to manufacture, obtain, distribute, or use fraudulent Social Security Number (SSN) cards. These cards are of particular interest and value to illegal aliens, as illustrated by the following instances:

One investigation exposed a four-year, assemblyline operation. The six conspirators included a Social Security Administration employee. The group printed SSN applications and documentation in a Los Angeles warehouse, processed them through an SSA data center, and then sold the cards to illegal aliens.

In New York, an auxiliary police officer pleaded guilty to selling counterfeit SSNs and bogus Puerto Rican birth certificates to illegal aliens.

Project Baltimore. An ongoing investigative effort by the HHS Office of Inspector General, the Immigration and Naturalization Service (INS), and the SSA. It focuses on criminal conspiracies to obtain SSNs for illegal aliens. This work has resulted in hundreds of convictions and deportation hearings for illegal aliens.

Project SSNAPBACK. Involves working with the Immigration and Naturalization Service to inform states of the particular SSNs that have been used by deported aliens to gain benefits or assistance to which they are not entitled.

"False Identification: The Problem and Technological Solutions" (April 1983). A report prepared as a technical assistance reference for state and local welfare agencies. It describes and analyzes the range of available identification and alternate issuance techniques and their usefulness in reducing fraud and abuse.

Project Clean Data. A computer application designed to detect false identities. It looks for invalid or fraudulently obtained SSNs. This program has been distributed to over 100 agencies in 43 states to look for erroneous SSNs and false identities, in their welfare rolls.

In addition, it should be noted that the Immigration and Naturalization Service developed Project SAVE, an online query capability that can be provided to states for checking alien status. INS estimates that $10 billion could be saved annually using this project nationwide. It is working with a number of states to implement the capability.

Another facet of the false identification problem involves people who use counterfeit degrees and certificates supporting their applications for professional credentials and/or licences. HHS' Inspector General is working with Postal Inspectors in their investigations of persons who have obtained medical credentials through such fraudulent methods. It has been estimated that thousands of "doctors" have phoney degrees from foreign universities. Two medical schools in the Dominican Republic, for example, were being investigated by that government for awarding fraudulent medical degrees. Disclosing such frauds protects both the public and the Medicare and Medicaid programs from any scams arising from billings by such people.

PROBLEMS AND ANSWERS IN IDENTIFICATION TECHNOLOGY

There are almost an infinite number of techniques and products currently available that can be considered when developing an identification card or system. These include a wide range of personal identifiers, document security methods, and machine-readable codes. Techniques vary greatly both in terms of cost and of the security provided. A thoughtful decision can be made as to an appropriate care configuration (i.e., design specifications) only through a comprehensive analysis of current losses, system needs (including administrative costs), and vulnerabilities.

ID Card Standards

While no national technical standards currently exist, a great deal can be learned from work done by several research groups and from the standardization activities of the American National Standards Institute (ANSI), the International Civil Aviation Organization (ICAO), and the American Bankers Association (ABA).

Burroughs Corporation, in a study conducted for the U.S. Passport Office, on magnetic techniques, identified aspects relating to the production of a machine-readable passport that are equally appropriate when considering ID card development.[4] Adapted slightly to identification card format or need, the considerations mentioned in that study included:

The question of size and physical format (card, tag, or book).

The type of encoding that should be used (bar code, magnetics, embossing).

Whether there should be a relationship between the ID and some national identity card.

The consequences of adopting a system which is implemented by some but not all the affected parties, that is, a voluntary versus mandatory system.

The format and layout of the card, including the information to be encoded.

The question of machine readability of the clear print zone.

The sociopolitical consequences of having magnetic encoded information visible to the human eye.

Basic antiforgery/counterfeiting provisions.

Measures to prevent obtaining valid ID cards by fraudulent means.

Design criteria and specifications for card manufacturing equipment, reader terminals, and related interfaces to computers (including the issuance process).

In 1974, the ICAO defined the qualifications of an identification document for passport purposes more concisely, detailing specific requirements.[5] Of the nineteen listed, twelve may be considered critical when designing a secure ID card. The card must be:

Designed to uniquely identify the bearer (in a simple and visual way).

[4]Burroughs Corporation, *Magnetic Techniques Study*, August 1977. Study work for the U.S. Department of State.

[5]International Civil Aviation Organization, *Working Paper on Passport Travel Document* (April 1974).

Difficult to alter, to deter, or to prevent unauthorized modification.

Difficult to counterfeit.

Easy to use and understand (use of standardized features).

Durable (3 to 5 years).

Designed for machine readability (optional, though clearly preferable).

Convenient to carry (that is, of a size, weight, and flexibility to encourage retention on one's person).

Designed to contain a unique identification number (necessary for the administrative aspects of issuing and handling the document in a secure and organized manner).

Cost competitive with other similar cards.

Capable of being produced under a secure production environment.

Nationally acceptable as a standard card configuration (optional though certainly preferable).

Designed to allow for a statement indicating special status of the bearer (for example, for the federal government, a food stamp authorized representative or public assistance representative payee).

Document Security

Generally refers to a system that will give a high probability of accurate identification while minimizing the likelihood of counterfeiting or tampering. While document fraud has an accepted meaning, the objectives of document security vary among groups (for example, banks, businesses, welfare departments, and military installations). Banks and retail outlets want assurance that bad or forged checks are not being passed. Welfare agencies want to be sure that benefits are being received only by those eligible for them. High security industries and government installations are primarily concerned with access control (that is, prevention of unauthorized intrusion) and protection of information and materials rather than personal data on a card. The common denominator for all of these organizations is how to keep their own costs down while increasing the cost and difficulty of defrauding the system.

Many techniques are currently available that make ID cards and systems harder to break, and others are under development. However, *there is no known ID card that is totally fraud or counterfeit proof!* It is up to each user to determine which combination of security features is best suited to his policy objectives, technical requirements, and budgets. An accurate assessment by the user of current losses and document security needs is highly recommended prior to selecting a system for identification.

In discussing secure identification systems, one must distinguish between (1) ID card technology and (2) the whole range of issues involved in document security. It should be remembered that false identification is a much broader issue. The relatively easy acquisition of fraudulent birth certificates and driver's licenses greatly complicates or impedes the utility of "secure" ID cards, which are issued based on those state-issued documents.

Observe what takes place the next time you renew your driver's license. It can, indeed, be a simple task to obtain a second or third license. One need, in many cases, only assert that the original was lost and then go through a relatively easy process to obtain a duplicate. Similarly, almost every municipality has a rather simple process that applicants may follow to get a new certification of birth, a facsimile, or a copy of the original document.

Requisites for an Adequate ID Card Design

These cards must be considerd "documents of value," and should be able to provide four critical features to protect both the cardholder and the issuance authority:

1. *Personal identification:* Guarantees the cardholder an identity and enables him to cash checks as well as participate in

a wide range of activities available to that group (for example, U.S citizens, students, membership clubs). Personal identifiers range from the most simple photograph or signature to the most elaborate laser-drawn image of the retina.

2. *Cardholder authentication:* Guarantees that you are indeed the individual to whom the card was issued and that you cannot cash checks or securities made out to someone else or gain access improperly to controlled facilities. The importance of a tamperproof card is particularly apparent here.

3. *Card validity:* Assures that the card itself is a legitimate article that has been produced by the particular bank, business, or government agency. It is capable of delivering whatever benefits or services are normally attached. Counterfeit cards harm both the legitimate issuance agent and the legitimate user.

4. *Benefits security:* Refers to the losses realized by both the issuance agent and the honest beneficiary and, in the case of government benefits, the public taxpayer, from the use of false identification cards. In the welfare arena, these losses include stolen and forged public assistance checks and Food Stamp Authorizations to Purchase (ATPs), cashing multiple warrants using several "identities," illegally obtaining employment benefits, etc. A secure card should guarantee that, to the degree possible, benefits will go to only those persons truly eligible for them.

Identity cards, with or without a photo, should be likened to security documents—the same as currency. Both identification documents and paper currency are subjected to more or less the same risks. Consequently, ID cards should be able to resist both accidental and intentional misuse. They should be designed so that even from cursory checking, the legitimate bearer can be "identified," while anyone misusing the card, fraudulently or not, may be intercepted and questioned.

Identification technology, as well as the public's recognition and acceptance of ID card use, has grown tremendously in the last decade. With the increasing reliance on electronics and the computer, technological advances in identification and benefits security can be expected to become even more sophisticated in the coming years.

Recently, a task force of concerned federal officials released a report on the Criminal Implications of False Identification, at the Fifth Conference of the Judiciary.[6] The report noted that the evolutionary changes taking place in the ways people transact business with one another as a result of computerization. It recognized that its recommendations had to be seen as part of the urgent need to control access to burgeoning computer based data. In this context, the report presented a number of practical recommendations in the following areas:

The Federal False Identification Crime Control Act of 1982 (Public Law 97-398) was passed in recognition of the growing problem of false identification and the need for specific legislation to deter crimes involving false identification. Thus it was recommended that increased emphasis be placed on investigating and prosecuting cases under this and other existing statutes. The report also urged development of improved investigative techniques and intelligence and information networks to aggressively ferret out identification fraud schemes and profiles.

Recognizing that technology does exist both to secure documents against counterfeiting and alteration and to provide positive personal identification, it was recommended that full dissemination be made of information about these techniques, cost-effective use of these techniques in document production, and a full public information campaign to educate managers and the public to recognize new document features.

The report stated that computer matching and other automated verification techniques were some of the most effective tools to assure against false identification crimes. Thus, it recommended that state and federal program managers maximize the use of automated techniques, where

[6]See Appendix VI excerpts from Fifth Conference on the Judiciary.

cost-effective, in lieu of manual document verification processes.

The birth certificate, a breeder document for almost any other kind of identification for citizens, is issued by over 7,000 state and local jurisdictions. The report urged a review and comparison of best issuance practices with a view toward development of minimum voluntary standards for the contents, formatting and quality of documents, and verification of applicants for new or replacement documents.

Prevention of false identification frauds in benefit programs should focus on the front-end or initial eligibility verification processes in these programs. Because of this it recommended a cataloging and exchange of effective automated front-end verification techniques for the common eligibility factors of federal and state benefit programs.

These recommendations reflect both the concern and the variety of ways that managers can use current technology and cooperative projects and approaches to address the problems of false identification. We all recognize, however, that support for these efforts and their goals is necessary not only at federal, state, and local government levels, but also among the public at large. Public awareness of the scope and impact of false identification and support for measures to counter the problem are essential if we are to check the pervasiveness and cost of false identification related crimes.

COUNTERMEASURE FOR BUSINESS

It is axiomatic to say "for every way that a businessman can make a buck, there are at least two ways that same dollar can be stolen by a crook." The balance of this chapter will address what business can do to protect itself against being ripped off by bad identification.

As was previously pointed out, we depend on documents for identification because we deal with strangers. Knowing how easy it is to obtain false identification alerts us to the vulnerability of that dependence. The further removed from our immediate environment, the greater the dependency on the documents being presented.

Therefore, the first lesson is to treat documentation with ever-increasing suspicion and scrutiny. This is particularly true when you are dealing with those pieces of paper called "checks." Extra care should be given to checks and supporting documentation when such checks are nonlocal. Look for inconsistencies in the supporting identification such as differences in names, addresses, and so forth. Any time a number is associated with an individual (such as, birth date, employee number, Social Security Number, license number) it should be noted.

Many kinds of documents are of poor risk as they are easily obtained, forged or duplicated. For example, the Social Security card was not designed or ever intended for identification purposes. Until quite recently, all such cards were easily duplicated, and only a tiny portion of the new cards that are less subject to tampering are in existence at this time. Other documents that are questionable because of the (1) lack of general recognition and acceptance, (2) common misuse, or (3) easy access or tampering include:

bank books
birth or hospital certificates
library cards
work permits
driver's learner permits
organization or business cards
voter's registration cards
selective service cards
credit cards

Needless to say, any identification bearing a signature should be compared to other documents and the individual's own signature done in one's presence.

PART FIVE

OPPORTUNITY

CHAPTER TWELVE

DENYING OPPORTUNITY THROUGH USING PROPER SETS OF RULES AND CONTROLS

Opportunity Defined

"1. A combination of circumstances favorable for the purpose.
2. A good chance or occasion."

WEBSTER'S NEW WORLD DICTIONARY

IN THE WORLD OF BUSINESS WITH INTERNAL CONTROL SYSTEMS

Thus far in the book we have observed there are (1) worthwhile targets all around us awaiting to be criminally attacked, (2) many people predisposed to criminality or under sufficient stress that they might engage in it, and (3) available access to those targets by those people. Therefore, fraud and other forms of criminality are an ever-present possibility in just about any setting. However, there still needs to be the invitation or the opportunity for the crime to take place. The organization's system of controls must be so poorly structured so as to provide the proper temptation for someone to attempt the crime with what they perceive to be reasonable chances of success, and a belief that they will be able to avoid detection and/or prosecution. Even otherwise honest, upstanding citizens have become criminals because the temptation was too great against the needs of the moment.

To one degree or another, we are all aware that to reduce the invitation to criminal behavior, organizations need to put policies and procedures into place to discourage would-be wrongdoers from engaging in criminality. This process is commonly called "Developing an internal control system." An internal control system can be defined as the plan of an organization to safeguard its targets and to assure that its resources and assets are used effectively and properly.

To reduce opportunities for would-be attackers to engage in criminality, internal controls need to be in place to ensure, among other things, that (1) there is proper authorization on the use of all resource and assets in accordance with applicable laws, ordinances, and regulations; (2) transactions are executed in accordance with management directions; (3) full accountability is maintained over all resources and assets; and (4) transactions are fully and properly recorded.

The whole area of internal controls is probably the most important subject now being wrestled with by investigators, auditors (internal and external), reviewers and management. Such controls (or rather sets of controls), consist of safeguards and personnel screening—all of which are inherent in every operational phase of any business operation, whether it be private or public. People at all levels of any industry must be concerned with internal controls.

Not the least of the problem in this vitally conceptual area is the ambiguity of the term "internal control" itself, and the varied interpretations and emphasis that managers give it. Furthermore, the concept of "materiality" as it applies to internal controls is also murky. We ought not be concerned with controlling trivia. Our emphasis must be placed on important assets and liabilities and the people who have the responsibility to account for them.

It is very difficult for individual professionals in the auditing arena to be fully competent, meet all required standards, be protective of clients' interests—and still be cost-beneficial and affordable. Two main thrusts appear to be the most responsive and workable, as large solutions.

1. There must be more interrelated and interdependent, combinative efforts, between all concerned parties. The focal point for this effort is seemingly self-evident: "management." Only management is capable of orchestrating and maximizing the efforts of all the other players. Only management can set the proper organizational attitude so vital for real internal control and accurate data bases. They can provide internal auditors with sufficient strength and competency to materially assist their external auditors in their periodic attestations.

2. The second, and probably more profound solution, lies in filling the fundamental need for better trained and educated independent auditors, who can cope with computer age complexities. This doesn't necessarily mean more specialization, for one can "buy" into that—statisticians, computer programmers, and the like. Rather, auditors are needed who have a firmer grasp of the fundamentals, more logical thinking and a global or renaissance outlook. These attributes will enable them to deal with the full range of business perspectives that management is vitally concerned with. After all, a really good auditor must know what good business practices are to begin with!

These are broad and basic general answers to the question— how does management act to restrain or impede a potential wrongdoer, and reduce opportunities for wrongdoing to a minimum? Effective *internal controls*, of course.

An organization with effective checks and balances that

internally harnesses its functions and processes can feel generally secure that few opportunities exist for wrongdoing. Well-controlled organizations function under pragmatic and cohesive sets of operational techniques. They should be pragmatic in the sense that the various systems and subsystems should be cost beneficial. More should not be spent in each situation than is at stake to control!

Informal controls need to be cohesive in that each organizational element should function in assisting and controlling each other's objectives. Opportunities for misdeeds can be contained. Wrongdoing can be limited to minor inadvertencies.

No matter which category they fall into, "problems" basically and fundamentally occur in an organization because of some critical breakdown that has occurred in its essential internal control system—either in the internal controls over its "Administrative Functions" or its "Accounting Processes." The distinction between these two aspects of internal controls must be considered in its most profound and broadest aspect.

Most internal control considerations or reviews to determine the degree of any organization's vulnerabilities or the adequacy of its mechanisms for data retrieval, center about its accounting processes. However, these are "processes," as distinguished from "functions." Processes are important; there is no attempt to minimize them or downplay their importance, and managers must have a healthy and natural concern for their impact. However, an organization's major and overriding concern should be centered on (1) the reliability of its administrative functions and (2) its own management's attitude toward honest and straightforward operations.

Walter E. Hanson,[1] in his "Focus on Fraud," describes how a company might contain fraud through three closely related functions: (1) a strong, involved, investigative board of directors, (2) a sound, comprehensive system of internal controls, and (3) alert, capable independent auditors. Hanson noted, "like the points of a triangle, if any function is not forcefully delineated, the entire structure becomes vulnerable."

[1]Walter E. Hanson, "Focus on Fraud," *Financial Executive*, 43 (1975).

The opportunity for wrongdoing is significantly reduced when top management is alert, active, and committed. The converse is true when management is negligent, lacks commitment, and is distracted by other duties and pressures. The ceaseless building of safeguards and the searching for weaknesses in internal control by frequent testing of those controls by independent auditors are the other two factors which must exist to make opportunity for crime difficult. Where any of these factors are weak, the environment is conducive to fraud and wrongdoing.

Whenever we refer to management, we are talking about those people in an organization who have the authority to create controls and, conversely, are not bound by or can override ordinary, day-to-day controls. They are the principal protectors of the target environment against giving opportunities to wrongdoers, as well as the potential weak link in any system of safeguards. When a manager disregards an internal control procedure, or permits or causes an employee to do so, an opportunity for some type of mischief is created.

The broad subject of internal controls can be summarized under the categories of: (1) the "concerns" (or why the subject is so critical); (2) the "fundamentals" (or what the basic tenets are); and (3) "practical rules of thumb" (for use by the professionals who are involved in the daily application and testing of the principles). These have been discussed in detail and in other contexts in all chapters of this book. Bear in mind, however, that our main preoccupation here, as elsewhere, is with white collar crime and all its ramifications.

The Concerns

1. The abilities and skills of treasurers and controllers, and their staffs, who are in particularly vital and sensitive positions of public trust. Similar concerns ought to be felt for those officials in the publicly held private sector organizations such as corporate directors, treasurers, and chief fiscal officers.

2. The difficulties of adequately controlling essential systems due to electronic transfer mechanisms and automation of basic data. Cash plus ADP equals a strong brew.

3. The wide scope of the fraud and abuse problem, in government and private sectors, as evidenced by many reports.

4. The inherent secrecy which prevails over the details and specific mechanisms used in prior abuses.

5. The paucity of practical training courses in traditional academic institutions on combatting white collar crime.

The first item in our concerns are the treasurers and controllers and others in particularly sensitive positions of public trust—be they in the public sector or the corporate environment. The manner in which they handle the recording and reporting of assets that are held or used, sold or bought is always of prime concern to anyone assessing an internal control system—and, of course, to the organization itself.

Secondly, and this point is becoming increasingly vital, modern internal control systems are difficult to maintain with integrity and assurance because of electronic transfer mechanisms and the automation of basic data. There is no question that these two considerations (particularly because of the depersonalizing effect and the related difficulties of pinpointing individual responsibilities) are very high on the list of concerns, when one talks about internal controls.

Next, the many reports of widespread fraud and abuse—even though they are just the tip of the iceberg—make this an obvious and important issue.

Fourth, if we knew exactly what the details and specific mechanisms used in prior abuses were, and if there were a full clearinghouse for this process, we would be much further along on the road to helping to restrict illicit opportunities. But inherent secrecy prevails over many of the details.

Finally, behind it all is the paucity of practical training courses available in traditional academic institutions—as well as the inability and short-sightedness of many organizations to adequately fund, prepare, and train their executives and employees for the difficulties in this major area.

Therefore, these are the five major concerns in a general way. This leads to the next section —fundamentals.

The Fundamentals

1. An important distinction exists between "administrative functions" and "accounting processes."

2. Periodic review of its own internal control systems (through internal audit and self-analysis) is an important inside managerial process. Regular independent audits to see that the internal systems are adequate are an important outside check.

3. Follow-up on defects disclosed—and taking the effective corrective action—is most important and closes the final loop. Top management's interest is vital here.

4. Organizations are responsible to provide assurance that

   a. Obligations and costs are maintained in compliance with applicable laws and management's policies.

   b. Funds, property, and other assets must be safeguarded; waste, loss, or misappropriation avoided.

   c. Revenues and expenditures must be properly accounted for, and recorded, to permit reliable reports by management and the maintenance of full accountability.

5. An internal control system is not a separate function in an organization; it is intrinsic to all its day-to-day operations.

In discussing the fundamentals as well as the concerns, one must begin with understanding the important distinction between administrative functions and accounting processes. This is one of the points highlighted frequently in the standards set by the American Institute of Certified Public Accountants

Standards, the Institute of Internal Auditors, and the government. It both sets the stage for an important point and deals with organizational attitude. The American Institute of Certified Public Accountants (AICPA) states in its Standardized Accounting Standards (SAS) No. 1, Section 320 that:

> Administrative control includes, but is not limited to, the plan of organization and the procedures and records that are concerned with the decision processes leading to management's authorization of transactions. Such authorization is a management function directly associated with the responsibility for achieving the objectives of the organization and is the starting point for establishing accounting control of transactions.
>
> Accounting control comprises the plan of organization and the procedures and records that are concerned with the safeguarding of assets and the reliability of financial records and consequently is designed to provide reasonable assurance that:
>
> a. Transactions are executed in accordance with management's general or specific authorization.
>
> b. Transactions are recorded as necessary (1) to permit preparation of financial statements in conformity with generally accepted accounting principles or any other criteria applicable to such statements and (2) to maintain accountability for assets.
>
> c. Access to assets is permitted only in accordance with management's authorization.
>
> d. The recorded accountability for assets is compared with the existing assets at reasonable intervals and appropriate action is taken with respect to any differences.

Separation of Duties

One must understand that when we talk about administrative functions, we are talking about a fundamental management division of responsibilities that serves as the basic counterpart for effective control processes. For accounting processes this would be the distinction between *who* records the daily time cards, and *how* they are picked up and posted on the payroll records. Separation of duties with respect to administrative functions is distinguished as between *the process* of daily recording of time spent on jobs and the maintenance of personnel and executive records. Each function is performed by a different organizational group that responds to a different chain of command. Frequently, different organizational chains of command handle different broad functions in companies with well-conceived control mechanisms. It is the overriding principle of not allowing one "corporate" group (or individual executive) to control a complete set of transactions.

Consider another example of how this works: The accounting functions and the data processing functions are staffed by entirely different organizational elements. There is a separate review process that takes occasional floor checks and performs the computer matching processes to see that the payroll is accurate and reliable. The distribution of the actual pay itself is a matter of concern in that cash methods are disappearing to a great extent—and check dispersal is handled either directly (person to person), or through the mail, or through electronic transfers to employees' bank accounts.

An excellent illustration of proper separation of administrative functions is (1) to have the group(s) who contracts for goods and services distinct and different from (2) those receiving these goods and/or services, such as on a loading dock, and to separate these two groups from (3) the project officers who are to use such goods and/or services in the first place.

The accounting process we refer to relates to records of obligations (commitments for goods and services to be bought)—how funds are obligated or set aside to pay for goods and services. What are the controls to ensure that these obligations are entered into the accounting records currently and accurately? Are all such obligations entered and monitored under proper accounting control? Are such records kept in balance with controlling general ledger accounts? Are there suitable processes in place to ensure that all commitments are obligated prior to commitment for their release/use?

Periodic and timely review of revenues and expenses are very important in helping management to keep its cash management flow and control timely so that major defects do not fester and become deeply ingrained.

Responsibilities

The responsibility for any internal control system should not be a separate function in an organization. Such intrinsic systems must be part of day-to-day operations. Management should not set a group aside, for example, and say "You are responsible for seeing to it that internal control in the system is working." Every manager, supervisor, and employee has the responsibility of seeing that control systems are working and responsive.

Front-End Controls

Another way of looking at the fundamentals in a general sense is to separate controls into several parts, the first part being "front-end controls." These are the ones you put into place to check and control operations before transactions begin. They tend to deny up-front many of the opportunities for misappropriation and misuse of assets. The absence of such front-end controls create opportunities for fraud and abuse. Inventories, for example, should be "locked and boxed" properly, so that things are not sloppy—and employees or outsiders cannot inappropriately take or mislay goods.

On-Line Reviews

On-line, ongoing review mechanisms are powerful controls. It is surprising how many times this concept of timeliness is called for by the standards in place for auditing and investigating. It is too late to come in at the end of the year to test these systems. Management has a *continual* responsibility for checking on its controls by using data analysis and/or internal audits.

Nowhere are on-line reviews more important than in processes involving computerized data. It has reached the point, for example, where many bank auditors are reviewing transactions behind the scenes as they occur. This serves the dual purpose of testing for accuracy and pinpointing responsibility—which is very hard to do in electronic data operations.

Consider what would happen in large insurance, government, banking, security operations, and the like if personnel dealing with computer data knew there was immediate and timely testing of the accuracy of what they were doing—item by item, on an hourly and daily basis. This in itself would deter many wrongdoers. The assets we are speaking about here are not tangible. Rather, they are other important matters sensitive to the internal control process such as

Directed purchases.

Purchases at other than fair prices.

Payment to unauthorized recipients. (This can be a particular problem in computerized operations covering payroll; for recipient roles of Federal public assistance, medicare, and social security programs.)

Accounts payable—all areas.

Dispensing information that is valuable, such as information as to stocks and bonds, or intended corporate, or organizational or government operations or decisions or plans.

Attempts to influence or peddle influence to hire friends.

Unauthorized free use of assets.

There are many other areas where on-line reviews are particularly valuable. Consider using this technique for testing incoming mail-room items. This should be a very important area for every organization to ensure that everything coming in is properly recorded—especially if there are checks, cash, or other assets or important information coming in the mail. Mailrooms are often not properly controlled by on-line techniques. It might be wise also to follow through on how well checks are controlled *after* they leave the mailroom.

A case investigated by HHS Inspector General staff illustrates this. Some 30 federal checks sent to an HHS grantee were diverted by one of their employees (a secretary), who altered these checks to make herself the payee. With just these details one might conjecture about the internal controls that would be lacking or circumvented in a situation of this type. In particular, a control should have been in place that would quickly identify a situation where incoming checks were diverted over an extended period of time.

A related area would be receiving docks. Incoming merchandise needs to be counted, tabulated and recorded. The paperwork must be compared satisfactorily with the original procurement and the accounts payable. As mentioned previously, these administrative functions ought to be separated and controlled. The accounting processes would be an adjunct to that procedure on an on-line basis. Management has the responsibility for internal controls. Auditors should be on-line and, after the fact, testing them.

Using Prenumbered Control Documents

One important technique of internal control that must be mentioned is the use of serially numbered forms, slips, sales slips, and inventory counters—any regular paperwork that organizations use both for assets, liabilities, processes, or operations in any manner, shape, or form. These should be serially controlled and prenumbered in advance. The batch numbers should be controlled and accounted for and it cannot be overemphasized as to how important this simple, straightforward mechanism is to proper internal control.

We discussed front-end controls and on-line reviews. There are also after-the-fact analyses which should and can link all these things together by analyzing trends, aberrations, distortions, and so on. An important example of these are modern computer matches that auditors employ to determine aberrant happenings. One set of data is compared to another by computer—with certain parameters stipulated beforehand.

Those not meeting the "norms" are set aside for individual sampling or testing. This is a powerful mechanism for after-the-fact review to see whether your front-end controls and on-line reviews are in place. For a further discussion of such computer record matching techniques see Chapter 19, Part VI.

Using Telephone Hotlines as an Information Source

One helpful tool in ferreting out fraud, waste, and abuse involving Federal funds has been the development and use of a telephone "Hotline." One such hotline is in use at the HHS Inspector General's office. It handles some 18,000 calls a year. The General Accounting Office, the FBI, and other Federal agencies have similar arrangements whereby concerned citizens may call in and report instances of suspected missuse of the public's trust, or funds. The form used to record such calls, showing the type of information requested from the caller, is shown in Figure 12-1 (page 188).

Some Practical "Rules of Thumb"

1. *Duties must be separated.* This cannot work in a one-, two-, or three-person organization. In such small organizations it is accomplished by attitude responsibility. There has to be some special measure of responsibility and reliance placed on employees in such small organizations. The owner or the manager, however, must know through on-line testing, day-to-day, that this reliance is justified and that this trusted employee is not abrogating that trust. So separation of duties usually takes place in a larger organization where, as a matter of practicality, they can be separated.

2. *Systems must be cost beneficial.* Stated otherwise, ". . . don't spend more than is at stake to control." Despite the emphasis about front-end, on-line and post review controls,

---

CONTROL NUMBER _____

NAME _____

Address _____

Call taken by: _____

Date: _____

_____ Time _____

Phone # _____

May we use your name? Yes

Your position _____

No

Government Employee? Yes ___ No ___ Location _____

Have you previously reported this? Yes ___ No ___ To whom_____

Names of individuals involved: _____

Agency/Office involved: _____

Do you have any documentation in your possession which could be used as evidence? Yes ___ No ___

Willing to put in writing and submit? Yes ___ No ___

TYPE OF ALLEGATION _____

_____

SUBJECT: _____

_____

_____

_____

_____

_____

_____

_____

_____

_____

_____

_____

REFERRED TO: _____

DISPOSITION: _____

FIGURE 12.1.   Inspector General's Hotline.

they should be applied with a sense of practicality. Standards themselves take account of this concept by specifying that things must be cost-beneficial. But the danger point here is that auditors, for example, torn between protecting clients' interests and trying to be cost beneficial and affordable at the same time, will often cut corners to make the two concepts compatible. So we hear frequently about the problem of standards overload and materiality and items that relate to this process. One might even relate it to the low bids that some CPA firms put in to do work and then make the work fit the low bid as tight as they can, still trying to be professional and minimally meeting the standards. So here again, management has the responsibility to see to it that there is a sufficiency of outside and inside audit regardless of how tight the cost beneficial and affordable concepts are:

3. *Vulnerability assessments should be made.* These are constantly needed efforts, not one-time chores. Thinking what could go wrong is everybody's job in an organization. This relates to quality control right on the manufacturing line. Many fine texts and articles and seminars discuss the usefulness of having every employee, every supervisor watch for what could go wrong and thinking about the quality control of every phase of the operation. These assessments are discussed in more detail in Chapter V, Part II.

4. *A key attribute of every strong organization is simply good supervision.* Hand in hand with this point is the delegating of responsibility. Who is responsible for what must be clearly set out, otherwise, nobody is responsible for anything.

5. *Technical assistance, on-the-job training, and personalized improvement investments are not discardable overhead.* Professional standards require them, good business practice dictates them. Not only is training a nondiscardable overhead, but the recruitment of what might be called more fully educated auditors is essential. This is a simple, but profound, point. There is a fundamental need for better and more fully educated auditors. It doesn't necessarily mean more specialized auditors, or more specialization in related fields, statisticians, computer programmers, or security wizards, and so on. Those can be bought. Auditors need a firm grasp of fundamentals and logical thinking, a global or renaissance outlook, to enable them to deal with all business prospectives of management which is the focal point the whole process is vitally concerned with. Really good auditors must know what good business practices are to begin with, otherwise, they will lack a benchmark for measuring adequate and controlled performance.

6. *There has to be an interrelated and interdependent combinative effort between management and auditors to make internal controls really work.* But the focal point for such an effort must be management. Only management is capable of orchestrating and maximizing the effects of all the other players and getting to perhaps the most important point of all, ensuring a proper organizational attitude. No system, internal control, no set of audit processes will make any business secure, if the organizational attitude is not honest and clean. Almost every major fraudulent situation we hear about has as its roots internal controls being overridden by a misguided, misbehaving management. What controls can be put in place if management overrides them that would be effective? Obviously, the outside attestation auditors are concerned with this. But there again, the problem relates to materiality. If what they find is not considered as material to what is being reported, then they are not directly concerned. They are concerned, however, when the testing process discloses an override capability—so that even what they see might appear to be legal is, in fact, incorrect. We are referring to counterfeiting or "cooking" whole sets of records for distorting the auditor's view.

Overall, management's "attitude" is the overriding key to a well-run organization with strong internal controls.

1. There must be clear prohibitions against purchasing agents getting favors from suppliers because they received a lucrative order.
2. Prohibitions must be spelled out in fine detail in the operations manual concerning gratuities (gifts, expensive luncheons, or dinners)—nothing above very minor courtesies exchanged during regular professional situations.
3. Tight cash or disbursement controls must be designed to preclude nonpermitted expenditures (buying special favors).

A good analogy can be seen everyday on the highway. It might be called the "Tone Setting Principle." Picture a three-lane highway loaded with cars—bumper to bumper. If all are proceeding at an even pace, then the scene will generally be regular and orderly. However, when one starts to move faster than the others the number of lane changers starts to escalate. If the road becomes absolutely clogged and unmoving, a high level of frustration starts to set in. Nerves start wearing thin, but motorists stay put. Then it always happens—almost like a force of nature. Someone starts to "ride the shoulder." It looks appealing because the car appears to be making great headway. Most drivers generally stay in their lane silently hoping that the violators will be caught by some highway patrolman. But what if this does not happen and nobody stops the first few lawbreakers? They will be perceived by others as getting away with it. And, if it appears that they will not be punished, the number of additional traffic violators will inexorably start to multiply—almost in direct geometric proportion to the time interval it takes to clear up the slowdown! Pretty soon, there is a steady stream of cars riding the emergency shoulder, feeling more secure all the time in the comfort of their numbers—and all doing the wrong thing!

So too with organizational performers. People are people no matter what the setting. When it is perceived that the powers that be are not concerned about corporate abuse, and worse, if they do it themselves and are seen to get away with it, there exists a heavy motivation and a fertile climate for ever-increasing wrongdoing. All the potential "shoulder riders" are just waiting to join the crowd. Remember, there are some who will never ride the shoulder; some who will always ride the shoulder; and most who will ride the shoulder only if it seems profitable enough after considering the absence of, or minimal chance of, risk, detection and punishment.

There is, however, another side to the coin—subtle, pervasive, and, according to many sociologists, inherently powerful for wrongdoing in any organization. One might call it the "Unfair Syndrome." One scenario in an organization arises frequently from misguided managers who are trying in a self-defeating manner to please their superiors or constituencies. They set up unrealistic targets and goals for subordinates. They respond, either out of fear or lack of insight, without useful rebuttal to unfair requirements put upon them by top management. They frequently want to establish a reputation for hard-nosed management, careful with the company's money or the public's exchequer. They might, for example, limit the reimbursement total (or maximum per diem allowance) to, let's say, $50 for each day's stay out of town. It is, of course, eminently "unfair" to ask a respected employee to stay in a large city on business with only $50 to spend on a hotel, meals, and so forth. Who is trying to impress whom? The organization's personnel will consider this to be patently unfair—and will look for ways to get even! (At the very least, it will surely adversely affect their work performance.) But, again, relating to our central theme, they will feel motivated to retaliate in some fashion. What's worse, they will feel justified in doing so!

The point here is top management's policy-setting role must include seeing to it that there is a logical, self-checking flow of control and separation of functions.

First to come to mind is the need for an executive selection committee, together with some sensible corporate policy setting edicts (will the organization buy talent, train talent, steal talent, and so on).

Wage scale determinations and a clear-cut view of who is responsible for the central personnel files should be set forth. Other considerations include: how union agreements are set; who are official negotiating executives; their responsibilities; what are the policies and techniques for testing and evaluating new employees? (Screening for sensitive assignments comes to mind as a potential source of later trouble if not handled right at the outset.) Clerical payroll data, ADP functions, time and attendance records, leave approval, medical testing (and how to keep them private), paying clerks (paymasters), etc., are all important functions that should also be considered.

Everyday influences that shape the mores of our national personality put our everyday social and business operations in a particular mode and setting, whether we like it or not. To illustrate the enormous negative backdrop to our working business arena, take a moment to retrieve from your memory the many cases you know about concerning our "ethical breakdown":

Supermarkets and retail fudging

Shoplifting/Inventory shrinkage

Counterfeiting

Credit card abuses

Tax cheating

Corporate espionage

Falsified research data

Medical malpractice (both medicine and economic)

Misrepresented advertising

Mechanics' short-shifting of service

Drug scene and all its ramifications

Quality control sloppiness

Kickbacks, embezzlements, payoffs.

All this makes us especially vulnerable in the age of electronic transfers and computer accessibility—right down to micro-computers in the homes of millions of students and users who have more than demonstrated their wizardry at tapping into the mainframes of every business and government entity in existence.

Management's attitude is the overriding key to a well run and internally controlled organization in every instance.

IN THE AREA OF PERSONNEL SECURITY

The problem of protecting executives against attack by denying would-be wrongdoers access to their quarry has previously been discussed. This section focuses on the same problem from the viewpoint of denying opportunities for attacks. The following list describes some preventative measures that can be employed under this principle:

1. Individuals considered suspectible to harmful actions should always keep alert for suspicious persons, vehicles, or circumstances, such as staged accidents or other hoaxes. Notes

should be taken of automobiles and plate numbers loitering in the area. Kidnappers and terrorists almost always place their intended victims under surveillance for at least several days prior to a planned attack. This gives them time to acquaint themselves with their victim's habits. In retrospect, released victims can often recall unusual circumstances that led up to the abduction.

2.   One should vary daily routine to avoid habitual patterns. This includes fluctuating time and routes. Isolated and unlit areas should be avoided.

3.   Both terrorists and burglars look for opportunities in the business and society sections of the printed media. Therefore, to reduce such opportunities for them, the executive should avoid advertising their activities and movements. These include items on such matters as weddings, travel plans, promotions, relationships, or other personal details. The limits of unnecessary personal details should be the rule with other publications as well, such as business directories, social registers, or community directories.

4.   Targets are rarely attacked when they are part of a group; therefore, being with other people where possible reduces opportunities for would-be wrongdoers.

5.   Many corporate and government organizations provide executives with specially designated parking spaces indicating the name and/or title of the individual. This provides great opportunity to the would-be attacker to learn the identity of the vehicle and target, as well as gain access to the car.

6.   Likewise, one should consider not advertising his residence by having unlisted phone numbers, no name identification on the house, and so on.

7.   When executives are being targeted, they are subject to individuals attempting to learn as much as they can about them for the purpose of detecting an opportunity for an attack. Therefore, it pays to be alert to strangers eliciting personal information. Avoid providing such information at parties. The telephone can be used in a wide variety of pretext calls in order to gain knowledge about their targets (telephone surveys, voter

registration, community service organizations, etc.). Instruction should be given to associates and family members, especially children, to follow the same rule. Under no circumstances should children ever indicate "no one is home."

8.   Opportunities for attack can be significantly reduced at the residence where the car is parked or at the job through the elimination of the kinds of shrubbery that can block one's field of vision or conceal someone.

9.   A business associate or family member should always be advised of destinations when leaving home or office and the time of return.

10.   Children should be carefully instructed on the importance of not entering into conversation with strangers or their vehicles. When children are visiting somewhere, have them call verification of their safe arrival or verify it yourself by calling them.

11.   Avoid obvious indications that you are not at home. Opened garage doors and newspapers left outside are telltale signs that the house is unattended. The same holds true for uncollected mail. At night have timer lights on in bathrooms, bedrooms, and so forth.

IN THE BANKING INDUSTRY

Nothing represents a more attractive target for would be wrongdoers than banks. Banks have cash—the most liquid of all assets. Therefore, banks must concern themselves with threats from both external and internal sources. Over 6000 external attacks, that is, robberies and burglaries, occur each year. The best defenses to external attacks are by denying *access* to the target through security measures, such as:

1.   Alarm systems that can be activated by tellers, guards, officers, and other employees.

2.   Alarm systems that can be automatically actuated when money is removed from a teller's cash drawer, and so on.

3. Alarm systems that can be actuated when the bank is unoccupied, such as from movement, heat, broken circuits, and the like.

4. Physical barriers that block access to customers (high counters, bullet proof glass, buzzer locked doors, and so on).

5. Closed circuit television to record events and monitor activities.

6. Booby trapped bait money (perhaps dye marked) that sends out homing signals, powder marks from anyone handling it, and the like.

The internal threat comes from employees who embezzle and misappropriate bank funds. This threat is much greater in terms of losses. At least five banks face bankruptcy each year as a direct result of fraud. In 1980, such *reported* losses involved some $160 million—four times the amount lost through robberies. Here are 12 routine preventative measures for banks:

1. There should be a careful selection of employees with appropriate background inquiries to verify personal history prior to giving them *access* through employment and to insure they have not demonstrated any predisposition to wrongdoing *(motive)*.

2. There should be a rotation of duties and assignments among employees *(motive)*.

3. There must be a policy of compulsory vacations (generally two weeks at a time) *(opportunity)*.

4. There should be a routine random sampling of all functions by audit on a periodic basis *(opportunity)*.

5. There should be a followup on all new accounts (i.e., a thank you letter, confirmations, checking references and verifying) *(opportunity)*.

6. There should be an independent review within the bank of all delinquent loans *(opportunity)*.

7. There should be a dual control on all transactions *(opportunity)*.

8. All systems changes should be reviewed for adequate controls *(opportunity)*.

9. Everyone within the banking institution must have a responsible superior *(opportunity)*.

10. There should be careful training and indoctrination of employees against circumventing controls *(motive)*.

11. A pro-active personnel policy to spot employees with problems and to counsel and otherwise assist them should be instituted *(motive)*.

12. The bank should have a personnel policy wherein performance reviews should be done so as to permit the employee to reconcile with the rater and have counseling thereafter *(motive)*.

CHAPTER THIRTEEN

DENYING OPPORTUNITY: BY UTILIZING AUDITORS, INSPECTORS GENERAL, AND OTHERS

THE CHANGING NATURE OF THE AUDITOR'S ROLES IN DETECTING AND DETERRING CRIME

The first part of this book discussed some of the consequences of the Protestant Reformation, the rise of commercialism, the Industrial Revolution, and the information explosion. Each of these events has had a great impact on the audit profession.

Early Audit Objectives

Until the mid-19th century the auditor's primary objectives centered around uncovering technical mistakes, violations of general accounting principles, and transgressions of the law. Simply, the auditor's job was to ensure the accuracy of records and the proper stewardship and accountability of monies, inventories, and assets entrusted to others for management. The demands for this kind of independent assurance has grown enormously.

Business Complexities Create New Needs

Dealing with strangers in an ever-growing complex society necessitated means by which banks, investors, and others could be assured of the true financial picture of business entities. The enactment of a federal corporate income tax in 1913 further accelerated this need. The American Institute of Accountants (AIA) was formed in 1916, about the same time that Robert Montgomery published his *Auditing Theory and Practice*, the first generally accepted auditing text in the U.S.[1] Montgomery's book, which became the AIA's bible, purported to educate auditors in a standardized examination of books throughout the country. The AIA grew into the American Institute of Certified Public Accountants (AICPA). The AICPA is now the most authoritative source of generally accepted accounting principles and auditing standards.

By the 1930s, there were increasing pressures to focus on the issues of (1) profit/loss statements, and (2) proper internal controls. Such pressure was spurred by the stock market crash. The expanded federal role in banking, commerce, and industry further accentuated this through the development of the Federal Deposit Insurance Corporation (FDIC), Federal Savings and Loan Insurance Corporation (FSLIC), Interstate Commerce Commission (ICC), Securities and Exchange Commission (SEC), and like agencies. In addition, the ever-increasing role of Internal Revenue Service (IRS) has enhanced the tax implications of accounting transactions.

[1]Robert H. Montgomery, *Auditing Theory and Practice*, New York: The Ronald, Press. 8th edition 1957).

In just the past several decades the scale of business activities and the amount of transactions has exploded so rapidly and on such a scale, that the auditing and accounting professions have undergone great changes. Educational prerequisites, skills, and requirements for practitioners have grown enormously. The public places great expectations and trust on the ability of audited statements. The role of the auditor, which was fairly comfortably that of a verifier, has become one of an attestor. It is no longer physically possible for an auditor to engage in verifying each transaction. Instead, auditors are limited to testing the financial system in order to attest to (1) the overall reliability of accounting treatment given individual transactions and (2) the reasonableness of management's financial statements prepared by management. With the auditor focusing on only limited samples of transactions and concerning themselves with the accuracy of profit and losses statements, the ability to detect criminality in the environment diminished greatly.

As the auditor's role changed a standard form of audit opinion evolved which minimized the auditor's responsibility for detecting fraud as an objective of financial statement audits. In this setting, the AIA issued its "Statement on Auditing Procedure (SAP) No. 33." Paragraph 5 of Chapter I is set forth below:

Detection of Fraud (including defalcations and other similar irregularities)

5. In making the ordinary examination, the independent auditor is aware of the possibility that fraud may exist. Financial statements may be mis-stated as the result of defalcations and similar irregularities, or deliberate misrepresentation by management, or both. The auditor recognizes that fraud, if sufficiently material, may affect his opinion on the financial statements, and his examination, made in accordance with generally accepted auditing standards, gives consideration to this possibility. However, the ordinary examination directed to the expression of an opinion on financial statement is not primarily or specifically designed, and cannot be relied upon, to disclose defalcations and other similar irregularities, although their discovery may result. Similarly, although the discovery of

deliberate misrepresentation by management is usually more closely associated with the objective of the ordinary examination, such examination cannot be relied upon to assure its discovery. The responsibility of the independent auditor for failure to detect fraud (which responsibility differs as to clients and others) arises only when such failure clearly results from failure to comply with generally accepted auditing standards.

As a result of such authoritative statement, many auditors felt relieved of responsibility to detect fraud, or other wrongdoing, as long as they complied with generally accepted auditing standards.

The prevailing attitudes of *caveat emptor* (let the buyer beware) and *laissez faire* (let business be) which prevailed in the 19th century seemed to be adopted by the audit community. The audit community was able to take solace in their abdication of responsibility in fraud detection in a landmark federal court decision rendered in 1931. This case, *Ultramares Corporation v. Touche* (255 N.Y. 170, 174 N.E. 441 (1931), involved a suit brought by a creditor who relied on an audit report in making a loan to the client without the knowledge of the auditing firm. In his decision, Judge Cardozo stated:

> If liability for negligence exists, a thoughtless slip or blunder, the failure to detect a theft or forgery beneath the cover of deceptive entries, may expose accountants to a liability in a indeterminate amount for an indeterminate time to an indeterminate class.

By this reasoning, Judge Cardozo concluded that the auditor could not be held accountable for detecting deception.

However, the 1950s and 1960s brought concern for the rights of consumers. This resulted in the courts progressively charging the auditing profession with legal duties. The decisions rendered in *Scott Bar Chris Construction Corporation* (283 F. Supp 643 (1968)) and *U.S. v. Simin* (425 F.2d 796 (1969)) established the liability of auditors to third parties. These cases demolished the defense of auditors who held they were not responsible for detection of fraud as long as they performed the audit in accordance with generally accepted auditing principles.

The disclosure in the early 1970s of additional major fraud cases, particularly those involving deceptive practices by management, created an atmosphere of great concern. This consternation extended from the financial community to the general public. The fact that many of the nation's most prestigious auditing firms, including members of the "Big Eight," were auditing these companies, certainly added to this feeling of dismay.

It was in this atmosphere that the AICPA began to shift from what might be described as a passive position on the auditor's responsibility to detect fraud to a more aggressive approach.

1. In 1974, the AICPA established the Commission on Auditor's Responsibilities (CAR), more commonly known as the Cohen Commission, for the purpose of developing conclusions and recommendations regarding the appropriate responsibilities of independent auditors. The 1978 Cohen Commission concluded that the auditor "has a duty to search for fraud and should be expected to detect those frauds that the exercise of professional skill and care would normally uncover." While not carrying the authoritative weight of the Auditing Standards Board, the Commission did have considerable influence on the profession. This report was further evidence that the audit community was reevaluating its position on the auditor's responsibility to detect fraud.

The Cohen Commission raises an interesting question as to whether the auditor, because of the current increased concern with white collar crime, should be viewed as a public agent committed to improve the enforcement system as it relates to the conduct of business. The Commission, although taking the position that the public accounting profession must be responsive to society's need for evolution of the services it provides, believes that "it would be inefficient and impractical for auditors to undertake responsibilities that require the knowledge, skills and experience of members of another profession."

2. The AICPA, in July 1975, issued Statement on Auditing Standards (SAS No. 6) on Related Party Transactions that set forth specific procedures: to determine the existence of related parties; to identify any transactions; to examine such transactions; and to properly disclose related party transactions that are material, either individually or in the aggregate.

3. In January 1977, the AICPA issued two other statements on auditing standards: SAS No. 16, The Independent Auditor's Responsibility for the Detection of Errors or Irregularities, and SAS No. 17, Illegal Acts by Clients. SAS No. 16 states that

> ". . . the independent auditor has the responsibility, within the inherent limitations of the auditing process to plan his examination to search for errors or irregularities that would have a material effect on the financial statements, and to exercise due skill and care in the conduct of that examination.

For purposes of SAS 16, the term "irregularities" refers to "intentional distortions of financial statements, such as deliberate misrepresentation by management, sometimes referred to as management fraud, or misappropriation of assets, sometimes referred to as defalcations."

SAS No. 17 states that it ". . . provides guidance for an auditor when a client acts that appear to him to be illegal come to his attention during an examination of financial statements in accordance with general auditing standards." This statement also discusses the extent of the attention the auditor should give, when performing such an examination, to the possibility that such acts may have occurred. The statement points out that although an auditor should be aware that some client acts might be illegal or unlawful, an auditor generally does not have the expertise to evaluate the illegality. Procedures for the detection of illegal acts and the reporting of such acts to management were also included in the statement.

In regard to the reporting aspects, SAS No. 17 states, "When an illegal act, including one that does not have a material effect on the financial statements, comes to the auditor's attention, he should consider the nature of the act and management's consideration once the matter is brought to their attention." If the auditor feels that appropriate consideration is not given proper attention, he should consider withdrawing from the engagement and/or disassociating himself from any future relationship with the client. The statement is silent on the auditor's responsibility on reporting such information to other parties except to say that it is management's responsibility.

All of this brings us back to where we began this discussion: The auditor still has the responsibility to ensure proper stewardship in every sense of the word. In January 1985, the news media reported on certain remarks made by James C. Treadway, Jr., an SEC commissioner. He suggested that the SEC could stop efforts by corporate executives to shop around for accountants who let questionable items pass and could also track down on sham transactions. Treadway called on the accounting profession to police itself and impose sanctions in individual cases. According to Treadway, the accounting profession needed to correct "the present public perception that much about accounting is flawed." He predicted that the public would demand that the SEC and the accounting profession work together to ensure that there would be no cases in which problem companies were not uncovered, despite the costs that are sometimes involved in such work.

In an article discussing damage suits against Big Eight Accounting Firms (Arthur Andersen, Arthur Young, Coopers & Lybrand, Deloitte Haskins & Sells, Ernst & Whinney, Peat Marwick Mitchell, Price Waterhouse, and Touche Ross) an article in the *Washington Post* of July 14, 1985 included a listing of judgments and settlements paid by these firms over the past four to five years. The *Post*'s source for these amounts was the Securities and Exchange Commission. While the amounts given were heavily qualified as to what they included, they were substantial in size, ranging from $1.4 million by Arthur Young to $137 million by Arthur Andersen. The others were in the $2 million to 19 million bracket. The accompanying text stated that attorneys for several of the Big Eight companies link the increase in cases (up to a dozen new ones each year) to "court decisions expanding the definition of an accountant's liability plus the fallout from the business recession of the early 1980's."

FEDERAL GOVERNMENT AUDIT STANDARDS

In 1972, the U.S. General Accounting Office (GAO) issued its "Standards for Audit of Governmental Organizations, Programs, Activities, and Functions." These standards have been generally accepted by all levels of government and conform in great part to those promulgated by the AICPA. The standards were revised in 1981 in order to make the auditor's responsibility for detecting fraud and abuse in government programs and operations more specific. The GAO incorporates the AICPA statements on auditing standards for field work in its statement for governmental financial and compliance audits. It then adds the following to the standard on examination and evaluation on field work:

> (4) Auditors shall be alert to situations in transactions that would be indicative of fraud, abuse, and illegal expenditures and acts, and if such evidence exists, extend audit steps and procedures to identify the effect on the entity's financial statements.[2]

In regard to standards on reporting, the GAO goes one step beyond the AICPA by requiring: "Copies of the reports should also be sent to other officials who may be responsible for taking action and to others authorized to receive such reports." The report shall include material instances of noncompliance and instances or indications of fraud, abuse, or illegal acts found during or in connection with the audit. Similar statements are also contained in the sections of GAO's standards covering economy and efficiency audits and program-results audits.

The GAO also imposes a reporting requirement on external government auditors performing an audit of a government entity. If the external auditor becomes aware of fraud or illegal acts, he is to notify the top official of the federal entity audited

---

[2]Comptroller General of the United States, *Standards for Audit of Government Organization, Programs, Activities and Functions*, (Washington, DC: U.S. Government Printing Office, 1981).

(unless that official is believed to be a party to the questioned activity), and the appropriate law enforcement authorities.

In regard to public accountants performing government audits, the GAO appears to defer to SAS No. 17. Public accountants are to discharge their responsibility by promptly notifying the entity arranging for the audit. It is then the responsibility of the receiving entity to notify appropriate law enforcement authorities.

THE CONCEPT OF AN INSPECTOR GENERAL

The concept of an Inspector General (IG) is not new. It existed in George Washington's Revolutionary Army. But it is nothing short of revolutionary itself in the civilian sector of the government. In 1976, Public Law 94-505 authorized the first statutorily independent Inspector General at the Department of Health, Education, and Welfare (now The Department of Health and Human Services (HHS)). The Inspector General was to be appointed by the President and confirmed by the Senate. A series of other legislation authorized 17 other departments and agencies to have inspectors general.

Behind the legislation was the Congress' desire to establish within the executive branch of government an independent arm of management within a department or agency that could focus on the problems of fraud, waste, and abuse and independently report to the top executive. They wanted an organization that could promote economy and efficiency in government. These offices would be staffed with auditors, investigators, and other reviewers of fact to ferret out the problems and expose them to management, Congress, and the public. They were to become organized bodies of "whistle blowers." To be effective, they had to be free of management retribution and influence.

Their stated purpose was to establish independent and objective units: (1) to conduct and supervise audits and investigations relating to programs and operations within the respective agencies; (2) to provide leadership and coordination and recommend policies to promote economy, efficiency and effectiveness, and to prevent and *detect fraud and abuse* in such programs and operations; and (3) to provide a means for keeping the head of the agency and the Congress fully and currently informed about problems and deficiencies relating to the administration of such programs.

The Acts require that each inspector-general: (1) comply with standards established by the Comptroller General for audits of federal establishments, organizations, programs, activities and functions; and (2) take appropriate steps to ensure that any work performed by non-federal auditors complies with the standards established by the Comptroller General.

This same Section requires that each inspector general report expeditiously to the U.S. Attorney General whenever there are reasonable grounds to believe a violation of federal criminal law has occurred.

The nucleus of the inspectors general were the preexisting audit and investigative staffs within the agencies. It was clear, however, that the mission for these entities had changed. Their new responsibilities required that they assume some responsibilities for promoting good management within their host agencies. The IGs were to become "agents for positive change," focusing on improving the processes of government so as to deny opportunity for fraud, waste, abuse, inefficiency, and so forth. This required changes in methodology and approach. New tools had to be invented for the new responsibilities added to the old roles. The concept is fast proliferating to state and local agencies. Even many private sector organizations are experimenting with it. It has worked well within the federal Department of Health and Human Services. See Figure 13-1, 13-2, and 13-3.

COORDINATING FEDERAL ANTI FRAUD AND ABUSE EFFORTS

The President's Council on Integrity and Efficiency (PCIE) was created by Presidential Order in March 1982. The PCIE was made responsible for coordinating Government-wide activitie

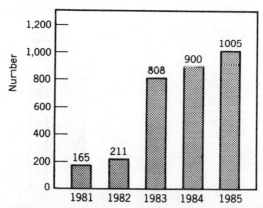

FIGURE 13.1. Department of Health and Human Services, Office of Inspector General (OIG). Successful Prosecutions culminating from OIG work. FY 1981 thru FY 1985.

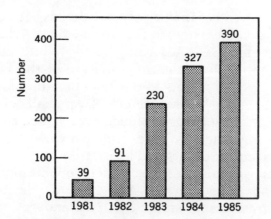

FIGURE 13.2. Department of Health and Human Services. Office of Inspector General Administrative Sanctions. Effected, FY 1981 thru FY 1985.

attacking fraud and abuse (and waste) in Government programs and operations. This high-level council includes top representatives from the Department of Justice, all statutory Inspectors General, and designees from the Secretary(s) of the Treasury, Defense, and the U.S. International Development Agency.

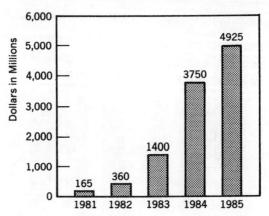

FIGURE 13.3. Department of Health and Human Services. Office of Inspector General Cost Savings, FY 1981 thru FY 1985.

Other Deterrent Actions Underway

The Federal Bureau of Investigation (FBI) has beefed up its war against white collar crime. In the last few years, it has *tripled* its resources in this area. According to the White Collar Crime Section, Criminal Investigation Division of the FBI in 1984, nearly 1700 Special Agents in the field, of a total force of some 7000, are devoted to the effort. Over half of them are accountants. A recent year included over 40,000 current white collar crime investigative cases under review.

Various executive orders and legislation, such as the Corrupt Practices Act, were also designed to deter or eliminate corporate kickbacks and bribes overseas. Also, the GAO, the investigative arm of Congress, issues statements on standards and internal controls that help set the ethical foundation for auditing and related efforts.

The Institute of Internal Auditors, representing the auditors of private sector organizations as well as federal, state, and local internal auditors, adopt more or less the same position as the AICPA statements and the GAO statements in their newly designed codes of ethics and standards. The internal auditors can be a powerful force for positive help in this area by providing on-line, current, and timely investigative and analytical techniques so that difficulties and abuses do not fester. These are all potentially major forces for deterrence.

Most major police forces have now instituted white collar criminal investigative programs. For the first time in the hundreds of years of constabularies, police department are now beginning to investigate these kinds of crimes that had never been part of the common law of England and America. Until the 1970s it was rare for local police agencies to investigate white collar crime. The notable exception to this was the New York City Bureau of Investigations. It was a unit set up outside the police department to act as a special investigative overseer of municipal practices. Its genesis extends over a 100 years. Today it prosecutes business entities dealing with the city and municipal employees who have engaged in corrupt practices. In the last decade a number of police departments began developing special white collar crime investigative units. One of the first major efforts was the Chicago, Illinois Police Department. During 1978–1979, one of the authors participated in the development of a white collar crime division for that department. Many other cities have followed suit.

CHAPTER FOURTEEN

TESTING CONTROLS THROUGH AUDITING

AUDITOR DEFINED

Much has been written here and elsewhere about the audit function. Ask the average layperson, to define the term "audit" though, and you will probably encounter a surprising lack of understanding about the function. Part of the reason for this is the fact that the term "audit" has become generic.

Most dictionaries simply define the term "audit" as being an independent verification of accounting transactions. Many people think of an audit as being some not-too-well understood method of finding deliberate careless errors or omissions. Some picture auditors as being ruthless technicians bent on discovering error. In reality, however, auditors wear many hats. Some are principally interested in accounting matters while others are involved in the whole business spectrum.

Writers have traced auditing back to its roots, when auditors orally briefed "clients" on the findings of their work. These oral presentations gave rise to the term "audit", that is, "to hear."

Modern auditing, however, originated in Great Britain in the late 19th century—a direct result of the Industrial Revolution. The concept came to the U.S. in the early 20th century with the arrival of young Scottish accountants.

Auditors Are Dispersed Throughout the Business World

Professional audit staffs may be found in the private sector as public accountants, in medium and large-sized organizations as internal auditors. Federal, state, and local governments in total employ thousands of auditors.

Essentially, public accountants on a fee-for-service basis perform financial (balance sheet) audits for their clients and/or provide management advisory services. Public accountants are called on to perform such tests and examinations as are necessary to determine whether management's financial statements "fairly present" financial position and operating results. Such unbiased, independent evaluations and reviews of an organization's reports are of great interest to the general public (stockholders in particular), government, employees and so on.

Internal auditors in both the public and private sector are a form of managerial control which, according to the Institute of Internal Auditors, operates by appraising the effectiveness of other controls. Internal auditors are concerned with the effectiveness of the controls over their employer's accounting and management (internal) controls. Auditors for the U.S. General Accounting Office act as the investigative arm of the Congress.

Attributes of an Auditor

What qualifies a person as an auditor? Many but not all are trained accountants. Auditors are considered professional in that their work to be acceptable must conform to standards set by the AICPA, the Institute for Internal Auditors, and/or the

Comptroller General of the U.S. As was observed in Kropatkin's *Audit Logic,* conformance to standards is "the crucial distinguishing factor that separates craftsmen, technicians, farmers and artisans from responsive professionals. . . ."[1]

Audit has moved from purely financial interests into operational areas, and other disciplines, such as computer specialists, have begun to occupy important roles in the audit function. Auditors within the Inspector General's Office at the Federal Department of Health and Human Services are largely accountants, but there are related disciplines, such as computer specialists, within that office to lend support, guidance, and advice. Regardless of discipline, though, auditor candidates need: intelligence; interest in, and curiosity about, ideas and things; articulateness in writing and in speech; and a good knowledge of people and their everyday business and social practices. This is a tall order. Auditors having all or most of these attributes are certain to have successful careers.

TIPS ON PLANNING AUDITS

Successful audits are those which are well planned. Auditing any business or government entity actually ought to be performed in an order that has a natural rhythm to it.

1. *Identify the audit target and the client.* That is, what are you going to look at, and who are you looking at it for?

2. *Decide on the scope and the audit period.* This is tied into the next point in that the survey may show internal controls to be so weak that an extended scope and audit period is called for.

3. *Survey the audit entity.* This is perhaps the least understood but most important audit phase. Surveys are the heart of the entire review process. Successful, cost-effective audits depend on good surveys. The verification phase is actually only the proving ground for those tentative audit opinions formed in the survey. The strategy for good surveys requires that the audit

[1]Philip Kropatkin, *Audit Logic* (New York: Ronald, 1984).

objectives are clearly and firmly in place. Each member of the survey team, and especially the leader, must be aware of the desired end product. In the private sector, the most common goal is the classic balance sheet and profit and loss attestation. In the public sector, the most requested audit is of the financial management and compliance tests of grants and contracts. This has changed, though, with the introduction of inspectors general into all major federal agencies. Federal audits are directed much more now to areas targeted as being susceptible to fraud, waste and abuse. The extent of audit coverage afforded previously unproductive areas (in terms of audit findings) is constantly reassessed.

A survey guide should be prepared to keep track of the items to be covered in the survey. This essential road map is often skipped. Surveys ought to be performed, or actively supervised, by senior personnel. Junior staff members do not have the experience to judge what items should be more deeply tested or decide which items should be quickly accepted.

4. *Evaluate the survey results and prepare a written guide for the use of the audit staff.*

5. *Complete the audit steps.* The most important thing to keep in mind is that the auditor doing this work should not follow each audit step blindly by rote.

6. *Relate the findings to the scope of the audit; summarize and report on what was right and what was wrong.* This is possibly the most difficult part of the audit. The auditor must stand back and impartially appraise what was found and compare it to what should have been found. Poor summations can effectively negate any meaningful results from an otherwise excellent audit.

TYPES OF AUDITS

There have been a great deal of thoughts, discussions, and decisions over the years concerning appropriate audit titles, scopes, purpose, deliverables, and methods. Within recent years, the AICPA and the U.S. Comptroller General have identified three major audit purposes:

1. Financial and compliance audit. Covers an examination of financial transactions, accounts, reports, and statistical data.
2. Economy and Efficiency audit. Reviews cost-benefit relationship in the use of resources to achieve intended program results.
3. Effectiveness audit. Reviews value created through the activity audited and measures that against organization's mission and/or objective. See Figure 14.1 for additional data.

Ideally, each management (i.e., non-balance sheet) audit ought to incorporate all three of these purposes. But due to simple economics, this can rarely be accomplished. However, audits should be tailored so as to be related to the needs of the users of the audit report. Their reliability and value depend in great measure on the professional competence of the individuals who direct and perform this work. See Figure 14.1 which is not all inclusive but which does cover many of the currently "popular" types of audits.

THE CONCEPT OF PROGRAM INSPECTIONS

Figure 14.1 contains a limited number of types of audits. This discussion concerns another method of conducting operational reviews. This method, developed by R.P. Kusserow[2] is known as "program inspection."

Case Example (HHS)

HHS is a department of 144,000 employees, 1600 sites, 250 programs, 100 mainframe computerized systems, and an

[2]Taken from an article by R.P. Kusserow printed in the *Government's Accountant Journal*, 23:1 (Spring 1984).

Type	Descriptive Statement	Audit Purpose	Deliverables	Audit Involves
Financial/ Compliance	Examine financial transactions, accounts, reports, statistical data.	Assess fairness of presentation of financial and related statistical data.	Opinion on fairness of financial and related statistical data.	Review and evaluation. Testing.
System Evaluation	Review systems of internal controls.	Evaluate organization's internal controls. Determination whether system of internal control is adequate.	Report on status of controls; areas where prescribed procedures are not followed; weaknesses exist. Recommendations for improvement.	System review and evaluation. Compliance testing.
Accounting Systems	Review accounting system(s) and procedures.	Assess appropriateness, economy and efficiency of accounting systems and procedures—validate consistency with accepted and established principles, practices and guidelines.	Report of findings, conclusions and recommendations.	System identification, documentation and appraisal. Compliance testing.

218

Compliance	Review compliance with applicable laws, regulations, and the like.	Assess degree of compliance with applicable laws, etc.	Report of finding and conclusions; may include an assessment of risks.	Identification and documentation of applicable laws, etc. Compliance testing.
Contract	Review of compliance with the contract provisions.	Assess compliance with contract; assess concomitant benefits, costs and risks.	Report of findings and conclusions. Assessment of risks and potential consequences.	Identifying applicable contract provisions along with contractor's degree of compliance.
Investigative Support	Investigation of alleged wrongdoing or possible fraud.	Documentation of facts and circumstances of possible fraudulent behavior (including improper cash generation and illegal payments).	Report of findings and conclusions as to actual extent of alleged wrongdoing and potential fraud. Report should include an assessment of risks and their potential consequences.	Development of a chain of evidence suitable for court by identification and documentation of facts and circumstances of alleged acts of wrongdoing or fraud.

FIGURE 14.1 Types of Audits.

FIGURE 14.1 *(Continued)*

Type	Descriptive Statement	Audit Purpose	Deliverables	Audit Involves
			Recommendations should be made as to how the system's weaknesses which give rise to the fraud might be eliminated.	This is done by compliance or substantive tests, personal interviews and appropriate investigative methods. Coordination and cooperation with legal authorities to focus this audit in a way that is admissable four court use.
Special studies	Reviews of specific systems or procedures, reviews of implementation status and assessment of effect of corrective action and the	Identification of facts and assessment of current situations.	Report findings, conclusions and recommendations.	Identification and documentation of existing situation. Compliance testing and follow-up to ensure organization has taken corrective action.

| Economy and Efficiency Audit | Review of cost-benefit relationship in the use of resources to achieve intended program results. | Provide assessment of the economy and efficiency in the use of resources to achieve stated or implied objectives. Assess existence and efficiency of systems and procedures. Identify operational strengths and weaknesses. Identify criteria for assessment of major issues and opportunities for improvement. Develop recommended priorities and timetables for future action (including estimated potential for costs and benefits). | Summary and detailed reports of findings, conclusions and recommendations. | Identify and document purported goals, objectives, and programs of organization, its resources, systems and procedures. Compare organization's results and resources utilized with the accepted norms. Develop criteria for assessing importance of issues and priorities. Develop estimated costs and benefits. Criteria for use in assigning priorities for corrective action; establish timetable. |

221

FIGURE 14.1 (Continued)

Type	Descriptive Statement	Audit Purpose	Deliverables	Audit Involves
Results and Effectiveness i.e., a Program Results Audit	Review the value created through the activity audited and measure that against intended organization mission/ objective	Determine assessment of program performance and identification of opportunities for improvement.	Reports of findings, conclusions and recommendations.	Identification, documentation and assessment of stated or implied program goals and objectives, program evaluation criteria, data accumulation and measurement methods and data collected. Development of recommendations for improvement in existing methods and for additional goals, objectives, revaluation criteria, data accumulation and measurement methods.

222

annual budget of $300 million. It represents about 70% of this country's nondefense budget. It is about one and a half times the defense budget. It is the third largest budget in the world after the U.S. Government and the Soviet Union.

Of the approximately 100,000 auditable entities, including 35,000 grantees and contractors, HHS auditors perform and/or manage 5000 to 6000 audits each year. It would take a great number of years to cover such a large turf creditably. The hard cold fact is that about 90 percent of the auditable activities had never been audited—and, with current resources, could never be audited.

Program inspections have been implemented in the office of the Inspector General at HHS and in other variants at other departments. Its concept is built on two separate disciplines: operational auditing and rapid feedback evaluations. A program inspection is a "quick and clean" inspection that examines an operation or program. It is used in place of an in-depth audit adhering fully to audit standards. Such inspections are a new type of tool intended to supplement traditional audit coverage.

By carefully studying a program in advance of initiating field work, many shortcuts can be taken to permit a very useful internal study. These inspections are studies by design and for specific limited purposes. They have proven extremely valuable to program management in their decision making. They are timely and relatively inexpensive. For the cost, time, and human resources it would take to conduct one full field audit of an entity, a dozen or more field inspections can be conducted. In a department with so many auditable entities, program inspections offer an attractive, economical, additional tool in providing proper oversight to an entire department. While each program inspection is tailored for quick turnaround, each includes the following five phases: (1) orientation, (2) field study, (3) analysis, (4) a report and (5) followup. Program inspections cover a wide area—any area, in fact, that has a potential for more economy, increased efficiency, or better effectiveness. This includes a review of programs, management, and regulatory processes. The inspection team itself is tailored to the problem being addressed. Although there may be audit presence on the team, a program inspection is essentially not an audit. The team is primarily directed and led by program analysts.

Orientation

The first step in operational inspections is to identify each organizational function. In doing this, a number of steps can be taken, depending on time constraints. These steps include:

1. A review made of program legislation, regulations, past reviews (audits, studies, evaluations, etc.), and existing data;
2. Discussions are held with program managers and staff (policy, evaluation, budget, personnel, etc.); and
3. Consultation with outside authorities (at the Office of Management and Budget (OMB), on the Hill, academia, professional associations, etc.).

The foregoing is particularly important if the inspection is at the request of or with the direct involvement of senior management. From this effort, issues, problems, and questions are surfaced. Decisions are made at this stage on the design of the inspection, the types of data to be collected, types and number of field sites to be visited, number and types of staff needs for the inspection team, and the schedule on which they will be operating.

Field Study

First-hand observations and a review of operations are made on site. The number of sites may vary according to the needs. The inspection approach uses the combination of qualitative and quantitative methods and, in many ways, is more suggestive of evaluation assessments than audit findings. Considerable time is spent in open-ended one-on-one discussions. Generally, this is in person but may be supplemented by telephone interviews. Analysis of program and site records and documents require a significant portion of the team's time. By focusing on fairly narrow management issues, predetermined on the orientation plans, this would be relatively limited by audit standards. Dependence on good random statistical sampling methodology is crucial.

Analysis

The third major phase in the inspection process is examination of the evidence gathered by the site visits and data collection. The issues, questions, concerns of management, as well as the inspection design, determines the type of analysis that will emanate from the study. Normally, the inspection report addresses how well the sites and programs are adhering to the objectives of senior management and the Congress. Comparisons of the sites are made with best practices being contrasted to those sites which lag behind. Emerging management problems are identified.

Report

All the findings are developed into a brief report for management. From the findings, recommendations rise for operational and systemic improvements. The findings are written concisely and without jargon. They are designed for the user, and they include all corrective actions taken by management during the course of the review. In addition to the written report, formal or informal oral briefings are offered.

Each of the first four phases is relatively equal in time and effort. The ideal time for each of these phases is about one week. The most significant fact in this process is the small amount of human resources involved. The inspection team is characterized not only by its quick turnaround, but the small number of people involved. The inspection team usually consists of four to six people.

Follow-up

The last phase of the inspection involves proper follow-up. A follow-up tracking system is necessary to ensure that management acts upon the recommendations on which they have agreed.

Examples of Program Inspections

Program inspections combine the best of both operational auditing and rapid feedback evaluation into a third new tool with many advantages. Inspections are targeted on specific issues of interest to top management and are conducted quickly. They are rigorous enough to provide solid, credible documentation while still allowing the flexibility to pursue promising leads during all stages of the work. Some examples of program inspections follow, which show rather convincingly that top HHS managers do, in fact, act on the findings and recommendations of these studies. Each example also illustrates how a program inspection blends entirely different analytic techniques—some from rapid feedback evaluation, some from operation auditing—into an appropriate methodology for studying the issues of interest in that particular study.

1. A program inspection of transportation charges for portable x-ray services involved reviewing the billings for seven portable x-ray suppliers doing business in three states. The review involved the verification of 2400 claims for portage charges that were paid during calendar year 1980. The portage payment policies of the 37 other Medicare carriers were also surveyed. Office of Inspector General staff found cases where (1) more than one patient was x-rayed during a single trip to a nursing home, and (2) carriers paid at a reduced rate. However, the aggregate amount of reimbursement for the single trip still exceeded the amount which would have been paid if only one patient was x-rayed. The recommendation was a change in Medicare carrier reimbursement for a multiple-patient visit so as to not exceed the reimbursement for a single-patient visit.

This inspection took 1317 staff hours and had a cost-benefit of $150 program dollars for each administrative dollar expended.

2. Another inspection focused on the rapid increase in reimbursement for respiratory equipment and the sale of oxygen. It involved reviewing a large number of beneficiary specific situations, and telephone price verification of six suppliers located within the Washington/Baltimore metropolitan areas. Telephone verification of findings were that more expensive oxygen concentrators were charging the Medicare program over 300% of the wholesale price for the rental of concentrators. OIG recommended that (1) definitive national guidelines on coverage of oxygen and respiratory equipment be issued to provide criteria for reimbursement for oxygen supplied by a concentrator versus the less expensive tank method and (2) a legislative change in the reimbursement methodology for oxygen concentrators be sought to bring Medicare reimbursement more in line with the supplier's cost.

This inspection took 400 staff hours. The cost-benefit ratio was determined to be $1400 program dollars saved for each administrative dollar expended.

3. A third inspection reviewed Medicare and Medicaid anesthesia billing for 15 physicians in one state. Results indicates problems with (1) disparity of the reimbursement rate for physician supervision of anesthesia performed by hospital-employed certified registered nurse anesthetists (CRNAs), (2) anesthesia groups billing the state for services provided by hospital-employed CRNAs as if they themselves performed the full range of anesthesia, and (3) some anesthesiologists not providing adequate supervision of CRNAs as required by Medicare reimbursement rules.

OIG recommended a reevaluation of policy on coverage and reimbursement for CRNA services under Medicare. One provider group was referred to the carrier and state agency for appropriate investigation and monitoring to verify that requirements relating to physician supervision of nurse anesthetists were met. This inspection took 1200 staff hours and the cost-benefit ratio was determined to be $3.50 program dollars saved for every administrative dollar invested.

CHAPTER FIFTEEN

INDICATORS OF CRIMINAL ACTIVITIES IN THE BUSINESS WORLD

INTRODUCTION

In the preceding chapters we have discussed the importance of denying opportunities for crime by building a system of rules and controls. We have also reviewed the auditors' role in ferreting out fraud and some of the methods they follow to achieve that end. Now, our discussion turns to the kinds of things that can and should "tip off" an alert auditor or manager that something may be very wrong.

Basically poor controls can be equated to high opportunity for wrongdoing. If these weaknesses are found, they do not necessarily indicate that a criminal act has occurred. Rather, there is a strong indication that vulnerability exists. It must be stressed that the act of searching for the indicators identified hereafter is not an acceptable alternative to a sound target analyses, vulnerability assessments, or internal control reviews. Such searches do provide a short cut method of early identification of some of the more serious vulnerabilities that require immediate attention. These searches, done in conjunction with the kinds of analyses described in each part of this book, are the best and surest method of reducing opportunities for wrongdoing.

DETECTING CORPORATE CRIMINALITY

If companies pay out large sums of money for bribes, gratuities, or payoffs, they cannot declare these payments as legitimate business expenses on their income tax returns. In nearly all cases, payoff money will be concealed in the books and records as some other kind of expense. If that expense account is identified the investigator's case is all but concluded. The trick is to find it. Normal audits will not uncover it. Bribes and kickback payoffs have been made to obtain new business, retain old business, cover up short deliveries or inferior products or service, secure figures on competitive bids, obtain approval or acceptance of work, influence legislation, obtain licenses, receive loans from banks, companies, or union pension funds, negotiate "sweetheart contracts," obtain proprietary information, influence law enforcement and regulatory personnel, affect zoning changes, induce purchases at inflated prices, prepare or approve false financial statements, and so forth. It is rare that a company would be willing or is able to include the payoffs out of their profits.

Hidden Payoffs

The sole purpose of an audit is not to detect fraud. While auditors are expected to—and do—look for fraud, the normal audit should not be relied upon to discover fraud or payoffs. For a fuller discussion of this point, see Chapter 13, Part 5. In most investigations there is little concern as to whether the company in question is following generally accepted accounting methods or whether the books balance or a profit is being realized. In determining the existence of criminality, one's primary concern (at least, in the context used here) is whether those books conceal hidden payoffs.

Books utilizing the double entry system of accounting should always balance, whether or not large illicit payments were made. Unless the company or individuals making the payoffs are very careless or not too bright, an examination of all their ledgers will not reveal anything untoward. After all, they are maintained as much for IRS scrutiny (by law) as well as for the company's operational purposes.

Many investigators have been pleasantly surprised, though, to find that some bookkeeper or secretary has routinely jotted down (on check stubs for petty cash) the name of an official who was to get the proceeds from that check. Any company involved in illicit payoffs needs to devise a method to generate the cash payment which will not be detected through a routine review of the books and records. Most often this is accomplished through the creation of a "conduit."

Hiding Illicit Business Expenses

In this sense, a conduit is an artiface by which company checks are recorded as business expenses—and can be converted into cash without an audit trail. There are many ways by which this can be done. Sometimes conduits, or those operating the conduit, are called the "middleman." If the conduit also passes the money to the bribed person, he is also called the bagman.

Payoff funds can be transferred without apparent trace by using a "conduit" or intermediary. Essentially, the party making the bribe enters it as a business expenditure in their accounting records. The conduit may be a professional (such as an architect, attorney, accountant) or another company. So, party A makes a payment to party B, who in turn passes the funds to party C, the recipient of the bribe. For acting as a conduit, party B will receive a commission, plus an amount to compensate for his income tax liability on the bribe funds. To illustrate, party A wishing to pay party B a bribe of $50,000 may end up sending $100,000 to party C; $50,000 in bribe money, and $50,000 as commission and reimbursement for income tax liability.

A similar arrangement can be set up with a company overcharging for goals or services; the differences less commission and taxes for payoffs. In either of these cases, the first party has merely passed the problem of concealing the payoff to the second party.

Sometimes, the company is either unable to find someone to act as a conduit or is unwilling to chance involving a co-conspirator. In such cases, there may be an election to create a conduit in the form of a ficticious company, employing the same general schemes as previously mentioned.

Conduits have one important problem: the IRS. They are required to report all income that passes through them, even if they pass on 90-100 percent to someone else. In such a case, expenditures are itemized against the income. The tax code requires that all income, and this includes bribes, be reported on income tax returns. Fictitious companies and individuals must file returns. If they do not, those operating the company are committing income tax crimes. If they file returns with all the income and write off the money passed on as expenses, they are in violation of the law. If they do not report their payoffs, they are in violation. No matter how they handle it, conduits may find themselves in a trap.

There are many different types of records that can be subpoenaed to uncover a conduit or concealed transaction, including journals (that is, general, sales, and purchase), ledgers (general and accounts payable), invoices (sales and purchases), notes and loans payable, purchase orders, bank records (cancelled checks, deposits, check stubs, bank statements), payroll records, cash receipts, disbursement ledger, and petty cash records. In addition, there are a number of internal documents on transactions, such as supporting memoranda, correspondence, minute books, contracts, articles of incorporation, and ownership records, that can be of evidentiary value. The problem is in knowing what to look for and what would be of evidentiary value. In the absence of that kind of information, a detailed review of all the records would have to be made in order to (1) verify the details on employees, customers, sales, purchases, commissions, loans, expenses, and the like and (2) determine whether these transactions were to legitimate parties in accordance with the going market. This would require an exceptionally large effort.

Of course, it would be much more desirable to develop a witness who could identify the *modus operandi* being used by the company to conceal the illicit transactions. However, if circumstances are such that a search of the records needs to be made, the indicators of criminal activity discussed below may help to expedite the process.

INDICATORS OF CRIMINAL ACTIVITY BY BUSINESSES

The businessman or embezzler who diverts assets for his own use, to pay extortion demands, or to make bribes can do it many ways: He can make loans at attractive rates or grant lines of credit to specified parties. He can employ people and pay them good salaries to do nothing. He can purchase tables at political dinners or pay for political ads. He can provide free use or make gifts of automobiles, boats, planes, apartments, resorts, tickets to special events, and so on. He can allow the purchase of stock, goods, real estate, and the like at below market prices. He can just pass cash to his public official beneficiary.

Regardless of the type or nature of the benefit, this type of businessman will always have the same two problems to overcome (1) how to generate the cash and (2) how to conceal the transaction within his accounting records. Indicators of possible schemes by a company to generate and/or hide cash to be used for illicit purposes include:

1. Indicators of "cash generation" which can be found by a cursory examination of company checking practices.

   a. Excessive appearing balances kept in noninterest-
       bearing checking accounts. This is not sound business
       practice, and it may suggest a readily convertible
       cash pool for payoffs.
   b. Payroll checks mailed to post office boxes instead of
       residences. This could mean "ghost payrolling"; that
       is, maintaining nonexistent employees on the payroll
       and using that money for payoffs.
   c. Cancelled checks on which the payee name has been
       left blank, or in which the payee name has been
       handwritten or typed in, using a different typewriter.
   d. Cancelled checks that have not been blockstamped
       (that is stamped for deposit only by the payee),
       warrant investigation, especially if they have been
       negotiated by an individual. Such checks could
       represent, among other things, a form of ghosting
       wherein the checks represent phony payments that
       can be cashed for use in payoffs.
   e. The frequent use of cashier's checks could indicate
       another means of generating cash.
   f. Any large checks payable to corporate officials should
       be considered suspect and reviewed further.
   g. Checks that bear variations of company names
       should be examined closely. It is a fairly common
       practice to set up phony companies with names
       similar to real ones. The checks sent to such
       companies would be used for payoffs.
   h. Checks cashed but not deposited.
2. Indicators of criminal action can be found in the types of
   transactions engaged in by a company, that is, the way
   they conduct business.
   a. Excessive bonuses to executives might mean they are
       kicking back into a secret payoff fund.
   b. A variation of this might be employees receiving
       excessive overtime payments or commissions. Part of
       such a payment could be kickback money.

c. Abuse of the petty cash account is the favored method of cash generation. By cashing an extra check now and again for "miscellaneous expenses," significant sums can be generated quite quickly.

d. Excessive and/or fake travel or entertainment expenses could serve the same purpose. Such false claims can be used to generate payoff money.

e. Phony or inflated promotional or advertising expenses. These expenses can usually be identified first as aberrations in the normal expense budget for that purpose.

f. Any large cash transaction should be suspect, particularly if it occurs frequently. Most companies, of course, rarely do business in cash.

g. Any large or unusual expense item such as for equipment rental or supplies of a questionable nature. As an extreme illustration, a retail bakery would appear to have little use for a shipment of construction equipment. In other words, any expenditure for items which appear to be outside of a firm's line of business could be questionable.

h. Any high discounts or rebates on billings or sales, particularly at below cost, purchases at higher than normal cost, and payments exceeding what is owed can be indicative of a conduit arrangement with the company that is paying the bills.

i. Delinquent accounts receivable being written off or payments for nonexistent goods or services can indicate a conduit arrangement. They are difficult to detect or prove, however, without inside information.

j. Investments, loans, stock and real estate sales, and so on, that appear to deviate from the normal business practice. Such transactions may be at a below market rate of return or written off as a bad investment or loan.

k. A company that has an unusually complicated

structure for its size warrants questioning, especially if some "profit unit" or subsidiary has minimal revenue against building deficits. The transferring of cash to these entities may be a conduit.

l.   Any large write-offs for spoilage or defects could be a means of generating cash by disposing of the property, that is, by entering it on the books as a write-off instead of a sale.

3.   The manner in which the record is kept can indicate possible criminal conduct.

a.   Any entry not in ink should be questioned, as should all unusual or unexplained journal or ledger entries.

b.   Any unusual, incomplete, improper, or missing documentation and/or authorization in the books warrants further examination.

c.   The appearance of a second set of books indicates criminal misconduct, as does the disappearance or destruction of records without cause. Also, any altered document or a document containing erasures demands additional inquiry.

4.   The manner in which the company deals with its professional help can be an "indicative" of potential criminal conduct.

a.   Anyone providing professional services is in an excellent position to be a conduit (that is, attorneys, architects, accounting firms, or consultants). Unusually high fees or charges for services rendered could be suggestive of this kind of arrangement.

b.   A company that has a frequent turnover of professionals in key management positions, (such as treasurer, auditor, or attorney) might indicate that someone high in the company is trying to prevent people in these sensitive positions from discovering criminal conduct.

c.   The manner in which a company meets with an investigator or creditors is a classical tipoff. That is, if an official is evasive or unresponsive to relatively simple questions, further investigation is warranted.

None of the preceding is a panacea for uncovering cash generation or record concealment. However they stimulate ideas when looking at company operations.

Dealings With Government Entities

In the generalized sense, there are certain indicators of misconduct concerning companies doing business with government entities. They include certain companies who (1) constantly get lower real estate tax rates, (2) operate without proper licensing or permits, (3) avoid contributing to public revenue, or (4) obtain large sums of money for public works and/or welfare programs (for example, housing, medical services, employment) while consistently demonstrating substandard performance.

Another warning signal is when certain contractors consistently win bids. This may suggest "rigged" bidding. Rigged bidding can be verified by checking with the losing bidders. Normally these bidders can provide valuable background on how the system is supposed to operate, how it is actually functioning, and who might be corrupting it. Also, a check of the losing contractors may show that (1) bids may have been submitted in the name(s) of firms that do not exist or (2) they are part of a scheme to rotate contracts among a select few companies.

Tracing Illicit Payments

Once the method being used to conceal the transaction is determined, it is much easier to examine the books for verification and documentation. The actual existence of employees, suppliers, subcontractors, clients, and so on, must then be verified by checking telephone books and the like.

Once their existence is proven, the next step is determining whether the money paid is commensurate with services provided. Time or commission records for employees could be checked against payment. The same could be done by comparing the records of service providers (such as attorneys, consultants, and architects) against payment records of the company. Unusual checks warranting further consideration can also be surfaced by arranging checks in numerical order. Checks that appear out of chronological sequence could indicate a problem. Additional unreported checks may be found by comparing the cash disbursement journal against the numerical listing of checks. Any questionable checks should have supporting data, such as invoices, vouchers, correspondence, purchase orders, contracts, receiving slips, inventory entries, and so forth examined. Lack of detail on any of the documentation should further suspicion of the transaction. The next step would be to carry the inquiry to the recipient company where suspected overpayments, and fictitious or overdiscounted transactions could be verified.

CONTRACTS AND PROCUREMENT FRAUDS: LESSONS LEARNED FROM THE DEPARTMENT OF DEFENSE

There is always a high vulnerability present in contracting for services or material and supplies in any business or government entity. No organization is more concerned about this fact than the Department of Defense (DoD). It is by far the largest purchaser of material and supplies in the U.S. Joseph Sherrick, the Inspector General at the Department of Defense, issued a publication in May 1984 on "Indicators of Fraud in the Department of Defense Procurement."[1]

The next few pages are excerpted from that publication. They describe some of the more common indicators of potential

[1]Office of Inspector General, *Indicators of Fraud in the Department of Defense Procurement*, (Department of Defense, May 1984), pp. 1, 3–9, 13–14, 17–19.

wrongdoing found in the DoD procurement process. These indicators, though, have wide application to almost any type of procurement system. A more complete discussion can be found by reading the entire publication.

Fraud in the Development of Statements of Work and Specifications

Bid specifications and statements of work detailing the types and amounts of goods or services to be provided are prepared to assist in the selection process. They are intended to provide both potential bidders and the selecting officials with a firm basis for making and accepting bids. A well written contract will have specifications, standards and statements of work which make it clear what the Government is entitled to. Sloppy or carelessly written specifications make it easy for a contractor to claim that it is entitled to more money for what the Government later defines as what it really wants. Sometimes, there is deliberate collusion between Government personnel and the contractor to write vague specifications. At other times there is an agreement to amend the contract to increase the price immediately after the award. One contractor actually developed a "cost enhancement plan," identifying all of the changes he would make in order to double the cost of the contract, before it was even signed.

Fraud indicators include:

1. Defining statements of work and specifications to fit the products or capabilities of a single contractor.
2. Advance or selective release by Government employees of information concerning requirements and pending purchases only to preferred contractors.
3. Using statements of work, specifications, or sole source justifications developed by or in consultation with a preferred contractor (institutional conflict of interest).
4. Allowing architect-engineers, design engineers or other firms participating in the preparation of bid packages to obtain those same construction or production contracts or to be subcontractors to the winning contractors.
5. Release of information by firms participating in design

and engineering to contractors competing for the prime contract.

6. Designing "pre-qualification" standards or specifications to exclude otherwise qualified contractors or their products.

7. Splitting up requirements so contractors each get a "fair share" and can rotate bids.

8. Splitting up requirements to get under small purchase requirements ($25,000) or to avoid prescribed levels of review or approval, e.g., to keep each within the contracting authority of a particular person or activity.

9. Bid specifications or the statement of work are not consistent with the items included in the general requirements.

10. Specifications are so vague that reasonable comparisons of estimates would be difficult.

11. Specifications are not consistent with past similar type procurements.

Fraud in Pre-Solicitation Phase

Fraud indicators include:

1. Unnecessary sole source justifications.

2. Falsified statements to justify sole source or negotiated procurement.

3. Justifications for sole source or negotiated procurement signed by officials without authority or the deliberate by-passing of required levels of review.

4. Placing any restrictions in the solicitation documents which would tend to restrict competition.

5. Providing any advance information to contractors or their representatives on a preferential basis by technical or contracting personnel.

Fraud in Solicitation Phase

Fraud indicators include:

1. Restricting procurement to exclude or hamper any qualified contractor.

2. Limiting time for submission of bids so only those with advance information have an adequate time to prepare bids or proposals.

3. Revealing any information about procurement to one contractor which is not revealed to all (from either technical or contracting personnel).

4. Conducting bidders conference in a way which invites bid rigging or price fixing or permits improper communications between contractors (See Chapter IV).

5. Failure to assure a sufficient number of potential competitors are aware of the solicitation. (Use of obscure publications, publishing in holiday season, providing a vague or inadequate synopsis to Commerce Business Daily, etc.)

6. Bid solicitation is vague as to the time, place, or other requirements for submitting acceptable bids.

7. Little or no control over the number and destination of bid packages sent to interested bidders.

8. Improper communication with contractors at trade or professional meetings or improper social contact with contractor representatives.

9. Government personnel or their families acquiring stock or a financial interest in a contractor or subcontractor.

10. Government personnel discussing possible employment with a contractor or subcontractor for themselves or a family member.

11. Special assistance to any contractor in preparing his bid or proposal.

12. "Referring" a contractor to a specific subcontractor, expert, or source of supply. (Express or implied that if you use the referred business, you will be more likely to get the contract.)

13. Failure to amend solicitation to include necessary changes or clarifications. (Telling one contractor of changes that can be made after award.)

Fraud in the Submission of Bids and Proposals

Fraud indicators include:

1. Improper acceptance of a late bid.
2. Falsification of documents or receipts to get a late bid accepted.
3. Change in a bid after other bidders prices are known. This is sometimes done by mistakes deliberately "planted" in a bid.
4. Withdrawal of the low bidder who may become a subcontractor to the higher bidder who gets the contract.
5. Collusion or bid rigging between bidders.
6. Revealing one bidder's price to another.
7. False certifications by contractor.
   a. Small business certification.
   b. Minority business certification.
   c. Information provided to other agencies to support special status.
   d. Certification of independent price determination.
   e. Buy-American Act certification.
8. Falsification of information concerning contractor qualifications, financial capability, facilities, ownership of equipment and supplies, qualifications of personnel and successful performance of previous jobs, etc.

Fraud in the Evaluation of Bids and Proposals

Fraud indicators include:

1. Deliberately discarding or "losing" the bid or proposal of an "outsider" who wants to participate. (May be part of a conspiracy between a Government official and a select contractor or group of contractors.)
2. Improperly disqualifying the bid or proposal of a contractor.
3. Accepting nonresponsive bids from preferred contractors.

4. Seemingly unnecessary contacts with contractor personnel by persons other than the contracting officer during the solicitation, evaluation, and negotiation processes.

5. Any unauthorized release of information to a contractor or other person.

6. Any exercise of favoritism toward a particular contractor during the evaluation process.

7. Using biased evaluation criteria or using biased individuals on the evaluation panel.

Fraud in the Award of the Contract

Fraud indicators include:

1. Award of a contract to a contractor who is not the lowest responsible, responsive bidder.

2. Disqualification of any qualified bidder.

3. Allowing a low bidder to withdraw without justification.

4. Failure to forfeit bid bonds when a contractor withdraws improperly.

5. Material changes in the contract shortly after award.

6. Advance information concerning who is going to win a major competition can give advantages to persons trading in the stock of both the winning and losing companies.

7. Awards made to contractors with an apparent history of poor performance.

8. Awards made to the lowest of a very few bidders without readvertising considerations or without adequate publicity.

9. Awards made that include items other than those contained in bid specifications.

10. Awards made without adequate documentation of all preaward and postaward actions including all understandings or oral agreements.

Fraud in the Negotiation of a Contract

There are a number of abuses which can occur in the negotiation of a contract. The first stems from the assumption of many personnel that once it has been determined that negotiated procurement procedures can be used (called procurement with discussions in the new FAR), that procurement on a sole source basis has also been justified. Whether a contracting officer is making the decision on a small dollar contract or a formal determination is being made by higher authority, competition is required unless specific justifications exist and are documented. Fraud indicators include:

1. "Back-dated" or after-the-fact justifications may appear in the contract file or may be signed by persons without the authority to approve noncompetitive procurement.

2. Information given to one contractor which is not given to others which give it a competitive advantage.

3. Improper release of information (e.g., prices in proposals, technical proposals or characteristics of proposals, identity or rank of competing proposals, proprietary data or trade secrets, and Government price estimates) to unauthorized persons.

4. Weakening the Government's negotiating position through disclosures to the contractor selected for award.

5. Contractor misrepresentation as to costs during negotiations (See Chapter III).

6. Failure of Government personnel to obtain and rely upon a Certificate of Current Cost or Pricing Data.

Defective Pricing Indicators

In September 1983, the Director of DCAA issued a memorandum to DCAA auditors stating guidance in the area of defective pricing where certain conditions exist which might indicate fraud. Auditors were instructed that when *indications* of fraud are found, the case will be referred to the proper investigative agencies. They include:

1. Persistent defective pricing.

2. Repeated defective pricing involving similar patterns or conditions.

3. Failure to correct known system deficiencies.

4. Failure to update cost or pricing data with knowledge that past activity showed that prices have decreased.

5. Specific knowledge, that is not disclosed, regarding significant cost issues that will reduce proposal costs. This may be reflected in revisions in the price of a major subcontract, settlement of union negotiations that result in lower increases on labor rates, etc.

6. Denial by responsible contractor employees of the existence of historical records that are subsequently found.

7. Utilization of unqualified personnel to develop cost or pricing data used in estimating process.

8. Indications of falsification or alteration of supporting data.

9. Distortion of the overhead accounts or base information by the transfer of charges or accounts that have a material impact on Government contracts.

10. Failure to make complete disclosure of data known to responsible contractor personnel.

11. Protracted delay in release of data to the Government to preclude possible price reductions.

12. The employment of people known to have previously perpetuated fraud against the Government.

These indicators should be applied as well by contracting officers and others involved in the procurement process. Particular note should be made in defective pricing cases that the "intent" of the contractor will be critical to a determination of whether a criminal act occurred. The deliberate concealment or misrepresentation of a single significant cost element could constitute a prosecutable crime. The establishment of intent should be the function of trained criminal investigators; auditors and contracting officials should make no assumptions that defective pricing results from unintentional conduct.

Indicators of Collusive Bidding and Price Fixing

The following list of indicators is intended to facilitate recognition of those situations which may involve collusive bidding or price fixing. In and of themselves these indicators will not prove that illegal anticompetitive activity is occurring. They are, however, sufficient to warrant referral to appropriate authorities for investigation. Use of indicators such as these to identify possible anticompetitive activity is important because schemes to restrict competition are by their very nature secret and their exact nature is not readily visible.

Practices or events that may evidence collusive bidding or price fixing are:

1. Bidders who are qualified and capable of performing but who fail to bid, with no apparent reason. A situation where fewer competitors than normal submit bids typifies this situation. (This could indicate a deliberate scheme to withhold bids.)

2. Certain contractors always bid against each other or conversely certain contractors do not bid against one another.

3. The successful bidder repeatedly subcontracts work to companies that submitted higher bids or to companies that picked up bid packages and could have bid as prime contractors but did not.

4. Different groups of contractors appear to specialize in Federal, state or local jobs exclusively. (This might indicate a market division by class of customer.)

5. There is an apparent pattern of low bids regularly reoccurring, such as corporation "x" always being the low bidder in a certain geographical area or in a fixed rotation with other bidders.

6. Failure of original bidders to rebid, or an identical ranking of the same bidders upon rebidding, when original bids were rejected as being too far over the Government estimate.

7. A certain company appears to be bidding substantially higher on some bids than on other bids with no logical cost differences to account for the increase, i.e., a local

company is bidding higher prices for an item to be delivered locally than for delivery to points farther away.

8. Bidders that ship their product a short distance bid more than those who must incur greater expense by shipping their product long distances.

9. Identical bid amounts on a contract line item by two or more contractors. Some instances of identical line item bids are explainable, as suppliers often quote the same prices to several bidders. But a large number of identical bids on any service-related item should be viewed critically.

10. Bidders frequently change prices at about the same time and to the same extent.

11. Joint venture bids where either contractor could have bid individually as a prime. (Both had technical capability and production capacity.)

12. Any incidents suggesting direct collusion among competitors, such as the appearance of identical calculation or spelling errors in two or more competitive bids or the submission by one firm of bids for other firms.

13. Competitors regularly socialize or appear to hold meetings, or otherwise get together in the vicinity of procurement offices shortly before bid filing deadlines.

14. Assertions by employees, former employees, or competitors that an agreement to fix bids and prices or otherwise restrain trade exists.

15. Bid prices appear to drop whenever a new or infrequent bidder submits a bid.

16. Competitors exchange any form of price information among themselves. This may result from the existence of an "industry price list" or "price agreement" to which contractors refer in formulating their bids or it may take other subtler forms such as discussions of the "right price."

17. Any reference by bidders to "association price schedules," "industry price schedules," "industry suggested prices," "industry-wide prices" or "market-wide prices."

18. A bidder's justification for a bid price or terms offered because they follow the industry or industry leader's

pricing or terms, this may include a reference to following a named competitors pricing or terms.

19. Any statements by a representative of a contractor that his company "does not sell in a particular area" or that "only a particular firm sells in that area."

20. Statements by a bidder that it is not their turn to receive a job or conversely that it is another bidders turn.

Collusive Bidding and Price Fixing Examples

The following sections describe common collusive bidding and price fixing schemes which DoD personnel may be able to recognize. These schemes relate to one another and overlap. Frequently an agreement by competitors to rig bids will involve more than one of these schemes.

1. *Bid Suppression or Limiting.* In this type of scheme one or more competitors agree with at least one other competitor to refrain from bidding or agree to withdraw a previously submitted bid so that a competitor's bid will be accepted. Other forms of this activity involve agreements by competitors to fabricate bid protests or to coerce suppliers and sucontractors not to deal with nonconspirators who submit bids.

2. *Complementary Bidding.* "Complementary bidding" (also known as "protective" or "shadow" bidding) occurs when competitors submit token bids that are too high to be accepted (or if competitive in price, then on special terms that will not be acceptable). Such bids are not intended to secure the buyer's acceptance, but are merely designed to give the appearance of genuine bidding.

3. *Bid Rotation.* In "bid rotation," all vendors participating in the scheme submit bids, but by agreement take turns being the low bidder. In its most basic form bid rotation will consist of a cyclical pattern for submitting the low bid on certain contracts. This rotation may not be as obvious as might be expected if it is coupled with a scheme for awarding subcontracts to losing bidders, to take turns according to the size of the contract, or one of the other market division schemes explained below.

4. *Market Division.* Market division schemes are agreements to refrain from competing in a designated portion of a market. Division of a market for this purpose may be accomplished based on the customer or geographic area involved. The result of such a division is that competing firms will not bid or will submit only complementary bids when a solicitation for bids is made by a customer or in an area not assigned to them.

APPLYING THE PRINCIPLES TO RETAIL SALES OPERATIONS

Nearly six million firms do business in the United States. Their assets, tangible and intangible, are prime targets for criminals engaged in white collar or felony crimes. The retail sales area is an excellent area for application and use of the principles of crime prevention illustrated throughout this book.

In this part, we discuss several of the major concerns that retailers must consistently consider: how to best ensure the honesty of their employees, ways in which shoplifting can be minimized through detection and control methods, and ways in which to guard against bad checks. We will relate these situations to the principles of crime prevention.

A price tag can readily be placed on one of the more easily identified crimes against retail business, the problem of "inventory shrinkage." This term simply implies that goods which should be on hand are not. Much of this shrinkage can be caused by criminal acts:

Shoplifting, whether it be done by impulse, or by a professional

Employee theft, carried out on an organized or impulse basis; or through collusion with intended recipients such as by deliberately undercharging, and/or overshipping orders and the like.

Other inventory shrinkage problems can be caused by careless or indifferent employees. Retailers lose over $6 billion in inventory shrinkage each year, or about two percent of their retail sales. Small businesses are the hardest hit since they usually lack the management skills needed to combat the factors which cause it. The Small Business Administration has attributed as much as 40 percent of small business failures to theft.

MOTIVATION AND YOUR EMPLOYEES

You should never underestimate your ability to influence your employees in the direction of honesty. Your use of good controls, stiff loss-prevention procedures, and cleverly located physical security devices are powerful reminders to employees that the boss does indeed care. The impact of all these good practices, though, can be wasted if the owner-manager fails to set a personal example of honesty and conscientiousness. You, as the owner-manager, should sign for items you take from the stockroom just like any other person.

The most successful crooked employees are those who have tested your control systems and are convinced that they can be circumvented. With every "score," their confidence increases, and along with it their danger to the company. The fear of being caught, a major factor in the decision to commit a crime becomes much less significant after every successful attempt.

Consider a plant where it is common practice for close relatives of the boss to help themselves from the stockroom without signing for the items they take. Soon it becomes a place where inventory shrinkage soars as employees get the message that recordkeeping is loose and controls are lax. In a manufacturing plant, no materials and no finished goods should be taken without a requisition or a removal record being made.

Nothing deters would-be thieves better than the knowledge that inventory is so closely controlled that stolen goods will be missed quickly.

Motivation and Shoplifting

All evidence suggests the most effective means to reduce shoplifting is through an aggressive policy of prosecution. This is particularly true among juveniles, who belong to one of the closest knit societies in the community. Kids spend time during the day together in school, and at play. They engage in mischief seemingly to test the limits of the rules that govern them. A store with a reputation for a no-nonsense attitude towards shoplifting is least likely to experience this problem among juveniles, once the "word is out." There are many other factors, of course, that weigh in this matter, such as the type of merchandise stocked, store safeguards in place, as well as the motivation of the latent shoplifter.

Losses from shoplifting have been estimated in the millions of dollars each year, representing an enormous economic abuse. A store operating at a three percent net profit on sales would, for example, have to sell over $1200 worth of merchandise to make up the loss for each $36 item missing from its counters. One may put shoplifters into five main categories: juvenile offenders; impulse shoplifters; alcoholics, vagrants, and drug addicts; kleptomaniacs; and outright professionals. All are differently motivated.

Youngsters account for about 50 percent of all shoplifting. They may steal on a dare or simply for kicks. Frequently they expect that store owners and courts will be lenient because of the offender's youth. They may enter stores in gangs in an attempt to further intimidate management. Shoplifting is usually the first type of theft attempted by juveniles, and it may lead to more serious crimes. Juvenile theft should be pursued and prosecuted through the proper legal channels.

Many "respectable" people are impulse shoplifters. They have not premeditated their thefts, but when opportunity and access suddenly come together (such as an unattended dressing room or a blind aisle in a supermarket), such people succumb to temptation.

Abnormal physical need such as those expressed by alcoholics, vagrants, and drug addicts, can drive people to theft, as well as to other crimes. These criminals are often clumsy or erratic in their behavior and may be easier than other types of shoplifters to detect.

Kleptomaniacs on the other hand are motivated by a compulsion to steal. They usually have little or no actual use for the items they steal and, in many cases, could well afford to pay for them.

The professional shoplifter is in the business of theft and motivated by desire for personal gain. He or she is usually skilled and hard to spot. They generally tend to concentrate on high-demand, easily-resold consumer goods such as televisions, stereos, and other small appliances which are later sold to fences.

Lastly, bad check artists are motivated by a desire for illicit gain that may be caused by any of the internal and external forces discussed in Chapters 4 and 5.

DENYING ACCESS TO WOULD-BE WRONGDOERS

Chapter 8 discusses in some detail the value of verifying the credentials of individuals applying for employment prior to their hiring. Corners are often cut in the retail field in verifying an applicant's credentials, since turnover is so great. This can result, though, in increased risk to employee theft, and is a dangerous short cut for even the most trained manager.

There is no company or organization immune to the continuing, massive problem of employee pilferage. Reliable observers estimate that as much as 40 percent of *all* company losses are perpetrated by employees themselves! While it is unrealistic to think it can be stamped out, it is possible and practical to institute attitudes and procedures to minimize its impact.

Overall, to prevent extensive pilferage, an owner-manager must recognize that some employees cannot be trusted. All employees should be aware that safeguards are in place to thwart dishonest personnel. Generally speaking, such steps include setting up a system of loss prevention devices and procedures, administering the system rigidly, and auditing it often to discourage dishonest employees who try to bypass the system.

To steal or not to steal? That is the question facing employees in the workforce. Many employees answer that question almost unconsciously. They see items lying around and pick them up for their own use. They slip small hand tools into their pockets, dip into the bin for a fistful of nuts and bolts, or snip off a few feet of wire for a home repair job. The question of what, if any, "pilferage" is allowable remains for the manager to decide. But this gate, once open, is hard to close.

One reason for employee pilferage is misplaced trust. Many owner-managers of small companies feel close to their employees. Some regard them as partners. These owner-managers trust their people with keys, a safe combination, cash, and records. Thus, these employees have at hand the access which a thief or embezzler needs for a successful crime.

Some of the "trusted" employees in many small businesses are larger partners than their bosses anticipate. Few indeed are the businesses in which dishonest employees are not busily at work. Usually, these employees are protected by management's indifference or ineptitude as they steal a little, steal a lot, but nevertheless, steal first the profit, and then the business itself.

One of the first steps in preventing pilferage is for the owner-manager to examine the trust he or she puts in employees. Is it blind trust that grew from close friendships? Or is it trust that is built on an accountability that reduces opportunities for thefts?

Employee Apathy and Bad Checks

Proper employee attitude is an all-important consideration for a successful, well-run operation. Employee apathy or carelessness towards accepting checks in payment for purchases provides opportunity for wrongdoers and is a big reason for stores being stuck with bad checks—as well as for unqualified credit transactions. It is axiomatic to note that the larger the operation, the more difficult it becomes to keep employees alert to company interests. As we know, one method that is being tried by many credit card firms is to pay a bonus to any employee who keeps a card proffered for a purchase, that can be determined as stolen, or owned by an unsatisfactory payor. Sales clerks must be trained and retrained to be alert to bad checks, and to make proper credit verifications. Additional training is needed also to alert clerks to possible shoplifters as well as to the characteristics of counterfeit money.

With Respect to Accepting Checks or Credit Cards for Payment

In accepting a person's check for goods and/or cash, experienced business people realize that the entire transaction may or may not be fraudulent, and that their business could very well be exchanging their things of value for a piece of worthless paper. Checks may be tendered that are fraudulent, written on no or insufficient funds, stolen, altered, post-dated (making them a promissory note), or improper in some other way. Much has been written about the criminal consequences of false identification in our society (see Chapter 11) and on the mechanical means of verifying identities (Chapter 10). You may wish to review and interpret these chapters, as they refer to this particular segment of the business world.

Suffice it to say, before giving access to your property, identification should be required with any check accepted as tender (two separate pieces are the general rule). Currently the most acceptable ID has been a state motor vehicle operators' license which generally carries the photograph of the individual along with his signature. National credit cards are another acceptable type of ID, as well as government or employee identification cards. The latter are of more use as identifiers, in that they contain both the photograph and signature of the bearer. None of these cards are easily obtainable because the issuing organization runs a check on the applicant's identity before the card is issued. Keep in mind that credit cards and IDs serve as access documentation to your property. Credit transactions should be considered as giving over access in return for a promise to pay based upon documentation.

Documents not meeting the above standards (that is, not containing a photograph, signature, restricted issuance practice) are poor risks. These might include various types of social club cards, library, voter registration cards, work permits, business cards and the like. None of these cards relate to credit history, are duplicated or forged easily, and cannot be checked for validity. A special note of caution needs to be made for Social Security Cards and birth certificates. In the former, federal law dictates that they are not to be used for identification purposes, and both are easily forged, altered and duplicated. They are the most abused documents in America today.

PART SIX

APPLYING THE FORMULA FOR FRAUD TO THE WORLD OF COMPUTERS

CHAPTER SIXTEEN

THE PROBLEMS OF RISING TECHNOLOGY

The computer is a great boon to government, industry, and science. It performs both mundane and sophisticated applications swiftly and truly. But life's good things are always accompanied by problems. With computers, one must consider the security of its operations, learn to deal with the growing problem of people gaining unauthorized access to computer systems (hackers) and continue to be aware of what can and has gone wrong with none-too-secure computer operations. Yet, computers have also become a major tool for use by auditors and investigators in the war against fraud and abuse.

The current information explosion is unparalleled in history. More information will be collected, stored, manipulated, and retrieved in our lifetime than all previous generations combined. Each period in our history has been accompanied by leaps in data storage. With the Industrial Revolution as a prod, vast increases of business information began to be collected. During the reign of Queen Victoria, auditors could no longer make 100 percent verification reviews and turned to sampling transactions (a shock that purists in the professions still abhor). Since then, major efforts have been made to develop, test, and implement techniques and strategies to detect weaknesses and ensure data security.

Who can deny that computer technology is here to stay and will become even more pervasive? This increase in the use of data processing is especially critical for auditors and investigators who are used to tracing transactions using paper audit trails. The crucial question for all of us is whether computers will become a beast of burden that serves us or an untamed monster that overwhelms us.

To make computers serve us, we must do two things. First, we must use computers to tame computers—using them as an audit or investigative tool, to search for computer stored data that appears inappropriate or illogical or duplicative in some sense. Later in this chapter is a discussion of such computer-record matching. Second, we must audit the computerized systems themselves to ensure that proper internal controls are being built into their systems designs and thus close off opportunities for illict ADP transactions.

Since there is such a need for this type of work, managers ought give every consideration to having an audit function available as needed to review new and existing ADP systems design and development; and to test the adequacy of the security systems in place over data, software, and hardware.

The continuing publicity and recognition given the problem of hackers confirms that management needs to recognize the vulnerabilities of computerized systems and implement safeguards to protect data bases from unauthorized intrusion. In recent years, mischief makers with knowledge of computerized systems have penetrated many such bases. This problem is growing at lightning speed. The following are but a few of a growing host of examples of attacks on computerized systems by hackers and others. It is worth noting that most were *motivated* by a desire for money.

An engineering student was able to steal and sell $1 million worth of equipment by manipulating a computerized supply system.

In Chicago a man substituted a stack of his own magnetically coded deposit slips for the blank ones used at the bank's service counter, causing all those deposits made by the customers using them to be diverted to his own account.

In August 1983, police agencies uncovered the "414s," a group of 10 young hackers in the Milwaukee area who had penetrated computer files of banks, hospitals, and even the Los Alamos National Laboratory in New Mexico, a center for top secret weapons research.

In February 1985, a California hacker who broke into a U.S. Department of Agriculture computer system in Colorado was the first person to be prosecuted under new federal legislation which outlaws unauthorized access to government computers.

A New York City bank teller used a computer to transfer $1.5 million to his personal account without trace in the computer system.

In Osaka, Japan, a female bank clerk and a male friend were co-conspirators in a scheme to defraud her employer. She opened savings accounts under a false name at five of the bank's branches. Later, she operated a terminal machine in a scheme that made it appear as if these accounts had received transferred funds. This person eventually fled the country after withdrawing a total of 130 million yen at three branches of the bank.

In mid-January 1979, an airplane with the Soviet Ambassador to the U.S. was landing at Kennedy Airport. An air-traffic control officer, not directly engaged in the control business, input illicit data into a computer. Such action caused a possibility of danger from an air-collision or a landing failure.

In 1973, a computer operator working at the Illinois auto driver registration bureau stole a reel of magnetic tape containing name and address data of registrants. As an address source for direct mailing, the tape was considered to be worth $70,000—the offender received $10,000.

A chief computer programmer with a chemical company in

Rotterdam (the Netherlands) stole a tape of data from his workshop and demanded a ransom for its return.

Two computer specialists working for a technical laboratory gained access to that firm's computer for a machine parts company and a trading firm. For this, they received $40,000. The operating cost of the computer for these illicit purposes amounted to over $200,000.

The director of development and the head of computer operations in a bank conspired to take advantage of a situation created by a computer system conversion that their employer was undergoing. During this period it was not uncommon for computer programs to be altered. The two, in conspiracy with an outsider, schemed to alter a computer program to make deposits flow from depositors' accounts into the account of the accomplice. The take for this scheme amounted to $137,000.

In October 1983 the FBI identified a group of intruders who tampered with the electronic mail of 18 corporations and government agencies that subscribed to the same communications service.

A physician used his own computer system to match diagnoses with all possible allowable charges to track drug allowances for each of his Medicaid patients. He generated false prescriptions and false laboratory reports to support the billings for those Medicaid recipients who had not reached their billing limit.

Scores of public welfare and Social Security Administration employees having access to payment systems are convicted each year nationwide for establishing false computer-based claim files or misdirected benefit checks to themselves. This continues to be a multimillion dollar problem.

Doctors, dentists, pharmacists, and other health providers are frequently found engaging in scams that involve inputting multiple claims for the same service to payment systems under different provider numbers.

A clerk typist was convicted for fraudulently obtaining and selling confidential information from a computer to which system she had access.

A telephone interviewer at a major insurance company submitted fraudulent requests for payment using legitimate names and numbers but substituting her address in the computer file.

One of the major concerns of banks has been employees independently identifying deceased customers or other inactive accounts and then manipulating the accounts to affect embezzlements.

RATING THE ADP ENVIRONMENT'S VULNERABILITIES

In Part Two, we rated the vulnerabilities of the environment to criminal attack. Below is a questionnaire designed to provide a similar "rough cut" evaluation of your ADP environment's vulnerabilities. Answers should be recorded on the answer sheet that immediately follows the questionnaire. Each question should be answered to the best of your knowledge. The questionnaire is scored by assigning value to the accuracy of each statement as it applies to your organization.

1 = Does not accurately describe
2 = Partially correct
3 = Generally correct
4 = Mostly correct
5 = Accurately describes

If you really cannot choose the most correct answer or if the question is inappropriate to your setting, then leave it unanswered and go on to the next.

1. ADP operations are separated from other business operations.

2. Guards or other designated employees are present at the terminals, storage areas, and so on, to limit access to only authorized individuals.

3. Data storage/utilities are secured and access is strictly controlled.

4. All access and authorizations are recorded for later review.

5. Any access or attempted access that was discovered results in immediate questioning of individuals involved.

6. Physical access to computer centers are barred by security devices (burglar alarms, card/key locks, logging-in procedures, and so on).

7. There are strict and published directives governing the use of all equipment.

8. Security and traffic control measures extend to and include unattended periods.

9. Passwords are randomly selected symbols that are frequently changed.

10. There are different levels of access granted to the data base, based on a need-to-have access basis.

11. Where terminal lines are used, the data is encrypted to prevent those who may access the information from easily understanding the data.

12. There are different levels of use assigned (such as reading certain types of files, adding or deleting from them, or creating new data).

13. Requests for data memory is limited to "need-to-have-access" rules.

14. A regular program to test the system's security through risk analyses, vulnerability assessments or security audit is enforced.

15. Prior to going live with a new system, a target analysis is conducted on a pilot basis.

16. The individuals who design new systems or programs are not allowed to be involved in their operation.

17. All phases of the system's design involve documenting transactions on appropriate flow charts.

18. Users of new systems are involved in designing the system to insure their needs will be met.

19. Electronic audit trails have been built into all the systems to indicate who has used the system, for what purpose, and under what authority.

20. User manuals have been developed for all systems and programs.

21. During the development phase there is ongoing testing, monitoring and evaluating that includes security measures.

22. There is an executive ADP management committee for strategic planning of equipment purchases and software needs.

23. The internal audit staff is involved in all phases of a new ADP system from its planning to the output.

24. The basic control of compartmentalization exists in that there is a separation of duties, processes, and checkout functions.

25. Audits of computer operations are ongoing and on-line.

26. Segregation of functions and responsibilities extend throughout the ADP operations.

27. Numerical (batch controls) have been set up for documents to be processed by the computer.

28. There are procedures in place to ensure that documents rejected by the computer are returned to the originator.

29. Followups are made to ensure corrections are made.

30. Sound editing procedures have been adopted to prevent incorrect data from being force-fed into the system.

31. The quality control system identifies individuals who are error prone.

32. Security is provided to the entire perimeter of the ADP center.

33. Positive security measures are provided at the entrance of the facility.

34. Positive security is provided at the entrance to the computer rooms, data storage areas, and so on.

35. Positive security is provided at the terminal sites.

36. Log-in and log-out records are maintained.

37. Discs, tapes, etc. are maintained in special safekeeping rooms.

38. There is a designated individual who is custodian over the safekeeping rooms, and who is accountable for them.

39. Access to safekeeping rooms is strictly limited to those who have prior screening and authority assigned.

40. Strict procedures are enforced for checking data in and out of the storage rooms.

41. Physical barriers are in force that require the use of identification badges, inspections and the like to limit access to unauthorized people, materials and supplies.

42. An emergency back-up system exists in case fire, water or damage to discs or tapes take place.

43. Alarm systems are in place that detect unauthorized intruders, heat, fire and water.

44. Restrictions against unauthorized use include limiting transaction privileges, log-in protocols and password access.

45. There are authentication procedures to verify the identity of the individual wanting access to the system, such as (a) a password, (b) a card or key, (c) a unique set of personal attributes (e.g., voice or fingerprints), or (d) a combination of the above.

46. Passwords given out to employees for access purposes are of such a complexity and length to limit the possibility of discovery by accident or systematic guessing.

47. Passwords are assigned by giving out random characters rather than using words or a system of words.

48. Employees do not pick their own passwords.

49. Random selection of passwords utilize suitable algorithms that mix letters, numbers and other symbols that are difficult to break by crypto analysis.

50. Each employee is held strictly accountable for misuse of their passwords.

51. The password issuance process is tightly controlled.

52. Access and dissemination of the password list is strictly controlled.

53. The password list is encrypted prior to storage.

54. When logging in, the password is suppressed so that it does not print or display for someone else to see.

55. Prevention of electronic eavesdropping or wiretappers from discovering the password is accomplished by causing it to be encrypted differently each time it is used.

56. No more than three password attempts are allowed an individual before automatic shutdown and alerting of security personnel that unauthorized access is being attempted.

57. Passwords are changed frequently.

58. Once the password is accepted, users log in the system to provide an audit trail on the user.

59. Your systems provide exception reports that are analyses of deviations from normal use, thus providing indicators of possible misuse.

60. Any evidence of possible compromise or attempted compromise of a password results in the issuance of a new one.

61. Any changes in access by users (such as reassignment or termination) results in the immediate invalidation of the password.

62. A workable system of controls exist over each step in the preparation, use, and storage of documents involved in ADP.

63. Published rules are applied to the use of equipment, terminals, and so on with strict enforcement of their infractions.

64. Employees are indoctrinated in the form of written reminders, warning signs, oral briefings, and so on, as to the rules governing ADP operations.

65. All equipment is identified and numbered for accountability by location.

RATING YOUR ADP ENVIRONMENT QUESTIONNAIRE

Point Value		Point Value	
1	_____	2	_____
3	_____	4	_____
5	_____	6	_____
7	_____	8	_____
9	_____	10	_____
11	_____	12	_____
13	_____	14	_____
15	_____	16	_____
17	_____	18	_____
19	_____	20	_____
21	_____	22	_____
23	_____	24	_____
25	_____	26	_____
27	_____	28	_____
29	_____	30	_____
31	_____	32	_____
33	_____	34	_____
35	_____	36	_____
37	_____	38	_____
39	_____	40	_____

RATING YOUR ADP ENVIRONMENT—Continued

Point Value		Point Value	
41	_____	42	_____
43	_____	44	_____
45	_____	46	_____
47	_____	48	_____
49	_____	50	_____
51	_____	52	_____
53	_____	54	_____
55	_____	56	_____
57	_____	58	_____
59	_____	60	_____
61	_____	62	_____
63	_____	64	_____
65	_____		

Instructions for Scoring

1. Add down the total number of points.
2. Divide the total number by the number of questions answered.
3. Evaluate the scores as follows:

4.1 to 5	=	Indicates environmental factor has low vulnerability to criminal attack
3.1 to 4	=	Indicates moderate vulnerability to criminal attack
3 to lower	=	Indicates high vulnerability to criminal attack.

THE ACCESS FACTOR

To gain access to a computer, an individual must first have the computer recognize him as a legitimate user. Thus, the first hurdle faced by a hacker is to log on the system. The computer asks the caller to type in the required identification code and personal password. Once this is done satisfactorily, the hacker is permitted to review some or all of the files in the computer's memory.

It is easy to learn the skills necessary to access most systems that are purposely designed to be "user friendly" (easy to access and use). Computer stores sell the basic hardware necessary to access systems, along with step-by-step instructions on how to use them. The same stores sell software in the form of magnetic discs or tapes with standardized programs that automatically direct computers to carry out various tasks. Once they master their own system, hackers can reach out to learn someone else's.

Fortunately secure systems of government and industry are isolated from outsiders and cannot be accessed via telephone. However, most systems are intended for routine, nonsecure information storage, and those systems are open to access by sophisticated hackers.

ACCESSING THE COMPUTER

The federal government alone has over 20,000 mainframe computerized systems with another half million mini- and micro-computers. The private sectors of North America and Western Europe have over 100,000 major computer sites storing and manipulating data on bank credit, medical records, confidential letters, defense secrets, and so on. By design, the majority of these computers are user friendly and can be reached by ordinary telephone lines. The would-be unauthorized user can find these numbers in a variety of ways, including published records from authorized users, by exchanging numbers through computer clubs and associations, or by just randomly dialing all the telephone numbers in a particular area.

To speed the process, a computer can be programmed to use an automatic dialer that can recognize a computer's answering tone.

Many computerized systems can only be accessed through pocket-switched lines, not directly by telephone alone. An amateur can call local telephone numbers that will plug him into such widely used pocket-switched lines or GTE Telenet and Tymet. (The 414s used such systems to access scores of computers.)

The hacker or thief may then make use of that information or change it to whatever purpose desired. Thus, school, hospital, financial, inventory, credit, and eligibility records can be altered or misused for a variety of motives: greed, curiosity, vandalism, revenge, industrial espionage, and so on.

As great as the problem may be, it can be readily arrested and perhaps reduced to nil proportions. Vulnerabilities to unauthorized intrusion could be quickly, easily, and inexpensively stopped with simple controls to insure computer security.

Three well-known cases highlight this problem. All were reported in the news media. The first case tried in Maryland involved the owner of a computer company who stole confidential software by tapping into the computer system of a previous employer from his remote terminal. Had the defendant not made 2 of the 50 access calls across state lines, there would have been no basis for federal prosecution. Only a state statute on theft of trade secrets would have remained as a possible recourse. The second case involved a defendant who was a former employee of the Federal Reserve Board, later employed privately as a financial analyst. He was apprehended after he attempted unauthorized access to information in the FRB's money supply (M-1) file. Any information he might have obtained would have been extremely useful in analyzing his client's holdings. As in the first case, the Government would not have been able to use the wire fraud statute if the access telephone calls had not gone across state lines. The defendant, though, would have been prosecuted for theft of government property which is the information he accessed. But fixing a value on the information obtained, a necessary element of proof, would have been very difficult. In the third case, a computer expert fraudulently used a bank's in-house access codes to transfer millions of dollars to accounts he controlled in another bank. As it turned out, the defendant was prosecuted in the California state court system. However, the facts of the case point up the potential gaps in the current laws that may be present in any case in which federal prosecution is considered. If the wire communications transferring the funds had all been in the same state, there is no apparent theory under which federal prosecution could have been undertaken. The 98th Congress, in its waning hours in 1984, passed the Computer Fraud and Abuse Act, which outlaws unauthorized access to federal computers. That Act may be the beginning of a series of new laws aimed at closing the loopholes in the law.

STUDIES ON TARGET VULNERABILITIES OF COMPUTERIZED SYSTEMS

For years, the Congress, the General Accounting Office, Inspectors General (IG), and outside consultants have stated that the government's computer systems are vulnerable. But there had never been a governmentwide study to confirm these beliefs. The President's Council on Integrity and Efficiency (PCIE), composed of the 18 Inspectors General and chaired by the Deputy Director of the Office of Management and Budget, was concerned over computer security and the need to upgrade the audit and investigative skills necessary to address them. PCIE commissioned the Health and Human Services' Inspector General to conduct the first governmentwide study on the extent and nature of computer-related fraud and abuse in federal agencies. Specifically, the Council wanted to know:

1. Is computer-related fraud and abuse a problem in the government?
2. If so, what are the characteristics?
3. What should the IG community do to detect and present future occurrences?
4. What additional computer security expertise and activity are required in the IG environment?

The findings of the first phase of the study, based on the analysis of 69 fraud cases and 103 abuse cases identified by the agencies of Agriculture, Commerce, Defense, Energy, HHS, Justice, Labor, State, Treasury, NASA, Office of Personnel Management, and VA are:

The scope of the problem is still unknown. Agencies do not systematically track computer-related fraud cases in their fraud tracking systems. Most agencies do not track abuse at all.

Most frauds involved theft through input manipulation of cash or assets. Most abuse cases involved theft of computer time for outside business or entertainment.

Computer-related fraud losses ranged from $0 to $177,383. Most were under $100,000. Many of these were probably understated. Agency responses on loss in abuse cases were very scant.

Insiders (that is, operating personnel) found over half of the frauds and over two-thirds of the abuses. More importantly, more cases were found by accident than by any other means.

Many of the respondents to the study questionnaire (who were primarily investigators) either did not answer or gave incomplete or illogical responses to questions on controls in victimized systems. The prevalence of accidental detection, however, is alarming because of the implied weaknesses in controls.

It is interesting to compare and contrast the PCIE's reported findings with two recent reports, one by the American Institute of Certified Public Accountants (AICPA) and the other by the American Bar Association (ABA). The AICPA published its report, "The Study of EDP-Related Fraud in the Banking and Insurance Industries," in April 1984. This study, which began in 1978, served as a model to the PCIE study. In fact, the survey questionnaire was patterned after the AICPA survey instrument. Appendix IV is a partial listing of the cases disclosed by this survey. Let us analyze one of these cases using the formula for fraud. Readers may make a similar kind of analysis of the

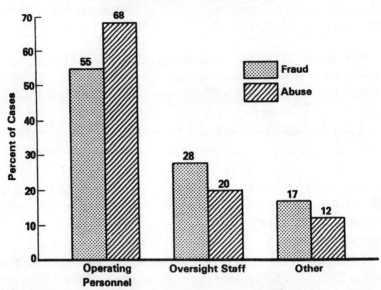

FIGURE 16.1. Computer-related fraud and abuse study: who detected cases. Source: PCIE study on computer-based fraud and abuse.

remaining cases—as a means for practicing the principles laid out in this book.

In 1974 when administration of cash assistance for the aged, blind, and disabled was transferred from states to the Social Security Administration (SSA), a Texas woman who had worked for the state program sought employment with SSA. She was hired as a clerk-typist, but soon became a service representative and later a claims representative. After five years on the job, she began, because of marital problems, to steal from the system by creating false aged SSI cases. Her scheme was more elaborate than most because she (a) falsely filled out application forms to create valid Social Security Numbers for her false cases, and (b) created false documents, such as school records and birth certificates, to put in the case file. The benefit checks were sent to post office boxes or to banks via direct deposit. She cashed the checks herself with false identification. She created 21 cases over six years and stole $309,000.

TARGET. The Social Security Administration with over $200 billion in outlays each year.

MOTIVATION. Predisposition unknown. However, situational stress provided the triggering rationale.

ACCESS. The wrongdoer gained access by following the transfer of the program from the state of Texas to the federal government. Because she was hired in a low level clerical position, no background investigation was conducted. Only cursory formal checks of prior employment were made. Thereafter, she worked her way up into a position whereby she could look for an opportunity to cheat the system. The triggering event was the situational stresses of marital problems which threatened her family support system and provided a rationale for engaging in criminal fraud. No one in her office, either peers or managers, seemed to take note of any changes of behavior until after she was caught.

OPPORTUNITY. After gaining a trusted position, she carefully developed a complicated scheme over a long period of time whereby she could generate false claim files and arrange for benefit checks to be sent to accommodation addresses. The system should not have allowed her to be able to complete and manage the whole case process. A simple system of segregating duties within the office would have prevented her from completing the whole process without implicating someone else.

The AICPA had more homogeneous study groups in the banking and insurance industries than one could ever find in the diverse functions and programs of the government. Nevertheless, the AICPA report of 119 fraud cases (85 banking and 34 insurance) does show interesting, and sometimes striking, similarities to the PCIE's study:

1. *The Wrongdoers:* In both reports, the primary objective, or motive, for the frauds was financial gain. Almost the same ratio (3 to 1) of nonsupervisory to supervisory employees were

involved in ADP-related frauds in both reports. Of even more interest is predominance of users, rather than data processing personnel, in frauds. In the AICPA study cases, over 80 percent (as opposed to 62 percent in the PCIE's study) of the perpetrators were users who committed frauds involving unauthorized file changes and transaction manipulation (lack of controls, leading to opportunity). Since the AICPA did not study what the federal (PCIE) study categorized as abuse, we cannot speculate if a similar involvement of data processing personnel is present in computer-related abuse in these industries.

2. *Losses:* Although the AICPA reported loss data in slightly different categories, reported cases with losses under $100,000 are the majority, as with the PCIE's study. It is interesting to note, however, that there were a higher percentage of cases over $100,000 (14 percent in banking cases and 21 percent in insurance cases) than the 8 percent found in PCIE's cases.

3. *Detection:* The AICPA study found that operating staff discovered over half of the ADP-related frauds (51 percent in banking; 68 percent in insurance cases); PCIE study results were similar. The AICPA also found that accidents or nonroutine events triggered the highest incidence of discovery, not the controls. In fact, the proportion of accidental/nonroutine discoveries in the insurance cases was close to half, as was the case with PCIE's study. This again reinforces the notion that the *opportunities* were great.

A third published study is also well worth noting. The American Bar Association's recent "Report on Computer Crime" discusses the work of an ABA task force which surveyed a broad range of private and public sector organizations on computer crimes, their causes and impacts. The ABA survey resulted in 283 responses from a broad range of organizations—including manufacturing, law enforcement, financial institutions, energy producers, and the computer industry.

The ABA definition of computer crime was deliberately broad to maximize response and minimize quibbling over narrow definitions. As a result, the respondents' answers indicated a wide range of abusive activities. While most of the ABA data is not comparable due to the presence of multiple answers, and other factors, several points are worth considering across all three studies:

The ABA respondents, as with PCIE and AICPA respondents, stated that when individual case loss was recorded or estimated, it was generally under $100,000. However, when asked their opinion regarding total annual losses due to computer crime, the majority of ABA respondents estimated between $100 million and $10 billion. More significantly, the ABA task force concluded that these estimates were probably conservative!

Based on the ABA respondents' experience with computer crime, most of the incidents were perpetrated by insiders who had been given access, and who were motivated by personal or financial gain—as was seen in both the PCIE and AICPA studies.

While acknowledging that reliable statistics do not exist on the incidence and losses of computer crime, the ABA report does assert that computer crime is significant and growing.

Finally, the ABA study underscores several points made by PCIE: (1) that problem awareness, particularly by top management, is not as high as it should be to focus on how to deny opportunity, and (2) that law enforcement personnel need more expertise to properly investigate and prosecute computer crime successfully in order to deter someone with a motive and opportunity.

COMPUTER RELATED CRIME IN JAPAN

The U.S. is not the only industrial nation plagued by concern for the problems of computer crime. In 1983 the Japanese government, in a White Paper on Police, devoted a special section to a study of Computer Crimes.[1] Their findings are

[1] 1983 White Paper on Police (published annually) by the National Police Agency in Japan.

remarkably similar to the U.S. studies noted previously. This suggests that the vulnerabilities arising from the information explosion and rising technology are generic. They know no boundaries between the public and private sectors, let alone among countries. The Japanese study focused on the 11-year period between 1971 and 1982. Their most serious difficulty in carrying out the study (as it was for the American studies) was being able to identify that criminal acts actually occurred. Although far more actual incidents were suspected, they were able to identify only 30 cases during the 11 years studied. In addition, over half the cases were in the two most recent years of the study. This, in turn, suggests that (1) the problem was growing and (2) the ability to identify the criminal acts was improving. Two-thirds of the cases involved manipulation of input data. This figure generally corresponds to both the PCIE government report (62 percent) and the AICPA report on the insurance and bonding industries (80 percent).

In December 1982 the Tokyo Metropolitan Police Department conducted an opinion poll on computer crime prevention measures among 500 computerized industries. They found that 70 percent of computerized facilities were not segregated from other business activities. (Note: This is a vulnerability since access is not limited.) Furthermore, a second finding was that over 40 percent of the facilities had no employees or guards for access control. Those that had some *access* control were broken down as follows:

22 percent at perimeter of the facility
55 percent at entrance/exit of the facility
15 percent near entrance/exit of computer room
 3 percent at terminal
 5 percent other or unstated

The Japanese study also addressed control systems which were designed to reduce opportunities for criminality. They concluded that controls in this area were not enough to prevent computer crimes. Only 17 percent were found to have crime prevention measures. The control-related procedures employed in operating computer operations break down as follows:

54.6 percent operated by plural full-time workers,

17.8 percent operated by plural nonfull-time workers,

10.9 percent operated by a single full-time worker,

13.1 percent operated by a single nonfull-time worker,

3.5 percent others.

Controls at the terminals among the industries were also surveyed, with the following results:

52.1 percent no access controls,

11.5 percent key access only,

22.4 percent access codes only,

6.3 percent required key and access codes,

3.4 percent other access restrictions.

Most of the several hundred companies surveyed had some control over data and programs, but those companies that maintain computers in a safekeeping room account for less than half. Even fewer companies keep in-and-out records of data and programs. The breakdown on those who had control over data/programs follows:

47.6 percent had safekeeping rooms,

35.4 percent had a person present who was in charge of storage.

60.3 percent had some limitation on access to data storage facilities,

23.4 percent had some procedures for checking data in and out of the room.

The study further noted that two-thirds of all companies do not have anyone specifically charged with crime prevention or have a training or awareness program on the subject.

A LOOK AT THE INDIVIDUAL WHO COMMITS ADP-BASED FRAUD

The results of some follow-up work done on the first PCIE study on government-wide computer fraud and abuse are both interesting and revealing. The report on that study is shown as Appendix 5. This work, which consisted of personal interviews with convicted perpetrators, was done in order to (1) develop a useful profile of such perpetrators and (2) understand the circumstances that made the crimes possible. It is also curious to note that the interview results were contrary to some of the findings of the first study, particularly as they related to whether the perpetrators acted in concert or alone. The PCIE study found that three-fourths of the wrongdoers acted alone, but the interviews demonstrated the reverse: 80 percent of the perpetrators acted with coconspirators. And most of the coconspirators were not discovered by the investigation. No conclusions can be drawn, though, because as the report explains the results obtained from the perpetrator interviews do not represent a statistically valid sample of government computer-related fraud cases. See Appendix 5.

CHARACTERISTICS OF COMPUTER FRAUD PERPETRATORS

Jack Molnar, lead analyst and principal interviewer on the PCIE project introduced the first public briefing on the report with the following narrative.

> Before I tell you a little about how we conducted this study of computer fraud perpetrators and share some of our early observations, I'd like to tell you about a guy—let's call him Bill—who I met early on during this study and also share with you his comments regarding computer-related fraud.
>
> Bill is 36 years old, married, with a six year-old daughter. He lives in his own home. He is very close to his parents and is an avid softball player. You'd like him if you met him. When he got

out of the service in 1973 he took the Federal Service Entrance Examination, got an excellent score of 103, and was hired by the Social Security Administration as a service representative. Bill, who finished third in his training class, soon became the office expert. Whenever anyone had a problem with the system that processed Social Security claims, they were told to "see Bill." Not surprisingly Bill got outstanding ratings and was soon promoted to claims representative.

After a few years Bill's wife became pregnant; it was unplanned. She had to stop working and their family income was cut by 60 percent. They had a mortgage on their home, payments on a new car, and another mouth to feed. In order to get some additional money, Bill submitted a suggestion to Social Security on how to tighten up on student claims to better find those that were fraudulent. He was convinced it would have saved a couple of million dollars a year. His suggestion was rejected and Bill became an unhappy employee with pressing financial problems. Had it been accepted, Bill could have expected a sizeable cash award.

Bill figured he needed about $300 a month, tax-free if he were to support his family. Bill set out to get it from the Social Security system. The next case that Bill got where a client's benefits were being terminated, he didn't terminate the case. Instead, he took some of his own money, opened a bank account in that person's name and then transferred the beneficiary's payment via direct deposit to the account he had set up. Bill told me that it was really easy to set up the account because banks don't ask too many questions when they are getting a new account. In fact, they gave him a toaster as he walked out the door. Over the next three-and-a-half years through this arrangement Bill stole about $15,000.

During the two-hour discussion we had that night in a small restaurant, Bill stressed two things that give some insight into this type of government computer-related fraud. The first thing he stressed was that virtually *everyone* in his office knew how to do what he did, because it is common to discuss "how to beat the system" during coffee breaks and at lunch. In fact, he wasn't sure that he was the only one in his office doing it. The other noteworthy thing he told me was that no one, until this study came along, had asked how he committed the crime. No investigator or anyone in authority with the Social Security Administration had tried to identify and fix the specific vulnerability (opportunity) in the system he had exploited. In fact, it wasn't until five months after the crime was identified and six weeks into his prison sentence that Social Security was able to stop the bogus checks. Quite a few useful and interesting facts were disclosed by the follow up work on this. Findings from the interview follow:

PERPETRATOR CHARACTERISTICS:

Average age	32 years
Average time in agency	5½ years
Average time on job	3+ years
Education	30 percent college degree
	40 percent some college
Prior record	25 percent (43 percent of state/locals; 15 percent of federals)
Performance rating	Almost all "Good"; in fact, 50 percent were "Excellent" or "Outstanding"
	Half of these got awards (4 for designing/ implementing system)
Motive	90 percent for money (two-thirds of these had specific problem creating need; situational stresses affecting motivation)

Modus operandi:

50 percent input directly from terminal vs. false coding of input document.

50 percent used ID code or forged signature of another employee.

50 percent created false beneficiaries, while 30 percent manipulated real beneficiary records.

30 percent destroyed hardcopy; many did not have to.

80 percent used co-conspirators—60 percent outsiders to receive/cash checks

20 percent insiders to bypass controls

20 percent both

External co-conspirators were used to receive and cash computer generated checks

Internal co-conspirators were usuall; needed to bypass separation of duties.

Duration and Loss:

Average duration—13 months before being caught

Average number of criminal acts—15

Average loss—$44,000

Controls and Environment:

75 percent said supervision weak (high opportunity)

75 percent said computer security weak (high opportunity)

Debriefing:

Only 20 percent had been debriefed by the authorities as to the nature and extent of the crime.

It is worth highlighting that two-thirds of the perpetrators had specific situational stresses affecting their motivation. Yet, in almost no instance had management taken such stress into account and tried to either (1) assist the employee through the problem, (2) remove the employee to a less sensitive area, or (3) place the employee under closer supervision. Some other interesting observations follow.

1. One out of six people interviewed refused to admit that they had committed the crime. In most cases they had even plead guilty to the crime, but they rationalized they were really victims of circumstances.

2. Most of the convicted wrongdoing was for fraudulent inputting into the system, yet several of these cases involved people who had responsibilities for designing and/or implementing the system. A fundamental breakdown in controls took place in these cases: no one who is involved in the design or implementation of a system should ever be in a position to operate it.

3. Nearly one-fourth of the wrongdoers had a history of felony wrongdoing. This is a basic breakdown in the principle of limiting access to individuals prone to wrongdoing. The question of how people with a history of breach of trust could be placed in a highly sensitive systems position is unclear. Was it a failure of properly checking the credentials of these people prior to hiring or assigning them to sensitive positions?

It is worth pointing out that a couple of these cases involved individuals who were known by their employers to have had a criminal history. They, in fact, were hired under a criminal offender program as part of their rehabilitation. One could question the employer's judgment in placing them in a position of special trust (high access), with high opportunity, and in a target zone with ready conversion to cash.

4. There was a general contempt of the systems controls by nearly all the wrongdoers. Only 30 percent even felt it was necessary to destroy the hard copy that could prove their guilt. Most engaged in their criminal schemes a relatively long time—an average of 13 months—before being caught.

5. Most perpetrators reported that immediate supervision was weak. They said that supervisors are most concerned with accuracy of claims and productivity. They noted that even when their work was checked no one was looking for crimes. Some mentioned that the massive caseload made it impossible for supervisors to truly monitor cases. Others said that because of the newness of automated program systems, their supervisors did not understand how they did their job on the computer system.

6. Many also reported that computer security was weak. They said that this was because either (1) computer terminal access was unrestricted, (2) ID numbers and passwords were

commonly known and shared, or (3) no one (namely their supervisor) ever spoke to them about security. In fact, about two-thirds of the perpetrators reported being aware of other "crimes like theirs."

7.   Only 20 percent of the perpetrators said that they had been debriefed to identify weaknesses in the program or computer system. In fact, when contacted for this study, several wondered when they would be asked about the system. The result was that a great many possible co-conspirators were left undetected—and presumably still working. Management missed golden opportunities to identify serious system problems!

8.   While 90 percent of the perpetrators reported "need for money" as their motive for stealing, two-thirds of those noted that a specific problem had caused that financial need.

CHAPTER SEVENTEEN

BASIC COMPUTER SECURITY MEASURES: DENYING ACCESS AND OPPORTUNITIES

INTRODUCTION

Computer security is an area concerned with those technological safeguards (denying access to unauthorized individuals) and managerial procedures (denying opportunity through an effective system of controls) which can be applied to assure the integrity, proper use, and confidentiality of computer facilities, hardware, programs, data, terminals, and operations. Good security planning encompasses ensuring the integrity of every facet of a computer's operations including data generation, access, input, storage, processing, and use.

PROTECTIVE ACCESS THROUGH PHYSICAL SECURITY

This involves the facilities that house computer centers, remote terminals, and storage of discs and tapes. Basic to such security are such measures as:

1. Physical barriers that require the use of identification badges, inspections, and the like to limit access to unauthorized people, materials, and supplies. Such access security may also include guard activated burglar alarms, closed circuit TV, metal detectors, card or code key locks, automatic door closing devices, logging-in procedures, emergency lighting back-up systems, an alternative power source, storage systems, and emergency preparedness.

Proper security and traffic control measures are needed over access to sensitive areas during unattended periods. One example of the need for tight security occurred a decade ago in Japan. According to a Japanese police study, six members of an "anti" group (the East Asian Anti-Japanese Armed Front) gained access to and blew up an area near the computer room of a large corporation, as well as the business department. Damages from these blasts totaled some 2 billion yen.

Formal fire protection/detection measures incorporating assessments of the adequacy of the number, kind, and location of (1) fire alarms and fire extinguishing equipment, (2) fire department notification methods, (3) controls over the use of nonflammable and nontoxic materials, and (4) safety inspections of cables and wiring used in the data center.

Also called for are annunciation panels for use to signal abnormal conditions and/or fluctuations in electrical and climatic conditions, the presence of water, possible unauthorized intrusions, and so on.

2. Access Security is important. It is not enough to limit access to the sites of computers and authorized terminals. Restrictions against unauthorized equipment use must be ensured. This involves limiting transaction privileges, log-in

protocols, and password access. This is most important when "dial-up" access via telephone is possible. In fact, most such unauthorized use arises from this situation.

Appropriate controls over access to the computer through terminals should be used as part of any comprehensive program in computer security. Such controls provide a degree of protection by verifying the identity of terminal users on the basis of a unique, secret, and protected identifier. Such identifiers, assigned to authorized users, authenticate the identity of the individual wanting to access the system can be based on (a) a unique set of characters called a password, (b) a card or key, (c) a unique set of personal attributes (e.g., voice or fingerprints), or (d) combination of any or all of the above.

3. Passwords are the most common means of gaining authorized access to a system. For most systems, passwords, unfortunately, may be the first line of defense against unauthorized access. Passwords can be any sequence of characters (for example, letters, symbols, or numbers). Personal identification numbers (PIN) are a form of password. They are used to gain access to bank cash-disbursement machines. When entered correctly, they serve to control access by verifying the user's identity. They must be of such a complexity and length to limit the possibility of discovery by accident or through systematic guessing. This is best accomplished by assigning random characters rather than using words or systems of words. This is particularly true where a would-be penetrator may have learned of one or more passwords used by the same system.

There is a trade-off between using passwords made up of a combination of letters or characters easily remembered and those randomly selected. In the former, selection of an easily remembered password by a user makes for less likely errors as a result of forgetting—or for the temptation to write them down for easy reminder. The danger of allowing a user to pick his own password is the tendency to choose familiar words such as family and nicknames, locations, and other nouns or words identifiable with his personal history.

The now-familiar cash disbursing machines (chargeable to your bank or credit card) require that one use a secret personal identification number (PIN). The Japanese government survey (see prior chapter) in discussing thefts involving such machines, reported that in 37 percent of the cases covered, the PIN number had been identified by the culprit through trial and error.[1] One such case involved an individual who stole the cash card together with the victim's ID documents. The thief took a chance that the victim's birth date was the PIN number. This proved correct.

Centralized generation of the password, especially where characters are randomly selected, creates a much higher degree of security but at the cost of making it more difficult for the user to recall. With the highly publicized "hackers," there has been an increased interest in developing suitable algorithms to generate passwords that are very difficult to break by cryptoanalysis. Consider that our alphabet uses 26 letters. A five-letter password derived from these 26 letters can create nearly 12 million possible combinations. Mixing letter, numbers, and other symbols, as well as varying the length of the password, raises the possibilities proportionately.

Each user should be assigned a unique password on a need-to-have-access basis. This permits an audit trail as to who is using the system for what purpose. It also develops accountability in users for securing their password, as well as making it easier to delete passwords when personnel change.

Of course, the password issuance process should be tightly controlled. Access and dissemination of the password list should be controlled. Indoctrination of the importance of password secrecy is a must. (Anyone in the audit or security field can surely cite experiences where passwords were found taped to terminals or in desk drawers.)

Efforts must be made to prevent discovery of passwords, particularly to prevent someone from observing the password

[1] 1983 White Paper on Police (published annually) by the National Police Agency in Japan.

as it is being used during entry. This can be aided by suppressing the password so that it does not print or display. Also, a system of encrypting the password using a secret code as it is entered so that it cannot be used by an observer is a valued technique. Prevention of electronic eavesdroppers or wiretappers from discovering the password can be done by causing it to be encrypted differently each time it is used.

Another method of discovering the identity of the password is by a "heuristic search." The would-be penetrator tries to gain access by repeatedly guessing the password using a computer to rapidly choose alternatives automatically. The easiest means to guard against this is by not allowing an individual more than three incorrect password attempts and for imposing time delays. After this, some sort of a security alarm may be generated. There should be a policy of frequently changing passwords and providing new password access to only that data the individual has current need to see or use. A minimum of changing passwords at least once a year would seem to be a basic requirement (or whenever it is reasonably believed that the security of the password has been compromised).

Once the password is accepted, the user logs on the system. This provides an audit trail on that user. Exception reports that produce an analysis of deviations from normal use provide indications of possible misuse. Periodic review by the user of the record of their most recent access or attempts at access might also reveal attempted improper access on the system. Any evidence to suggest a compromise or possibility of compromise (e.g., user forgetting or losing the password) should result in delisting the password and reissuing a new one. Any changes in access by users (such as reassignment or termination) should also result in invalidating the password.

4. Pass cards and keys require a user to give identity or verification of identity by means of machine readable identity card and access keys. Inasmuch as they may fall into unauthorized hands, it is advisable that these be used in conjunction with some type of password to limit the vulnerabil-

ity to misuse. To limit opportunities for duplicating or counterfeiting by penetrators, such cards or keys should be replaced/updated on a frequent basis. Each access card or key should be unique to the user, with an audit trail of use.

5.   Personally unique identifiers are measurable attributes unique to the authorized user, such as voice prints, fingerprints, hand characteristics, and handwriting. A password, identifier card, or any other method can introduce the individual; verification of the claimed identity comes from the password attributes selected and on file.

6.   The term "authorization" means that each user has an associated set of privileges to which they are authorized to access specified types of data. In turn, there are also certain requirements over actions that may be taken (such as reading the file, adding to the file, creating a file, carrying out a transaction, compiling or executing a program, and so on). Users who have access to the system may be (and generally are) limited to what they are authorized to use. Thus, there are "levels of use" or access authorized.

System access may be limited to regions of the data or memory. Various regions may be walled off from someone not authorized to use it. This "storage partitioning" protects information from unauthorized use. Also, there may be limits on the use of programs and procedures (i.e., calls, returns, and passing of parameters).

One uncomfortable underlying thought, however, is that organizations are faced with a continuing dilemma—that is, how to make their computer systems useful, workable (friendly to insiders), yet generally secure and materially free from unauthorized intrusions. To illustrate, one Social Security Administration claims representative (responsible for authorizing Supplemental Security Income (SSI) claims) obtained fraudulent SSI payments of over $104,000 over a year and a half by reinstating closed accounts, reactivating records of deceased recipients, and creating fictitious accounts.

TARGET ANALYSIS: ASSESSING VULNERABILITIES/RISKS AT COMPUTER INSTALLATIONS

Internal controls and security measures at computer installations may be measured by the use of vulnerability assessments and risk analyses. (See Part II on targets for additional discussion.) Essentially vulnerability assessments can be used to rank or prioritize programs for functions for subsequent internal reviews. Such assessments are used to determine what needs to be looked at in terms of its vulnerability; first, second, and so on. The end result is that the most sensitive programs/operations will be looked at initially. The studies of computer operations discussed in the previous chapter are a means towards this end. The PCIE study (appendix 4) confirmed once again that federal programs are susceptible to computer fraud. One reason are the scores of people with legitimate access to federal data banks. Review of those with lesser significance are deferred until resources for their review become free or until they in turn move up in terms of vulnerability. These assessments provide a broad coverage of ADP activities.

Risk analysis is probabilistic in the sense that it evaluates loss before it occurs. Problems with it relate to establishing valuations on hardware assets and software; the values of both are subject to change because of obsolescence, depreciation, and the like.

DENYING OPPORTUNITIES THROUGH EFFECTIVE CONTROLS

Definitions

Data security considerations include the manual handling of data before and after computer processing. Most losses are a result of false or improper handling of data prior to its entry. Such precautions help ensure that files belonging to a user are accessed only by those persons authorized to do so by the originator of the file. Careful consideration must be given to proper control over each step in the preparation, use, and storage of documents involved in processing.

Consideration of *operations security* means that sensitive computer production jobs must be isolated and compartmentalized to minimize exposure to unauthorized modification, destruction, exposure of data, or to unauthorized equipment use. Production and testing activities especially should be segregated. Restrictions against unauthorized access and/or use must be insured by:

Appropriate storage partitioning

Installation of protected or privileged modes for operating systems programs

Installation and use of trouble logs and activity records

Appropriate ID safekeeping and backup of all tapes/discs/ output documents

Input data validation

Exception reporting

Appropriate cryptographic and live security protection

Adequate system of employee ID/electronic audit trails and use records.

Encryption is a means to deny opportunities for electronic eavesdroppers, wiretappers, as well as those intent on injecting, deleting, substituting, or modifying data. As in access, encryption data can be encoded. Suffice to say that data being transmitted can also be encoded in a process specified in a set of rules or steps called algorithm, with decoding merely a reversal of the process. Because the authorized terminals have the means to translate these encoded messages, it is essential to secure the terminal against tampering or unauthorized access. By this means, any wiretapping would net only meaningless data.

TEN ADDITIONAL SECURITY RULES FOR THE MICROS, MINIS, AND PCS

Rising computer technology has come about so rapidly that the federal government alone has over 500,000 micro, mini, and personal computers (PCs). Almost daily, a smaller, more powerful model comes on the market. Their portability and easy adaptability to a myriad of personal, business, resource, and recreational purposes make them an attractive target for theft and misuse. The uniqueness of size and relative high cost warrants some special notes about their security.

The target could be the entire system or only selected components or accessories (such as printers, disc drives or circuit boards). The proliferation of computer networks also makes it possible for wrongdoers to use the desk top or portable computer and their programs to access them. Protective measures that can be taken include the following.

1. *Target Analysis.* Limiting this vulnerability requires a target analysis of the environment in which they are used. Companies and agencies might permit removal of the units to the residence or road worksite. Good judgment should prevail in balancing the organizational advantages of allowing these units offsite against the risks associated with increased opportunity to theft. The same balancing considerations need to be made of all the security measures.

2. *Publicize Restrictions on Use.* As has been consistently pointed out throughout this book, any program designed to deter the motive element must involve publicizing the rules and those who violate them. This means that whatever measures that are employed to control theft should be well-publicized. Everyone using one of these computers should be well-indoctrinated in what the rules of use are. There should be no surprises or embarrassing misunderstandings later. The rules must be clear, concise, to the point, and with published consequences for their violation. Transgressions of these rules should thereafter be dealt with aggressively, consistently, and with no exceptions.

3. *Publicizing Other Preventive Measures.* Publicizing how seriously the entity looks upon computer fraud/theft abuse is a rule that should run throughout all preventative measures. Security personnel should be uniformed and obvious. This deters the motive factor by making a statement of how serious management is about securing the area and creates a sense of deterrence from the threat of being caught.

4. *Indoctrinate Employees.* Any security measure requires indoctrination in the form of written reminders, warning signs, oral briefings, and perhaps even signed acknowledgement of limiting instructions.

5. *Build Personal Accountability.* The most effective control to reduce opportunity for theft is to have a firm set of rules concerning accountability. Someone should feel and must be held strictly accountable for every valued piece of property subject to theft. In the case of mobile property, such as mini computers, a system of tracking use and accountability needs to be developed so that at any given point in time (1) the whereabouts of the property is known and (2) the individual responsible for it can be identified.

6. *Take Random Inventory.* The accountability of mini computers can be developed within any existing inventory system. Some modifications may be necessary to account for some of their unique characteristics. Although most companies have annual inventory taken of property, consideration might be made to modify this into a more random process. Employing this variant where there has been loss or misuse of mini computers has been quite effective in surfacing the problems.

7. *Lock Units to Work Location.* Other effective measures include (1) securing each unit to a desk and (2) controlling the key or combination. The tradeoff is sacrificing one of the PC's attractive features, that of mobility.

8. *Increase Security Force.* Depending on the vulnerability analysis and the degree to which theft problems have surfaced, consideration might also be given to increased guard services, such as increased fixed guard posts, patrols, car searches, and so

forth. All these have positive deterrent effects but may be costly in terms of expense and employee good will.

9. *Tag the Equipment.* All equipment, including the portable computer, should be identified and numbered for purposes of accountability, location, and all its major component parts. But its label or serial number is not the only method of tagging the items. It is quite common to exit department stores through special sensors. All items with a magnetic tag sets off the alarm. This same technology is available for portable computer units.

10. *Alarm the Equipment.* Technology provides more sophisticated methods of protecting equipment of this type from unauthorized removal. Various types of signal-generating devices are now marketed. Some are like transceivers sending out a specifically identifiable signal that is interrupted if removed from its power source. This, in turn, alerts the monitoring equipment that provides an alert to possible theft of a specified unit at its exact location. Other technology may provide for unique homing signals if a unit is removed and plugged back into a new power source.

CHAPTER EIGHTEEN

INSURING
SYSTEM INTEGRITY

INTRODUCTION

No computer system is invulnerable. However, the extent of vulnerability can best be limited by front-end review of new systems in the design phase. The Department of Health and Human Services houses some of the best—and some of the worst—examples of vulnerable systems. In the latter category one would certainly include the systems that operate the Social Security Administration (SSA). Over 200 million active files exist at SSA, with over $200 billion in benefits being paid out to 35 million Americans in monthly installments each year. The job of making these systems work with antiquated hardware and software is horrendous. As each new generation of computers is adopted, the system is modified to permit manual override of the controls in order to make the operation work. The result is near chaos.

THE DESIGN PHASE

Commencing in 1981 SSA began a half billion dollar process to revamp the entire system. We have learned the hard way that securing a system once it is operational is nearly impossible—at least on a scale as large as that of SSA. The best and most economical approach to minimize risk must come in the design stage. To insure any measure of security with SSA necessitates on up-front approach.

In designing a new system there must be, in addition to controls and audit trails, user manuals to explain how human computer operators will interface with the machine. Each step in the transactions must be documentable if users and reviewers are to understand how everything is supposed to work.

In addition, there must be ongoing testing, monitoring, and evaluating during each development phase. The purpose of such testing is to keep track of the accuracy of the data output, identify any potential weaknesses requiring attention, and take the "bugs" out of the system.

THE TARGET ANALYSIS

A preimplementation target analysis should be made during the design phase and tested more comprehensively during a pilot effort. In this way problems can be anticipated, encountered, and dealt with prior to the system's going "live."

The proposed system should undergo a security review at the earliest possible time. Such a review should involve documenting the flow of information through the new system. This is best accomplished by talking with the users, managers, and programmers on the project. All the acquired information should be incorporated into flow charts that visually depict the kinds of data to be inputed and stored, the programs and formats to be used, as well as the types of data and reports to be generated. From these detailed charts, logical points should be identified that would ensure sufficient controls in the system.

The review should then be compared against the project plans to make sure these controls are being built into the system, along with the audit trails that will maintain the history necessary to document what is happening at each step of the cycle. When information is transferred from a printed medium to an electronic one, the audit trail must also change from a paper one to one that is electronic. Such a trail must allow all transactions to be traced back to their source. If there is no such trail, there cannot be a proper audit later.

CONCLUSIONS ON OPTIMAL ADP SYSTEMS SECURITY

Since the federal government is an enormous user of ADP in its operations, the President's Council on Integrity and Efficiency (PCIE), which consists of all the Inspectors General, recently undertook a cold, hard appraisal of what was needed for optimal ADP systems security. In order to improve their integrity and auditability, PCIE wanted to increase audit's effectiveness in reviewing ADP systems as they were being developed. This massive undertaking, which included people from a number of federal agencies, and was chaired by HHS' Inspector General, received substantial input from the private sector. PCIE invested the time and resources in this project since:

1. Current ADP systems can be characterized to a great extent as being uncontrolled, undocumented, and unauditable.
2. Systems upgrades and redesigns proliferate; the state-of-the-art continues to advance as do ADP applications.
3. Policy, standards, and guidance for ADP applications in the federal sector exist in a briar-patch of statutes, regulations, and guidance.

There were three components to this PCIE project: (1) determining what the responsibilities and critical documentation would be for a model "ADP system life cycle," (2) surveying and reporting on the state-of-the-art in the private sector, and (3) developing of a work priority scheme for ADP auditors.

An important product of this work was the development of an Automated Information System (AIS)—Responsibility Matrix, shown in Figure 18.1. Quite a bit of data has been packed into this matrix which is intended for two audiences: managers and auditors.

As you review Figure 18.1, there are several points to keep in mind:

1. This is a model system with all requirements and all players carefully defined. The six phases shown here as comprising systems development can be condensed; the roles of the various actors can be merged; and the documentation called for can be abbreviated.

2. While this matrix is designed for federal in-house ADP operations, it can be adapted and used by state and local operations, as well as by the private sector.

3. With respect to the column headed "Responsible Participants": The titles shown have value only as being critical identified functions. While these are mandatory functions, in some places the same individual may perform multiple functions.

Going down the list of titles:

Information Resource Manager: Actually conceptual, but relating to an individual response for approval of all management information systems.

System Security Officer etc.: An individual, at a headquarter's location responsible for a ADP security program.

Internal Auditor: Sees that new systems meet criteria, oversight review of existing systems.

Sponsor/User: One who initially identifies need for new system.

Project Manager: Sees that system is properly designed and on time.

System Security Specialist etc. Individual at a sub-head-quarter's location responsible for ADP system's security.

Contracting Officer etc.: Self-explanatory; used only for contracting out situations.

ADP Manager: Responsible for data processing center

Quality Assurance Specialist: Actually conceptual. Would be responsible for quality control for system.

4. *For the column headed "Initiation":* This phase of the development stage begins with recognition of a problem . . . identification and validation of a need, and . . . the exploration of alternate concepts.

5. *For the column headed "Definition":* This phase involves defining function requirements . . . starting detailed planning, and . . . identifying internal control/security problems.

6. *Column headed "System Design":* Includes refining and resolving deficiencies . . . defining additional details and . . . packaging solution.

7. *Column headed "Programming & Training":* At this stage programs are ready for testing, evaluation, certification, and installation. User and maintenance manuals are prepared.

AUDITING EXISTING SYSTEMS

Auditors must learn to audit computerized systems. There is no other way to trace the millions of transactions that flow through a computer. The Inspector General at the federal Department of Health and Human Services recognized this and established the first full data processing audit division in the Inspector General Community. It is located at a vast computer complex in Baltimore servicing the gigantic Social Security and Medicare programs. Auditors must become thoroughly knowledgeable in computers to perform their work. This is one of the few instances where an auditor must become skilled in a technical area under audit. Checking security methods, operating controls, programs, transactions, and the like cannot be left to computer wizards and technicians.

Phil Kropatkin in his book *Audit Logic* (also published by John Wiley & Sons' Ronald Press) covered this important issue. The highlights of this subject are stated here for emphasis and handy reference. Keep in mind, however, these thoughts:

> . . . there is a gross lack of tight experience (or confidence) by the average auditor (be he staff or supervisory) in this arena . . .

> . . . No longer is computer expertise concentrated only in a relatively few "computer rooms." With the development of the integrated circuit (a complete electronic circuit on a small silicon chip), computer capacity and availability has soared and prices plunged—causing them to sprout up throughout the country in large and small offices *and the home.* One serious problem with this widespread availability is "networking" through which "everyone can get into the act" with few if any audit trails to analyze and retrace transactions.

LESSONS FOR THE AUDITOR

First, stay cool! The basic objectives of an audit—whether it is computerized or manual—remain the same. Management's internal controls must be reviewed and tested to see if they are effective. The records produced (however recorded) must be examined for accuracy and reliability. Nothing is new about that.

What is the auditor trying to accomplish in his review of any automated (ADP) system of records? Answer: The same objectives as if operations were manually kept.

Internal controls—Are they really working?

Physical safeguards—Are they fully adequate?

Operations—Are they economical and efficient?

Data—Are they meeting managements' operational needs?

Reports—Are they accurate and descriptive?

These items should sound familiar. The main distinction,

however, is that our ADP environment causes the whole process to be many times more intense and vulnerable. For example:

> The possibility for large losses are far greater, can occur instantly, and the fast moving ADP machinery can be used to gulp whole chunks of a company before management is aware of it.

> Even if not deliberate, inadvertent clerical or procedural mistakes can be very expensive (For example, customers can be inaccurately charged $.09 for an item that should go for $900 each.) It is hard to effectively program ADP machinery to automatically recognize obvious mistakes—mistakes that are normally spotted in an instant by humans.

> Companies experiencing even brief equipment breakdowns cannot really function manually. (Imagine ticket counters or supermarkets hobbling, manually, through a day's business). Even if they somehow keep going (slowly) through an afternoon's business, what happens to their high-geared inventory control, internally?

With some clear thinking, imagination, and knowledge of ADP processing (though no more than necessary to exist in our computerized age), auditors can (1) reach a conclusion as to whether each significant part of the accounting system is controlled and (2) provide reasonable assurance that the system is free of material weaknesses. But what are the possibilities for abuse in the current atmosphere of proliferating computers? The majority of computer frauds (at least those detected) are, as one researcher has pointed out, "old wine in new bottles." These brands were not particularly new or supercreative other than the fact that the *computer* was used to provide a smokescreen.

1.   Internal controls for ADP systems fall into three general categories: management practices, physical security, and system security. In reviewing each of these areas bear in mind that the threat of the "human factor" also includes programming flaws, data entry errors, and other plain old human mistakes.

Many experts recommend—and one must surely agree—that the first step is to start with a look at the mission and objectives of the organization under review and its reliance on ADP to achieve those objectives. They also say to read all prior related audit reports, both internal and external, and see what previous reviewers had to say. Inventory the equipment, hardware, software, terminals, and the like.

2.   An organization should have written records of their ADP hardware and software. It is also helpful to have a written record of planned acquisitions. This is basic accounting, of course, but, as other authors have noted, with so many branches of an organization nowadays purchasing computer hardware and software, some companies have literally lost track of how many they have at any one time.

Next, find out what kind of top management oversight controls are in place: Is there an executive ADP management committee for planning equipment purchases and software needs? Are the organization's own internal auditors involved from the planning to the output? (They should be.) Are policies and procedures in writing? (They, too, should be.)

3.   What kind of operational controls are in place? Because of the concentration of functions brought about by the computer, make sure the data processing function is really separate from (1) other agency functions and (2) the ADP procurement and programming departments. What kind of authorization is needed for system and program changes?

4.   Do different people or groups handle: Systems analysis? Application programming? Acceptance testing? Program change control? Data control? Systems software maintenance? Computer files maintenance?

5.   What kind of personnel background check is made? Is there a personnel rotation plan in effect within the different functional areas in the ADP department? Is this rotation plan in writing?

6.   Look, too, to the user—is he satisfied with results? If not,

why not? What are the problems? Who knows about them? All too often computer or ADP-related problems are kept in management's own ADP family and not shared in, or considered properly, by the general executive group. This is a bad oversight that auditors should be alerted to.

7. What physical protection controls are in place over the hardware, software, tapes, and discs, to protect against natural disasters, power failures, sabotage, and other threats? Are duplicate files maintained in a separate, secure location? Are security devices changed frequently? Is a risk analysis performed both before the approval of design specs for an installation and whenever there is a "significant change" to the physical facility, hardware, or operating system software?

8. Are good system controls in place? Does the system software contain a complete audit trail feature that records all changes to application programs, including ID-ing the programmer(s) making the changes? Is there strict security over the passwords, authorization codes given out for on-line access? What about that on-line access? Are passwords changed frequently? Are users only able to access certain data? What about transaction logs for on-line use—namely, who accesses what?

As you can see, the questions that can be asked are only limited by the imagination of the auditor.

In the final analysis, it will be the ingenuity and logic of the practitioner that will offer breakthroughs and practical tests in the modern audit environment. No one can tell you what the whole set of problems are likely to be. The computer part of this world may be the toughest challenge. You must be prepared to match wits with the ADP specialists.

Where does this leave modern auditors? How can they evaluate the auditee's books and records and assert reasonable assurance of reliability and do it on a timely basis? Before answering this, think about compartmentalization of the computer system for the purposes of both efficiency and security.

A NEW AND LOGICAL APPROACH TO ADP REVIEWS

Think about spy networks. What single process ensures their invulnerability to overall and complete penetration? It is the individualized cell approach! Breaking down one spy (on interrogation, if caught) or breaking into one whole clandestine operation (if exposed) does not usually destroy the whole interwoven organization. This same notion can be applied analogously to the general study of computers. Thus, consider the constant need for: (1) physical security (compartmentalized hardware) and (2) process segmentation (separation of duties and functions).

1. **Physical Modularization.** This safeguard can take a variety of well known forms (passwords, locked rooms, cryptological scrambling, separate air conditioning, heavy fire walls, storm protection, burglar proof tape and reel storage, earthquake springs, dust filters, window-free buildings, human guards, patrol dogs, duplicate data banks, and so forth). All of these must be persistently, if not fanatically, adhered to by all employees, or they become merely fragile, falsely-comforting, screens for everyone in the company.

2. **Process Modularization.** The much more subtle, more difficult, but far more potent second aspect of compart-mentalization is the concept of "procedural security through separation of duties, processes, and checkout functions—*all related to people.*" This is where real internal control begins—and sometimes prematurely ends—in the computer business. One of the most important facets of an effective review process is up-front, design study. Consider again the age-old logic used by spy networks the world over. If one cell breaks down, or its secrecy is destroyed, the entire cellular network is not destroyed. In other words, no one individual or group operator, programmer, analyst, maintenance person, and

so forth should have access to the whole process. If they do, the system becomes wholly vulnerable to abuse. Look for real separation of ADP functions in a similar mode. It should, of course, vary from place to place depending on the extent and complexity of the operations, amount of hardware, and sheer volume of operations—all of which dictated the use of ADP equipment in the first place.

AUDIT REVIEWS MUST BE ON-LINE

One extremely important aspect, if the function of audit is to be intrinsic and useful to the internal control (processes), is the absolute necessity for it to be on-line, or timely in the examination of the ADP processes. Procedures have to be checked almost literally while they are happening, in the ADP area. You cannot come in later and expect to be able to effectively check ultra high speed runs, printouts, or most data analyses. Arrangements have to be made, and audit techniques have to be employed, on a very current basis. Absolute timeliness is essential!

Samples have to be drawn almost as quickly as the data is generated, or the bookkeeping will literally get away from you. Computers keep updating current accounts and dropping off old entries. There are no ending control balances with starting points that have details on them showing all the additions and subtractions, or debits and credits to any summary accounts. That's not to say that one could not reconstruct prior balances from the piles of daily runs; but at what a cost!

Early audit involvement is needed here to see if all practical internal controls and possible checking points have been incorporated into the whole operation. This provides timely, before the fact, useful audit help.

In auditing a computer center, one must think like a manager. That's the simple part. Think in terms of traditional management objectives. The "merging" process is simple, too, if you have done a good job in learning the technical part about computers. For example, it is common knowledge that it is a good practice to make duplicate copies of important master files that are kept on a computer. The key word here is "important." Which master files are important? One could exercise his "judgment"—whatever that is intended to mean. But there is a better way. Master files pertaining to a company's primary objectives are surely important. (How would you like to lose the only reliable file that records sales on account or the key coding on retail inventories?) Files pertaining to indirect support objectives should rank below those relative or pertaining to primary functions. See how it works? The judgment process is a convenient mechanism for logical thought.

The best approach to a simplified, generalized, and logical approach for effective computer auditing begins with a proper game plan. The auditor must think like the chief executive. Then, he must get sufficient detailed technical knowledge. (None of that "confined to the classroom" knowledge or two-day insight refresher, either—become a computer programmer! Junior high school students are learning programming every day. The small, powerful, personal computer is not just a fad. Programming is not for the strictly scientific-minded. Major universities are requiring all freshmen to have their own personal computer. Not a little hand-held calculator, but something like a 16-bit, 64K RAM rig with video screen and all. Think like a top level manager, learn the basics of computer programming, and, above blend your top level management thinking with your technical knowledge. A good basic checklist of do's and don'ts might include these items.

1. *Do* have an up-to-date and formal organizational chart and written statements of functional responsibilities. A computer is a magnet—it attracts all kinds of data from every department in the organization. People in the computer center are charged with making sure that data is processed accurately, swiftly, and economically. And that's why it's so important to have good, strong organizational policies, in writing, of who is responsible for what. Otherwise, nobody is responsible for anything!

People must know what they are responsible for—in clear terms. A computer center is no place for guessing!

2. *Do* segregate incompatible functional responsibilities. Don't let computer programmers (who design and write computer programs) operate the computer. If you do, the programmers have complete control: they can do anything they want with the input—such as adding, say, an extra $1000 to their paychecks—and you will have a hard time in finding out that (and even if) it happened.

3. *Don't* let computer operators have authority to change computer programs. If you do, you are back to the computer programmer-operator problem.

4. *Do* require prior approval by management before a computer program can be changed.

5. *Do* use passwords and account numbers to restrict computer access to only authorized persons—and protect those passwords and account numbers.

6. *Don't* let ADP personnel have authority to authorize transactions. ADP personnel are data processors—and that's all they should do.

7. *Do*, if possible, segregate the responsibilities of design, writing, and application of computer systems.

8. *Do* be careful in transcribing documents that are to be processed by the computer. The computer will blindly process anything clerks give it.

9. *Don't* assume that every document that the system calls for processing by the computer *will* be processed by the computer. Documents get lost. Set up some type of numerical or batch control to be sure that what you send to the computer gets to the computer.

10. *Do* be careful in designing the forms that will be used for transferring the data into a form the computer can read. Carefully design input forms—they are important. Be sure to make them simple! Relatively low paid clerks will run them into the records *as they are!*

11. *Don't* assume that your input files are important only to

the person or persons who sent them to you. Protect them, in a secure place! It is expensive to recreate data files. And much of the data is sensitive and valuable to "outsiders."

12. *Do* follow up on input records that the computer does not process. Something is wrong on every record that the computer does not process. Too often, thousands upon thousands of records get "lost" in this manner. Input records must be in the exactly correct format before the computer will process them. If the records are wrong, procedures must insure that they be sent back to the originator and a follow up is made to be sure that corrections are made.

13. *Do* build sound editing procedures into computer programs—to be sure that the computer or programmers cannot "force-feed" obviously incorrect data into the system. For instance, overtime hours that exceed regular hours; excessively high rates of pay; two time cards for the same employee for the same pay period; inventory balances that show negative quantities on hand; Social Security numbers that are all zeros; and people's names that have numbers in them.

14. *Do* set up a quality control system to pinpoint people who continually make large numbers of errors in preparing input for the computer. This could be one of management's most profitable tasks. Remember, most computers catch, or are programmed to reject, the most obvious errors. It is the ones that are not so obvious that get through the computer and into your data bank— with damaging results.

CHAPTER NINETEEN

INSURING DATA INTEGRITY

Using the Computer
to Tame the Computer

Matching or comparing one set of records with another is one of the most basic auditing processes. The fact that most businesses—government or private—are computerizing their records (or have already done so) opens the door to an automated application known as "computer matching" which is essentially no different than any of the so-called "old fashioned" methods of audit pursuit.

THE CLASSIC AUDIT APPROACH

This can be illustrated by a long-time area of audit attention: payroll. These audits involve a variety of "matching" steps—on a test basis—starting backwards from the issuance of a check to a specific employee:

1. Personnel records are verified to test whether selected persons to whom checks are addressed are listed there.

2. A physical floor check is made of the passing of the check to these selected recipients to determine that a real or actual person "matches" the payee name.

As a further comparison the auditor could ask to see the person's credentials—are they really who they say they are? Another step would be to have a supervisor vouch for the identity of the person receiving the check; again, usually on a test or sampling basis of a relatively small number of recipients.

Selected salary or wage payments can be matched against subsidiary leave card records to see if employees are being improperly paid for periods of absence.

Time cards could be matched on a selective basis (again) against leave records to see if people are lying for each other in order to get paid for days when they were absent.

Checking into the accuracy of accounts receivable is another example of what might be done in a matching process. Sales slips can be compared to entries on sales journals, and then both of these can be matched against entries on subsidiary journals and ledgers. Another "match" involves connecting shipping records to completed sales, vouching them to sales journals, and so on.

These types of matches, even using scientific sampling methods, can never equal the completeness and validity of a 100 percent verification, as is possible when using computer record matching. An organization's entire set of records can be matched against other sets. Relatable data from federal and local agencies can be run, one against the other, and by setting certain parameters in advance, aberrant data can be sifted out for further study and testing.

While the extent to which this valuable computer verification is used in the private sector is not known, one could easily surmise, for example, that major insurance companies could, if they wished, run (match) their dormant accounts against any of their disbursement runs, including claims, premium rebates, and closeouts. Much more is known about the actual details of such matches emanating from public audit and Inspector General reports. These will be discussed later.

AN OVERVIEW OF COMPUTER MATCHING

What precisely is computer matching? It entails comparing different lists of files to see if identical, similar, or dissimilar items appear in them. It is a simple, quick, and accurate crosschecking method. Such comparisons can involve names, social security numbers, addresses, government contract numbers, invoice or billing numbers, and so on. What happens, of course, is that the computer merely establishes that an apparently common or related item occurs in the compared information—a "hit!"

For example, the same name, social security number, address, or telephone number appearing on two sets of tapes being compared would be a "hit." Also, two different names appearing with the same social security number would constitute a "hit." At first, it would be considered a "raw hit"—information that seems to match.

Computers are no more accurate than the information people have stored in them, and people make mistakes. Names can be misspelled, digits in social security numbers can be transposed, and birth dates can be inaccurately recorded. Mistakes like these can lead to erroneous matches or the appearance of impropriety. Decisions cannot be made on the basis of a computer match alone because all that a computer match can show is that the same, similar, or contradictory information appears in the compared files. Verification of the match and investigation into the case are necessary before any tentative conclusions can be drawn.

If, for some reason, inquiry into the case does not resolve the errors found, a person still has the legal right to challenge erroneous data. There are, in fact, ample opportunities for such challenges to be made in the federal sector—before decisions are made that effect an individual's status, rights, and benefits.

Computer matching can also include other uses of computers, such as screening or scanning. In computer screening, for example, the general characteristics of cases in which fraud and abuse have occurred are identified by analysis. Comparisons are then made with the program case rolls. Any cases found can be set aside for further verification analysis and investigation. Examples of this occur in the Federal Aid to Families with Dependent Children (AFDC) Program. Many cases of fraud have been found whereby the recipients of benefits of this program have listed nonexistent sets of twins. These AFDC cases can be screened or scanned for cases in which twins are listed. When they are identified efforts are made to establish whether these twins exist or not. Such screening can and does take place at the state level.

The use of computer matching has increased for several reasons. First, it is a fast, efficient, and accurate means of reviewing large amounts of data. For a person to go through thousands of cases manually would be extremely tedious, time-consuming, and nearly impossible. High-speed computers can process voluminous files comparing elements and records quickly. Because computers are not subject to human fatigue, the results will be more accurate than manual processing.

Secondly, computer matches have proven to be an excellent starting point in the detection and prevention of mistakes or fraud. Once similar, identical, or apparently contradictory information comes to light through these matches, verification or investigative efforts can then determine whether possible error or fraud exists. The match provides clues that can improve efficiency, correct mistakes, cut down on waste, or uncover possible fraud.

Computer record matching is cost beneficial. In fact, the cost to benefit is quite lopsided:

1. The State of New York has been matching its records of welfare recipients with quarterly wage reports from New York employers. They estimate that they will save $95.2 million from 1978 to 1982 from the system which cost $28.1 million—a return of almost 340 percent.

2. The Small Business Administration matched its farm disaster loans with Farmers Home Administration emergency loans (1977 crop year) and found that 123 borrowers had received over $2.3 million in duplicate loan benefits. Recoveries of almost $1.3 million have been made from this match which cost $50,000.

3. California uses computer matching to find people who have been ordered by a court to repay overpayments from the AFDC—those who are *also* due state income tax refunds. The tax refund is applied instead to the debt the individual owes the state. Over $200,000 was recovered in the 1981 tax year. The match cost $6000.

4. Through a quarterly match of wage records and unemployment insurance benefits, Kansas recovered $750,000 in overpayments a year, is discovering over 300 cases of fraud a year, and is saving $1.2 million by offsetting or stopping benefits.

5. Data on Food Stamp recipients has been matched against other data relating to wage information and the roles of certain other benefit programs by the U.S. Department of Agriculture. For every dollar of computer and investigation costs, $20 in overpayments has been recovered from people first identified by the computer matching as possibly not fully reporting the benefits they were already receiving—when they applied for food stamps.

6. In just one nine-day period, the Illinois State Employment Security Agency saved over $1.5 million in state funds by detecting fraudulent documentation presented by aliens applying for unemployment compensation benefits. A simple hot line telephone inquiry with the local district offices of the U.S. Immigration and Naturalization Service (INS) resulted in a quick computer match of alien identification numbers. INS costs for this were virtually nil.

Besides dollar savings, the deterrence factor is inestimable. Other examples of good case histories, well known in government circles, are discussed briefly later in this chapter.

While there are literally thousands of state and federal prosecutions every year for fraud against government programs, it is impossible to say how many have resulted from leads obtained from computer matching. Most computer matching is conducted by state governments and little data on matching results have been collected in the past. There is reason, though, to believe that a substantial number of criminal prosecutions have resulted from this work. In Memphis and Nashville, Tennessee, for example, 89 federal and 114 state indictments followed investigations of leads from matching involving the Food Stamp, AFDC, Medicaid, and HUD housing programs. Of even greater importance and savings effectiveness is that such matching helps in fraud prevention for initial eligibility determination. This prevents money from being misspent in the first place. Cost savings and overpayment prevention are the two most important objectives of conducting computer matching.

Computer matching techniques do detect overpayments made through error or fraud, but often recovery of misspent money has proved difficult, if not impossible. Thus, *prevention* of fraud before payment occurs is a far more effective approach to saving money. Techniques of computer matching are still developing and more attention is being paid now to verifying eligibility at the time an application for government benefits is made. This is called "front-end" matching.

As mentioned, another important factor in computer matching is deterrence. There is evidence that public knowledge of matching being done acts to deter possible fraud attempts. Shortly after the appearance of newspaper reports that state and federal officials were cooperating in Memphis and Nashville (see above), local welfare offices received a large number of phone calls from people asking to be removed from Food Stamp rolls because they had just found work. The joint effort by Illinois and the INS to stop illegal aliens from receiving unemployment benefits caused a dramatic statewide drop in the percentage of illegal aliens applying for assistance (46 percent to 25 percent in less than two weeks).

Federal agencies have used computer matching for many different purposes. Matches have been developed to detect conflicts of interest, indebtedness, or possible fraud among government employees. For example, in matching lists of individuals with delinquent debts against lists of federal employees, the Veterans Administration uncovered 66,000 federal employees who owed some $37 million. In similar efforts, Health and Human Services (HHS) matched overdue school loans to health professionals with departmental employees—and medical professionals receiving payments from the Medicare and Medicaid programs. This work disclosed nearly 7000 accounts ($5.2 million) that were delinquent by 90 days or more. Over 3000 new loans could have been made if these loans had been repaid on time. Many of the professionals had the ability to pay; as an example, 442 borrowers had received $12.4 million for Medicare/Medicaid services in 1980 and 1981.

Other matches have been made to uncover tax frauds; possible double billings on the part of medical providers; to make sure that earmarked grant funds have been spent legitimately for the purposes intended; that various government loans are not duplicative; that defense and other contractors are charging time and other costs to the proper contract accounts. Currently, government is actively seeking to expand the instances in which matching techniques might prove to be an effective management procedure.

From another perspective, it can be argued that even matching in assistance programs is hardly designed to penalize the poor. One should recall that people who need assistance and legitimately apply for help are not the targets of matching and will not show up on match lists unless through error. Saving funds through the reduction of error and fraud makes more money available to assist those who are legitimately in need.

CONCERNS ABOUT A PERSON'S RIGHT TO PRIVACY

The Federal Privacy Act of 1974 safeguards the individual's right to privacy and specifies how the government may use the information it gathers. There are strict limitations and procedures included in the law and there are severe penalties, including stiff fines for violations of privacy on the part of government officials. To make sure that government agencies understand that the law also applies directly to computer matching, the Office of Management and Budget (OMB) in the Executive Office of the President has issued specific guidelines on how computer matching is to be conducted. These guidelines apply all the requirements of the Privacy Act to matching activities. Information in computer records can be used for matches only if notices, subject to public comment, are published in the *Federal Register*. Safeguards over how the information is used, stored, and disclosed must be maintained. Notice must be given to the Congress, OMB, and the public on any matching that will be undertaken by an agency. Individual privacy is protected. For practical and procedural reasons this computer matching activity will not result in huge government master files of information on private citizens. First, government records are dispersed through numerous files and records systems in large numbers of separate government departments and agencies at federal, state, and local levels. To bring them all together would not only be unwise, but also would probably be impossible. Moreover, the way matching must be done will not permit the gradual accumulation of files in what could become a master file.

When a matching effort takes place (according to the OMB guidelines on computer matching just discussed) the files being matched remain the sole property of the separate agencies which supplied them. After a match, the agency conducting it must either return the tapes to the agency which makes them available or destroy them. The record of the hits will be kept only so long as an investigation is active and will be disposed of thereafter. As a result, no permanent files identifying individuals exist and, therefore, no master file can develop over time.

MICROCOMPUTERS ARE A DEFINITE BOON

Certainly this whole discussion assumes that the reader with an interest in this validation-and-discovery technique has a capable computer staff available, but this is not always true. While development of this capability takes time, payoffs from using computer matches have been most cost effective for federal departments.

As an example, the HHS Office of Inspector General has

computer specialists assigned to all its regional offices. They provide computer support to the IGs audit and investigative staff. These experts, using a mainframe computer exclusively, had designed complex computer programs to perform a variety of sophisticated data processing tasks. However, this meant that detailed computer knowledge was being confined to a small part of the professional staff.

As time passed, the demand for the services of these computer specialists increased. They were working on data processing tasks ranging from the simple to the complex. In part, this problem was resolved by making field professional staff more knowledgeable in data processing, particularly in those instances where their needs did not require the use of a (large) mainframe computer. One particular application was to be computer record cross-matching.

The start of a typical match may involve working with 10 million records. Perhaps 20,000 of these may result in "raw hits" or possible matches. Since even these 10,000 cases would be too great to work with, the next step called for the computer programmer to begin refining the criteria for "hits." To illustrate:

> First match (20,000 hits). All persons named "John Quincy Doe."
> Second match (5000) hits. All "John Quincy Doe(s)" born in 1930, and so on.

This procedure took time, particularly if the computer specialist was doing matches and rematches for five to ten people. Delays in this work were commonplace.

The introduction of the microcomputer to this environment made the difference. The computer specialist can now give the requesting staff member the raw hits produced by the first match in the form of a floppy disk. The staff member puts the floppy disk into his or her microcomputer and reduces the list to a manageable size. In the meantime, the computer specialists are able to process millions of records for others.

The benefits of this are obvious:

Workloads of individual computer specialists have been sensibly reduced.

Computer literacy is now spread throughout the organization.

The field staff can do analyses that previously had gone undone, either because of a lack of time or resources.

You may wonder how the size of an organization dictates the use of microcomputers. Organizational size is not the *best* criterion for measuring the potential for applying microcomputer technology. Rather, this decision should stem from your answers to two very fundamental questions about microcomputers:

What productive work are you doing now that could be done more efficiently (cheaper, quicker, and maybe of better quality) with the aid of a microcomputer?

What productive work are you not doing but that needs to be done and that you could do with a microcomputer?

Analyses coming from these two questions should lead us in the proper direction. But there is a danger here. We must approach the answers with an open mind. Too often, especially in large organizations, one may be tempted to dismiss the microcomputer with the rationale that the mainframe computer is already available for ADP needs. Married to that approach though is usually a heavy and worrisome dependence on a small staff of computer technicians.

1. Many large organizations (and some small ones, for that matter) are fortunate enough to have already made extensive use of large mainframe computers. Thus, the introduction of micros is easier. The big advantage in this area comes from a "relaxed resistance" to computer technology.

2. Many large organizations usually have some staff already proficient in the application of computer technology. This staff can be a valuable catalyst in training and in initial microcomputer applications. Once the general staff understands how the

micro can help them, they are usually anxious to learn about micros in general and apply this technology without technical assistance. This has been the HHS experience. Its short-term objective is to use the computer specialist as a catalyst. The ultimate objective: to place the microcomputer in the hands of the professional field staff, with minimum technical assistance.

COMPUTER RECORD MATCHING BY FEDERAL DEPARTMENTS
SELECTED EXAMPLES

Federal Office	Method and Purpose of Match	Results Now Known
Agriculture	Match rolls of food stamp recipients between several adjacent jurisdictions to see if people were participating in more than one jurisdiction.	Hundreds of cases found.
	Match USDA employee records with names in one state's insurance department's master file. Sought to identify employees involved in USDA loan making who were also selling insurance to USDA borrowers.	Results being analyzed.
Education	Match names in Federal Insured Student Loan default files against various federal employee payroll records to locate defaulters.	Thousands found. Estimated savings projected in millions of dollars.
HHS	Match names of individuals shown as deceased on Medicare Program rolls to names of current beneficiaries of SSA's Title II survivors and disability insurance program (Title II benefits cease, of course, when recipient dies).	Many thousands of cases found; savings in millions of dollars.

| HHS | Two-stage match. Involves benefit payments for Federal Aid to Families With Dependent Children (AFDC) program. Question: Were benefits being claimed for nonexistent children? Matches involved checking AFDC rolls against payments for Medicaid services to claimed dependent children, as well as to school enrollment and birth records. | Thirty targets identified in first state checked; seven indictments and two convictions. |
| HHS | Medicaid payment data for a several year period analyzed to detect payments to nursing homes for durable medical equipment for specified individuals. (Payment not allowed except for such equipment in an individual's residence.) | Over $243,000 in misspent funds identified with $81,000 recouped. |

APPENDICES

APPENDIX I

THEORY OF DIFFERENTIAL ASSOCIATION

ABSTRACT

Following is an outline of Professor Edwin H. Sutherland's genetic approach (that is, theory of differential association) as presented in the 1955 edition of *Principles of Criminology*.

1. "Criminal behavior is learned" (and not inherited).

2. "Criminal behavior is learned in interaction with other persons in a process of communication."

3. "The principal part of the learning of universal behavior occurs within intimate personal groups." Other areas of communication (other than the personal and intimate), such as radio, television, motion pictures, magazines, and so forth are all minor in the development of criminal behavior.

4. The criminal learning process involves not only techniques of committing crime, but also the shaping of motives, drives, rationalizations, and attitudes.

5. "We have culture conflict in relation to our legal

codes. . . . The specific direction of motives and drives is learned from definitions of the legal codes as favorable or unfavorable."

6. The core of Dr. Sutherland's theoretical position for his famous principle of differential association rests on this following point: "A person becomes delinquent because of an excess of definitions favorable to violation of the law over definitions unfavorable to violation of the law."

7. Differential association may vary in frequency, direction, and intensity.

8. The process of learning criminal behavior by association with criminal and anticriminal patterns involves all of the mechanisms that are involved in any other learning.

9. "Though criminal behavior is an expression of general needs and values, it is not explained by those general needs and values since noncriminal behavior is an expression of the same needs and values."

CONVICTED PROVIDERS IN MEDICARE AND MEDICAID

Report of Inspector General
Richard P. Kusserow,
Department of
Health and Human Services

ABSTRACT

Fourteen practitioner-providers convicted of fraud against the Medicare and/or Medicaid program in four states agreed to discuss their perceptions of program vulnerability, detection and deterrence of fraud, and sanctioning. Although not a random sample, the group did not differ statistically from the total universe of convicted providers on demographic characteristics, the circumstances of their fraud, or the sanctions applied. They may have differed on attitudinal characteristics which we were unable to assess for the full population.

The convicted practitioner-providers generally seemed to be open

*during the discussions, but there was a good deal of self-justifica-
tion in their responses.* The majority had a surprisingly common
view of their experience. They saw the line between fraud and
abuse as very thin and considered themselves guilty only in a
technical sense. They felt that they had "slid over the line" into
fraud and that other providers were doing similar things but
had not been charged with fraud.

There was no general agreement about the extent of fraud. The
convicted practitioner-providers were unable to provide much
specific information about patterns of occurrence. They thought
that the structure of the Medicare and Medicaid programs
encouraged providers to seek opportunities to maximize
income and that it was easy to move from there into fraudulent
practices.

*Most convicted practitioner-providers had little or no knowledge
about how fraud or abuse is detected.* They indicated that they
understood little about the mechanics of pre- or post-payment
screens or utilization review and that they had little or no
preventive contact with the carriers.

*Convicted practitioner-providers stressed the need for early
intervention by the carriers and the government prior to the time
abusive practices become fraudulent.* They stressed the need for
the carrier to develop a "sense of presence" so that providers
understand what is required of them and become aware that
there are real people watching over their shoulder.

*Fear of the available sanctions (arrest, conviction, financial
penalties, jail, loss of license, and suspension from the programs)
had little impact on the behavior of the practitioner-providers prior
to conviction.* They felt these penalties would only be applied to
someone else and that they were not in a situation where they
would be vulnerable to them. Fear of sanctions was seen as
having an impact only when brought very close to the
immediate situation of a particular provider.

As a part of the Inspector General's initiative to increase the
identification of fraudulent providers in Federally financed

health programs, this study is directed at those practitioner-providers who have already been convicted of crimes against the Medicare and Medicaid programs. The purpose of the study is to identify *vulnerabilities* in the reimbursement system by determining those things which providers have been caught and penalized for; to identify *deterrence* methods that would have prevented convicted providers from committing these crimes or would deter others from engaging in fraudulent actions; and to identify elements of the *detection* systems that worked for those who got caught and that would better identify others who are attempting to defraud the system. The study would be accomplished by discussing these issues with individual convicted practitioner-providers as well as by reviewing available case files on them.

This initial phase of the study was directed primarily toward the feasibility and worthwhileness of speaking with individual convicted practitioner-providers (physicians, dentists, psychologists etc., not pharmacists, nursing home administrators, etc.).

This report then provides findings on the following questions:

1. Would convicted providers talk with us? If so, what level of effort was required on our part?

2. What types of providers agreed to talk with us? Were they representative of convicted practitioner-providers in general?

3. What was the quality of the discussion?

4. What did they tell us about vulnerability, detection, deterrence and sanctioning?

In addition, consideration was given to how the Office of the Inspector General might, in the future, routinely and systematically gather information from convicted providers.

FINDINGS

1. **Would convicted providers talk with us? If so, what level of effort was required on our part?** During the period October 13 to

November 1, 14 convicted practitioner-providers of Medicare
and Medicaid services met with Service Delivery Assessment
(SDA) staff from Regions I and V. The convicted providers came
from a potential universe of 70 persons who had been convicted
in four states: New York, New Jersey, Michigan, and Wisconsin.
These states had 34% of total U.S. convictions.

In order to select candidates most likely to agree to
discussions, SDA staff reviewed Office of Investigations (OI)
regional files, state Medicaid Fraud Control Unit (MFCU) files
and met with OI investigators, state MFCU investigators and
single state agency personnel. After these meetings, 29 of the 70
were selected for preliminary contact. Those who were excluded
on the first cut included persons who were involved in pending
cases, who had moved long distances, who were suing state
and/or Federal officials, who in the past had exhibited
extremely hostile attitudes toward state or Federal officials or
whose cases represented very unique circumstances.

There were discussions with state and Federal officials as to
what incentive could be provided to encourage convicted
providers to cooperate in the study. It was decided that the
letter to the convicted providers requesting an interview would
include the sentence:

> If you are willing to participate in this study, we will report your
> cooperation to the Health Care Financing Administration for
> consideration in their determination as to the length of your
> suspension from the Medicare/Medicaid program and/or in
> reviewing your application for reinstatement to the Medicare/
> Medicaid program.

The letter was drafted in cooperation with Health Care
Financing Administration (HCFA) Central Office Program
Integrity staff. It should be noted that some state MFCU and
HCFA regional Program Integrity staff had concerns about the
letter, fearing that it would be used to reduce suspension
penalties that the providers well deserved.

In the letter, the convicted providers were given a telephone number where they could contact the SDA Regional Director for an appointment. SDA staff followed up with telephone calls to those convicted providers who did not respond. In many cases it took three or four telephone calls to establish personal contact with the providers, and many of them were made after normal business hours. Of the 29 persons selected for participation, 20 were actually contacted and 14 agreed to meet with us. Those who refused were "too busy", not interested in further Medicaid participation, or gave no reason. Again, it must be emphasized that those who agreed to participate were selected from the group thought likely to cooperate.

Prior to the study several people questioned whether the convicted providers would agree to participate without having their lawyer present. Although a number indicated they had contacted their lawyer about the study, only two asked that a lawyer talk with SDA staff and in no case did one attend the actual meeting.

The cost and level of effort required to carry out these interviews proved to be greater than for a normal service delivery assessment. Because of the small universe, the scattered location of the respondents, and the difficulty in substituting providers who might drop out, it was necessary to make every effort to meet with the convicted providers at the time and place of their choosing. Optimal air transportation was difficult to schedule. For two sets of interviews there were driving trips of up to 1000 miles in 36 hours, and there were a number of day trips for only one interview. Interviews were generally 2 to 2½ hours long, much greater than in normal assessments.

In order to guard against later misinterpretation or legal questions, it was decided that 2 SDA staff people would be at each discussion. Because many of the meetings were held in the evening in hotels, offices, and private homes, the inclusion of the second SDA interviewer had added value for safety and security.

2.   What types of providers agreed to talk with us? Were they representative of convicted practitioner-providers in general? The 14 providers comprising our sample break down as follows:

Sex:	13 Male, 1 female
Discipline:	9 physicians (3 psychiatrists, the rest mixed), 1 dentist, 4 allied health professionals.
Place of Training:	9 U.S., 5 foreign
Offense:	12 cases of billing for services not rendered, 2 each of misrepresentation of services (upcoding) and duplicate billing, 1 each of overcharging, back billing, billing without a physician's order, running an employment scam with Medicaid recipients, and theft of a Medicaid authorization stamp (cases add to more than 14 due to multiple offenses).
Amount Defrauded:	Median estimated amount—$3,159
Program:	10 Medicaid, 2 Medicare, 2 both
Sentences:	5 received jail or prison terms. Median restitution—$3,226
Sanctions:	8 had their professional licenses suspended or revoked, and 2 more are still under review by authorities. 8 were suspended from Medicaid/Medicare, 4 are awaiting suspension, 2 are ineligible under current regulations.

The figure for median estimated amount defrauded must be qualified and should be used only with caution. There was a similarity between the value for this variable ($3,159) and median restitution ($3,266), along with a general similarity in the discussion responses. However, data for this variable was available for only half the sample population and was usually drawn from the amount included in either the indictment or a plea. Discussions with investigators and U.S. Attorneys indicated that for a number of reasons the dollar amounts of fraud included in an indictment or a plea often represent only a small proportion of the total suspected amount defrauded. Restitution amounts are usually tied to the amounts in the counts on which the provider is convicted. Therefore this figure may significantly underrepresent the amount the providers actually stole. Data for all other variables was available for the total sample.

Explicit demonstration of representativeness of the sample is warranted because (a) the sample was small, and (b) not picked at random. Statistical tests indicated that the sample was comparable to the general population of convicted practition-er-providers with respect to the following characteristics (see Appendix A for a description of tests):

Age, sex, and proportion FMGs

Distribution of disciplines, specialties, and urban-rural mix

When case was opened, distribution of offenses, proportion Medicaid vs. Medicare, and estimated amount defrauded

Proportion sent to jail or prison, amount of restitution, and amount fined

Proportion suspended by HCFA and length of suspension.

They differed significantly only on method of detection; specifically they were less likely to have been initially identified by an informant than convicted practitioner-providers generally. This may reflect the aggressiveness of the MFCUs in our sample states. The general lack of observed differences between the sample and population does not guarantee representativeness of the sample. They may still differ on characteristics we are unable to assess for the full population (e.g., belief in their own innocence), and these characteristics could have influenced their responses. On those characteristics we were able to measure, however, the support for representativeness is strong. (See Appendix B for a comparison of the sample of convicted practitioner-providers with the universe for selected variables.)

3. What was the quality of the discussion? The convicted providers generally seemed to be open during the discussions and there appeared to be few obvious attempts to provide misleading information. There was, however, a great deal of self justification in their answers. They seemed most interested in talking about their own cases and several expressed their appreciation at having an opportunity to tell their side of the story in a fairly neutral setting. Their views of larger systems issues are best understood and interpreted in light of their perceptions of their individual experiences in the Medicare and Medicaid programs.

From a majority of the convicted providers there emerged a surprisingly common pattern of viewing their experience. They:

> Saw the line between fraud and abuse as very thin.
>
> Did not consider themselves guilty of fraud except in a technical sense.
>
> Felt that they had "slid over the line" from abuse to technical fraud.
>
> Felt that other providers were doing similar things, but had not been charged with fraud.

Only two of the convicted providers indicated they had consciously set out to steal from the Medicaid program or from clients. Both of them felt that they had been on a compulsive "self destruct trip" which motivated their behavior. What may be significantly missing in the observations which follow are the views of persons who saw themselves as cooly, rationally and systematically developing schemes to defraud the programs.

4. What did they tell us about vulnerability, detection, deterrence and sanctioning?

A. VULNERABILITY There was no general agreement about the overall amount of fraud in the Medicare and Medicaid programs. In part, this was because the convicted providers had no clear understanding (or perhaps acceptance) of the differences between fraud and abuse and also because most were solo operators with little awareness of the broader health care delivery system. Some thought that fraud and abuse were more prevalent in the Medicaid program, particularly in urban clinic settings, among foreign medical graduates, in hospitals, and in conjunction with laboratory services. Others felt that the problem cut across all types of providers and practice settings. There was some general agreement that:

Whether you label it fraud or abuse, other providers are doing what the providers in the sample were convicted of.

The rules governing reimbursement are unclear and are interpreted inconsistently over time. You never know what will be paid and the carriers provide little clarification or assistance.

There is considerable dissatisfaction among providers with the level of reimbursement, particularly for Medicaid. This dissatisfaction encourages providers to seek various ways of presenting claims to maximize income.

It is easy for a provider to move from looking for loopholes to submission of obviously false claims.

Billing for services not rendered and upcoding for services that are provided are the most frequent types of fraud.

Kickbacks, gang visits, double billing and billing for services to ineligible clients are much less frequent.

B. DETECTION Most of the convicted providers felt that the reimbursement system was inconsistent and that they knew little about how the carrier handled routine administrative matters, let alone specific detection policies. Before they were arrested, most had little or no knowledge of how their fraud was detected. They were almost universally surprised when a case was brought against them. They:

Reported there was little or no preventative contact with the carriers. No one ever warned them that their actions were improper.

Were almost totally unaware of the pre or post payment screens used by the carriers to audit their activity. Where utilization review was understood, it was seen as a procedure to control hospital inpatient utilization and quality.

Two physicians working in clinic settings indicated they had neither seen the bills which the clinic owners had submitted

under their names nor had they personally received anywhere near the total amount that had been billed for their
services.

The one provider in the sample who had purposely submitted
numerous false claims and had systematically milked the
Medicaid system for large sums indicated that because it was
so easy for so long, he thought no one was ever reviewing
anything.

C. DETERRENCE Convicted providers stressed the need for early
intervention by the carriers and the government to change
provider behavior prior to events reaching a crisis state.
Provider education and establishing a "sense of presence" on
the part of the carrier were seen as more effective in preventing
fraud and abuse than reliance on penalties and sanctions to
frighten people away from committing fraud. They recommended that there should be:

Early and frequent contact between the carrier and the
provider so that he/she fully understands the process and the
responsibilities of participation in the Medicare and Medicaid programs.

Improved consistency in claims processing so that a provider
knows what to expect and does not see a lot of slack in the
system.

Increased highly visible administrative oversight by the
carrier including use of screens and routine audits; the
carriers develop a quick personal response so that problems
which are identified are dealt with immediately.

Increased use of experimental delivery systems, case management experiments or percapita payment methods to take the
profit out of billing for services not rendered or of upcoding
services provided.

Use of peer groups to educate other providers about the
problems and pitfalls of fraud and abuse.

Use of selected convicted providers to spread the message of
what can happen to a doctor or other professional who "slides

into fraud". The message should not be to inculcate fear of sanctions but rather for one provider to tell another "you may not think you are doing anything wrong, but look what happened to me."

More convictions and more general publicity about investigations and convictions were seen as having a lesser deterrent effect. Convictions may be a useful means for punishment, recovery of funds or getting providers out of the program. But the average doctor or other health professional does not identify with the person who gets caught unless it is brought very, very, close to home. The two convicted providers who compulsively set out to rip off Medicare and Medicaid said essentially that nothing would have deterred them.

D. SANCTIONING   Fear of the available sanctions, (arrest, conviction, financial penalties, jail, loss of license, and the HCFA suspension) appears to have had little impact on the behavior of these providers prior to their conviction.

None of the convicted providers thought they would ever pay a penalty for their actions except for a routine financial adjustment or repayment.

None conceived they might be convicted of a crime or go to jail.

Fear (or even understanding) of HCFA suspension was almost totally absent. Several of the convicted providers didn't even understand the suspension process or issue prior to being contacted for participation in the study.

For many, the lack of concern may have been because they did not perceive they were committing fraud (or abuse). The two who admitted intent felt they could always evade detection or could work their way out of anything.

For most, the loss of license to practice their profession was considered so serious as to be "almost life threatening." Most thought that licensure should be only related to medical practice and not to financial matters. None thought that this was a penalty that was likely to occur.

FUTURE DISCUSSIONS WITH CONVICTED PROVIDERS

In order to determine how, in the future, the Office of the Inspector General might routinely and systematically gather additional information from convicted providers, discussions were held with U.S. Attorneys and Probation Officers in five Districts. The U.S. Attorneys indicated that there are three primary potential points to access to the provider: between conviction and sentencing, between indictment and conviction and after conviction while still under supervision. They generally agreed that between conviction and sentencing is the point of greatest leverage, because the convicted provider is then under some obligation to show remorse and has additional incentive to cooperate at that time.

The U.S. Attorneys contacted were generally enthusiastic about cooperating with OIG efforts to gather additional information about Medicare and Medicaid vulnerabilities and on the detection, sanctioning and deterrence of fraud. But, because there are special circumstances in particular cases which would make contact with the provider more or less appropriate, the U.S. Attorneys suggested that all contact should be made through them on a case by case basis. This would require that representatives of the OIG establish contact with individual U.S. Attorneys to make known what data was to be sought and what would be its potential uses.

U.S. Attorneys vary in their policy on influencing presentence reports and their degree of cooperation in working with the OIG is likely to vary. And where the provider intends to appeal a case, cooperation from him is likely to be limited.

APPENDIX A

Tests

To test the representativeness of the sample, the following statistical tests were done:

For 2-category variables (e.g., sex), exact binomial probabilities were computed and tested against population proportions.

For multiple category variables (e.g., discipline), chi-square approximations to multinomial probabilities were used.

For continuous variables, differences between sample means and population means were assessed with z-tests. Because of skewness in their distributions, estimated amount defrauded, restitution, and amount fined were reexpressed as log transformations, and suspension length as a square root transformation, prior to statistical testing.

Power

The "power" of a statistical test refers to the likelihood of detecting differences that truly exist, or stated more formally, the probability of rejecting a false null hypothesis. The lack of a significant difference cannot be construed as indicating that a sample represents a population unless the test has reasonable power to detect otherwise. Power is of some concern here because it is partly a function of sample size, which is small (N = 15).

On the basis of its distributional properties, year of birth (age) was selected as the best variable to use for a power analysis. The observed population mean for all providers was approximately 1933, with a standard deviation of 10.2 years. It is assumed that the hypothetical population of cooperating providers has the same standard deviation (this is a standard assumption); our interest is in differences between *means*.

Over repeated samples of cooperating providers of sample size 15, the power to detect a population difference of 7 or more years in either direction would be .60. In other words, a difference of this size would have been detected in 60% of the samples. Smaller differences would have been detected less frequently. If age is typical, the tests for representativeness had reasonably good power to detect large differences, but may have missed some small ones.

APPENDIX B

Selected Characteristics of Convicted Practitioner-providers in the Sample and the Universe.[1]

Variable	Sample (N = 14)	Universe (N = 310)
Sex - % male	93%	95%
Type of practitioner - % physicians	65%	50%
Physician training - % FMG's	36%	29%
Program defrauded		
Medicaid only	71%	75%
Medicare only	14%	19%
Medicare and Medicaid	14%	6%
Median amount defrauded[2]	$3,159	$5,088
Offense [3]		
Billing for services not rendered	85%	75%
Upcoding	14%	14%
Duplicate billing	14%	13%
Other	35%	28%
Sentences		
% sentenced to jail	36%	28%
Median restitution	$3,226	$2,610

[1] Statistical tests indicate that the sample and universe were comparable with respect to each characteristic indicated above (see Appendix A for description of tests).

[2] Files often did not indicate the method for estimating the amount defrauded. Where estimates were derived from amounts included in an indictment or a plea, they may significantly underrepresent the actual amount stolen.

[3] Percentages add to more than 100 because some providers were convicted of more than one type of offense.

APPENDIX III

PREVENTING SEXUAL ABUSE IN DAY CARE PROGRAMS

Report of Inspector General
Richard P. Kusserow,
Department of
Health and Human Services

ABSTRACT

A challenging by-product of the changing composition of America's workforce is the increasing need for day care. In 1980, there were 19.6 million children under five, and 8.7 million of them had mothers who worked outside the home. By 1990, these numbers will increase to 23 million and 12 million, respectively.[1] There are more than 11 million employed mothers with

---

[1] *Families and Child Care: Improving the Options*, A Report by the House Select Committee on Children, Youth and Families (September 1984), p. 12.

children between six and 18. It is projected that by 1990, the number of six to nine-year-olds alone will total 15 million. Traditionally children's primary caretakers, employed mothers must turn to others for child care.

Day care is needed for children of all ages, but is absolutely necessary the younger the children are. An estimated two to seven million school-aged children are left alone after school each day.[2] A 1982 study shows that 36 percent of mothers working full time outside the home had their three- and four-year-olds in the care of a relative, 32 percent placed these preschoolers in day care and nursery schools, and 18 percent placed their children in nonrelative family home settings.[3]

Within recent months, the tragedy of child sexual abuse in day care settings has garnered public attention. The problem is being discussed by parents, teachers, physicians, therapists, day care providers, law enforcement officials and law-makers. Within the public forum, Congress took action by enacting P.L. 98-473, which provides supplementary funding to the Social Services Block Grant program for training, including prevention of child abuse in day care settings. In order to retain all of these training dollars, states must implement by September 30, 1985, procedures to screen specified child care personnel through employment history, background and nationwide criminal record checks. In addition, Congress required the Department of Health and Human Services to draft model licensing and registration standards for day care centers, group homes and family day care homes.

In October 1984, the HHS Under Secretary requested the Inspector General to conduct a national program inspection on the issue of prevention of child sexual abuse in day care programs. Accordingly, staff from the HHS Office of Inspector General and the HHS Office of Human Development Services talked to 300 persons from 49 states and the District of Columbia. Participants in the study included state child

[2]Ibid. 23.
[3]U.S. Bureau of Census, "Child Care Arangements of Working Mothers," *Current Population Reports* P-23, No. 129, (June 1982).

protective staff and social workers, state licensing officials, city and county licensing officials, state criminal identification system directors, physicians, sexual assault therapists, child psychologists, district attorneys, police investigators, other experts in the field of child sexual abuse, day care providers, parents of children in day care, and special interest organizations. The results of this review follow.

MAJOR FINDINGS

1.   Most known sexual abuse of children occurs in the home. There is a clear cycle of abuse begetting abuse: abusers who were abused as children, and mothers allowing their children to be sexually abused because their own fathers did it to them.

2.   There is no profile or predictive model of child molesters. A number of professional studies, some funded by the National Institute of Mental Health, are underway on the identification and treatment of sex offenders.

3.   Pedophiles can be attracted to day care programs, can abuse hundreds of children without being caught, are often not convicted after being arrested, and may have no criminal records even if they plead guilty to sexually abusing children. Experts estimate only 1% to 15% have any criminal records, and not necessarily for sex crimes.

4.   Experts unanimously agree that education of parents, children, teachers, and day care providers to recognize, resist and report sexual abuse is the most effective method of preventing sexual abuse, both in the home and in child care programs. Employment screening techniques, including background and reference checks and criminal record screens, are seen as desirable but no guarantee that child molesters will be identified.

5.   Twenty-four states currently screen some day care operators and/or staff against state criminal record files, but only California, Georgia and Minnesota have statutes for national criminal record screening of such employees. Only

California and New York City have undertaken extensive fingerprinting of day care employees.

6. The only feasible approach to nationwide criminal record screening is the FBI fingerprint screen authorized under P.L. 92-544, which usually needs to be supplemented with a state criminal record screen. The cost of this dual screen is estimated at $25 per person screened.

7. To screen all licensed day care providers and employees would require screening half a million persons in each of the next three years. This would exclude about 350,000 unlicensed providers and all volunteers, even though in many of the known abuse cases the perpetrators were not direct program employees, but volunteers, relatives of providers or peripheral employees.

8. Licensing and employment screens typically reveal 5-8% of the applicants with *any* criminal record whatsoever. For many reasons it is quite likely that only a minuscule number of sex abusers with criminal records would be detected by screening all day care employees.

9. There are substantial timing, technical and due process problems with implementing the screening provisions of P.L. 98-473.

RECOMMENDATIONS

Education

1. As a first priority in prevention of child sexual abuse, HHS should support education of parents, children, child care providers and staff in how to recognize, resist and report child sexual abuse.

2. HHS should promote more nationwide television educational spots and programs raising adult and child awareness of these methods.

3. HHS should prepare and distribute to appropriate child

care grantees and to the public written information on this subject.

4. HHS should prepare and disseminate to appropriate grantees and other child care providers educational materials on how to (a) screen, check on and hire child care employees, (b) arrange facilities and staff, and (c) supervise staff so as to avoid child abuse in child care programs, as well as materials on how to handle reported abuse.

Research

HHS should continue to fund research into the profiling, detection and treatment of child molesters, and should assure that NIMH research currently underway finds practical application in effective public education materials.

Screening

1. HHS should require appropriate grantees to:

    a. Explicitly advise every employee and volunteer that sexual activity with children is illegal.

    b. Obtain from every employee and volunteer a signed declaration of prior criminal arrests, charges, and dispositions.

    c. Conduct background and former employer reference checks for all prospective employees.

    d. Obey state laws applicable to licensed or registered child care programs for screening or criminal record checks of current or potential employees.

    e. Have a plan for responding to suspected or reported child abuse whether it occurs inside or outside the program.

2. The Secretary should publicize that criminal record screens of child care employees are desirable but are no

guarantee of safety from child molesters (who seldom have criminal records) even in licensed centers; rather, that the best protection of children in child care depends on (a) education and alertness of parents, staff and children, (b) careful listening and observation by parents and staff, (c) child care participation and monitoring by parents, and (d) parent networks within programs.

3.   HHS should encourage states to screen child care staff and employees first within their state criminal record systems and then against the FBI nationwide file. HHS should seek a technical amendment of PL 98-473 if General Counsel advises this is necessary to allow states to retain 98-473 funding while using the FBI nationwide user-fee screening process for targeted sub-groups rather than for 100% of all prospective employees of child care programs.

4.   HHS should rapidly advise the states as to the nature and scope of child care staff screening which must be instituted by September 30, 1985, to retain full funding under P.L. 98-473.

COST IMPLICATIONS

Without this flexible interpretation, we estimate that $12.5 million will be lost to the states which Congress intended to be spent for preventive education. These funds would be either (a) wasted on low-yield fingerprint screening of an unnecessarily large number of day care employees or (b) recouped by HHS for technical state noncompliance with the screening requirements.

If all states were to comply literally with full FBI fingerprinting of all licensed day care employees, an estimated outlay from government or private funds of some $37.5 million would be made over three years. At least half of this would be wasted on extremely low-yield fingerprint screening.

We've had only one day care case—a man who molested preschool boys. When asked how many boys he had assaulted during his life, he said, 'You don't have a piece of paper long enough to write down the names.' He is 28 and had no prior record.

AN ASSISTANT DISTRICT ATTORNEY

BACKGROUND

The extent to which child sexual abuse occurs is unknown. Most of the national experts contacted in this study emphasized that no one really knows because most abusive incidents are not reported. Of those who ventured an estimate, the most common figures were 1 in 4 or 5 girls and 1 in 9 or 10 boys are sexually abused before age 18. Although the age of greatest risk is estimated to be between 8 and 13, children of all ages are assaulted. In one program treating assault victims, one-third of the children treated are under age 6.[4] Professional research is increasing and offers heightened understanding of the problem's magnitude. Data gathered from the sexual offenders program at the Oregon State Hospital reveal that 35 men admitted responsibility for 20,276 separate sex crimes. Of these, 18 men admitted more than 5000 assaults of 1000 children. One offender alone admitted abusing 500 children before being caught.[5] In an ongoing study of sex offenders, Dr. Judith Becker, Columbia University, found that 659 men admitted committing 280,000 sex crimes, of which the number committed against children is unknown. However, 58% of these offenders began their assaults while still in their teens. These figures are startling, but provide a glimpse at the extent to which a few offenders can abuse so many different persons.

Formal crime reports of abuse and clinical work with convicted abusers reveal that most sexual abusers are known by their victims. According to reported data on known abusers compiled by the American Humane Association (AHA), the federally-funded national reporting system on abuse, 95–98% of

[4]Lucy Berliner, Sexual Assault Center, Harborview Hospital, Seattle, WA.
[5]Unpublished data provided by Robert Freeman-Longo, Director, Sex Offender Unit, Correctional Treatment Programs, Oregon State Hospital.

known abuse occurs in the home, by close relatives, family friends or neighbors—that is, by someone whom the child knows well and trusts. AHA statistics reveal that 77% of the known abusers were parents (fathers, stepfathers, foster fathers), 16% were other relatives (grandfathers, uncles, cousins, brothers), and 6% were others (including both strangers and persons known by the child). Although most known data indicates that men are the primary perpetrators, researchers and clinical therapists are now learning that there are more female perpetrators than ever realized. Some experts estimate that women may comprise as high as 20–30% of abusers.

Although there are problems about using such statistics, there is common agreement among the experts that much of the abuse goes unreported. In addition, most research done to date tells us more about intrafamilial abuse than it does about extrafamilial abuse.

Nationally recognized experts contacted in this study agree that *no applicable profile of sexual abusers exists*. Five experts said explicitly:

"Don't believe anyone who says there is an abuser profile. There simply is no such thing."

"There is no profile—that's part of the problem."

"There is no sex abuser predictive model. Most studies of abusers are of incarcerated individuals and statistically invalid."

"The typical psychologist cannot spot a sex offender. Sex offenders can even pass polygraph tests."

"A trained psychologist can't identify an abuser easily. Even after treating 300-400 sex offenders, I would pick up a lot of 'false positives.' "

In an effort to develop predictive as well as treatment information, the HHS National Institute of Mental Health, through its Rape Center and its Center for Antisocial and

Violent Behaviors, has funded the following recent and/or current studies:

1. *Evaluating Sex Offender Treatment Programs,* Mark Weinrote, Evaluation Research Center, Eugene, Oregon. (5/79–3/81.)
2. *The Rapist's Social Background and Criminal Career,* James Galvin, National Council on Crime and Delinquency, San Francisco, California. (5/79–3/81.)
3. *Subtyping of Sex Offenders,* Raymond Knight, Brandeis University. (4/80–3/87.)
4. *Sex Aggression: Constructing a Predictive Equation,* Clarke Institute of Psychiatry, Toronto, Canada. (5/81–4/82.)
5. *Incarcerated Rapists: Exploring a Sociological Model,* Diana Scully, Virginia Commonwealth University, Richmond, Virginia. (9/81–4/83.)
6. *Prevention of Relapse in Pedophiles,* Richard Laws, Specific Professional Association, Morrow Bay, California. (1984–present.)
7. *Evaluation and Treatment of Child Molesters,* Gene Abel and Judith Becker, Columbia University, New York. (1984–present.)

Although there is no predictive model or abuser profile to aid in identifying child sex abusers, there are some common descriptors. Sex abusers come from all socioeconomic backgrounds. As a police investigator noted, "They are beggars to bankers." There is a victim cycle, both of the abuser himself and the child's mother or guardian who knowingly does nothing to stop the abuse. Study respondents cited that as many as 75% of offenders have been victims themselves. Although female victims are less likely to become abusers, they often become covert perpetrators who fail to protect the child. As an investigator summarized, "An abused girl becomes the mother of an abused child and then the grandmother of an abused child. She rationalizes, 'It's not so bad—my father did it to me. It's expected.'"

Most abusers maintain otherwise responsible lives. They are often considered "real nice guys," whose friends and neighbors are shocked if they are caught and publicly identified. Although some are psychotic or mentally ill, many more have cognitive distortions. They rationalize their behavior as "sex education." "The kids like it." "Kids are consenting." "It doesn't hurt them."

The research of Dr. A. Nicholas Groth was referred to frequently by study respondents, as the state-of-the-art in describing child sex abusers. He describes two types of pedophilic behavior:

Fixated

Primary sexual orientation is to children.

Pedophilic interest begins during adolescence.

No precipitating stress/no subjective distress prior to the assault.

Persistent interest—compulsive behavior.

Preplanned, premeditated offense.

Equalization: offender identifies closely with the victim and equalizes his behavior to the level of the child; offender is a pseudopeer to the victim.

Male victims are primary targets.

Little or no sexual contact with agemates; offender is usually single.

Usually no history of alcohol or drug abuse.

Characterological immaturity/poor socio-sexual peer relationships.

Offense = maladaptive resolution of life issues.

Regressed

Primary sexual orientation is to agemates.

Pedophilic interest emerges in adulthood.

Precipitating stress usually evident.

Involvements may be more episodic.

Initial offense may be impulsive, not premeditated.

Substitution: offender replaces conflictual relationship with involvement with the child; victim is a pseudo-adult substitute.

Female victims are primary targets.

Sexual contact with child co-exists with sexual contact with agemates; offender is usually married/common-law.

In more cases the offense may be alcohol related.

More traditional lifestyle but underdeveloped peer relationships.

Offense = maladaptive attempt to cope with specific life stresses.[6]

Study respondents also agreed that *there is no such thing as an abused child profile.* Children frequently do not tell when they are sexually abused because they are afraid that (a) they or someone they love will be punished or killed, (b) no one will believe them or (c) they are responsible in some way for the abuse. Also, children may not be able to tell someone directly, either lacking the language skills or being too young to verbalize. There are, however, signals or "red flags" that *may* indicate that a child has been assaulted. The following *signals may help* in detecting sexual abuse in children:

Inappropriate sexual knowledge or behavior, e.g., preschooler knowledge of sexual intercourse

Sudden withdrawal, passivity or depression

Sudden active or violent behavior

Fantasy or infantile behavior

Poor peer relationships

[6]Adapted by Robert E. Freeman-Longo from *Sexual Assaul of Children and Adolescents,* by Ann W. Burgess, A. Nicholas Groth, Lynda Lytle Holmstrom and Suzanne M. Sgroi (Lexington FMA: Lexington Books/D.C. Heath, 1978).

Self-mutilation

Suicidal actions or discussions

Reluctance to go certain places, e.g., neighbor's house

Change in eating habits or gagging around food

Multiple personalities

Psychosomatic disorders

Nightmares, fear of the dark, or sudden bedwetting

New fears

Dislike or avoidance of someone previously liked, including a parent

* Bodily bruises

Irritation or pain in genital/rectal areas

Venereal disease, especially under age 13

Difficulty in walking or sitting

Torn, bloody underwear

Early pregnancy

Truancy or runaway behavior

Of all of these, the most telling sign of sexual abuse is *unusual sexual behavior beyond the child's age level* in both verbal and action cues. "All sexual behavior is learned. Children either observe it or experience it," reminded Lucy Berliner of the Seattle Sexual Assault Center. In sum, any sudden and/or unusual behavior in a child *may* be caused by sexual assault and should be investigated.

Generally, the best advice offered to detect sexual abuse is to educate parents, teachers and caretakers to watch children carefully, listen to what they have to say and recognize the signals or indicators of possible abuse. Then, the key is to believe the child when abuse is asserted.

There are several reasons why abusers avoid detection. Historically, society collectively has been unwilling to recognize or talk about child sexual abuse, making it easier for abusers to evade discovery. With few exceptions, child sexual abuse is not observed by witnesses. It is performed in isolation, in secrecy, and the victims are reluctant to report it. The child may not know or may be convinced by the abuser that nothing is wrong with the act. Children, especially the very young, are too trusting and are easily manipulated. Some abusers convince their victims to assume the responsibility and/or guilt for the abuse. In other situations, abusers intimidate their victims, coercing them into compliance by threatening to harm them or a loved one, "If you tell, your mother will die." In some cases, they try to target children who are neglected or whose parents are having life adjustment problems, such as death, separation or divorce. Even when detected, they frequently move on and with the absence of an interstate tracking system easily avoid detection.

As little is known about the cause or deterrence of child sexual abuse, little is known also about treatment for abusers. Some believe that incarceration is the only answer, that the pathology of a pedophile is so intractable he must be taken out of circulation. A few respondents suggested self-help programs like Parents United, wherein support groups of former abusers work with current abusers under supervision of trained psychologists. Others suggested use of medication (to lower the level of the male hormone testosterone and reduce the abuser's sexual drive) or aversion therapy. Dr. Vincent Fontana, Chairman of the New York City Mayor's Task Force on Child Abuse and Neglect, summarized the views of most respondents, "We can't determine effective treatment until we know more about the problem."

> The amendment . . . is a modest first step that would help states establish and improve child abuse prevention programs.
> SENATOR LEVIN, INTRODUCING P.L. 98-473

THE NEW LAW AND THE FBI CRIMINAL RECORD SYSTEM

New legislation enacted as part of P.L. 98-473, continuing appropriations for fiscal year (FY) 1985, (a) requires the

Department of Health and Human Services to draft a Model
Child Care Standards Act for states' consideration by January
12, 1985, and (b) authorizes (without an appropriation)
challenge grants to the states for child abuse prevention
activities with federal funds to accrue the year following that in
which the states earmark their own funds.

   This act also *authorizes and appropriates* $25 million under the
Title XX Social Services Block Grant, to be distributed to each
state proportionate to its other Title XX funding for the purpose
of training (including training for child abuse prevention)
providers, operators and staffs in *licensed or registered* child care
facilities. To keep from losing one-half of these funds in FY 1986
and FY 1987, however, states are required to have in effect by
September 30, 1985, (1) procedures established by state law or
regulations to provide for employment history and background
checks and (2) provisions of state law consistent with P.L.
92-544 requiring nationwide criminal record checks for all
current and prospective operators, staff, or employees of child
care facilities and juvenile detention, treatment, or correction
facilities. The child care facilities are defined to include any
facility or program having primary custody of children for 20
hours or more per week.[7]

   The only feasible way for a state to conduct a "nationwide
criminal record check" on any person is to access information
contained in the computerized criminal history file of the
Federal Bureau of Investigation. P.L. 92-544 authorizes the FBI
to exchange identification information from this file with duly
authorized officials of state government, "if authorized by state
statute and approved by the Attorney General."

   In fact, the Attorney General, through the FBI Identification
Division, has screened and approved over 500 state statutes
requiring FBI fingerprint checks for employment or licensing
purposes. Last year, out of a total of 6 million fingerprint cards
submitted for all criminal and other screening purposes, the
Identification Bureau screened 697,000 fingerprints for licens-

---

[7]*Congressional Record* (October 2, 1984); S12710.

ing or employment purposes. Screening is free of charge to
authorized law enforcement agencies in return for their
cooperation in supplying arrest and disposition information to
the FBI. However, the FBI collects a fee of $12 per screen (i.e.,
per fingerprint card submitted) for licensing/employment
checks. Fingerprint cards are submitted to the FBI via the single
approved state identification bureau, such as the state police,
and are returned to that bureau or directly to the state licensing
or social service agency authorized in the state statute.

A state statute is accepted by the FBI for inclusion in the
process so long as it (a) does not violate public policy (e.g., Civil
Rights) and (b) clearly shows that the state legislature intended
that a nationwide check be conducted. The FBI is prepared to
screen any state laws submitted in accordance with P.L. 98-473
and to accept fingerprint cards on child care staff accordingly
for the $12 fee. However, our discussions with the FBI's
Identification Bureau indicted that they do not intend to review
compliance with P.L. 98-473, i.e., the FBI will not determine
whether the scope or coverage of the state statutes with respect
to the type of staff or facilities involved is sufficient to qualify
the state for continued training funds under Title XX. The FBI
considers such determinations to be the responsibility of HHS.

The FBI's National Crime Information Center (NCIC) is
currently developing a new criminal record access system
decentralizing all record-keeping to the states. Under this new
Interstate Identification Index, states will maintain their own
statewide records, which will be accessible through a computer
query of the FBI file. Only 15 states are now participating in
demonstrations of the new system. While this system conceiv-
ably might reduce the necessity for fingerprint checks, the NCIC
Policy Advisory Board strongly opposes its use for employ-
ment/licensing screening because of the wide divergence of state
laws concerning the dissemination of criminal history information for such purposes. Some states even deny federal
agencies, such as the Office of Personnel Management, access to
state criminal record information for federal employment
screening. Both the FBI and state identification bureau officials
emphasize that name checks or any other screening without

fingerprints are subject to error and misapplication when used for licensing/employment screening purposes.[8]

> We can do thousands of criminal record screens by name, but when you tell us to fingerprint lots of employees is when I start hollerin' and stompin' my feet.
>
> STATE IDENTIFICATION BUREAU CHIEF

CURRENT SCREENING PRACTICES IN THE STATES

The FBI has approved licensing/employment screening statutes for all but nine of the states in one or more areas of employment. Forty-one states and the District of Columbia require FBI checks for employment in the banking and/or securities industries, and 37 states require FBI screening for federal employees. Over half the states require such screening for private investigators and/or gambling establishments, and many states require such screens in conjunction with gun permits and/or alcohol distribution. In New Jersey, one must have an FBI check to run a bingo or raffle, do acupuncture, be a firefighter, plumber, undertaker or cigarette salesman. In Texas, such a check is required for junk dealers, pest controllers, union business agents and marriage counselors. In the District of Columbia, an FBI screen is required to operate a bowling alley or a massage parlor, or to be a cab driver, pawnbroker, fortune teller, clairvoyant or medium.

In professional occupations, such screening is required less frequently. Only 12 states require FBI screens for teachers, doctors, dentists, nurses and/or lawyers, with California, Minnesota and New Jersey requiring the most screens. *Only three states have approved statutes requiring FBI screens for any directors or staff of day care programs: California, Georgia*

[8]Robert A. McConnell, Assistant Attorney General, Office of Legislative Affairs, U.S. Department of Justice: Memo of June 11, 1984, to the Honorable Strom Thurmond, Chairman, Senate Judiciary Committee, with reference to S. 1924.

(directors only) and Minnesota. Minnesota's authorized use of FBI screens has not been implemented because of budget limitations.

States vary considerably on (a) what sorts of child care they license or register, (b) whom they screen: whether operators, teachers, peripheral staff or volunteers, (c) how they screen: whether by fingerprints, name checks or reference checks, and (d) what records they screen against: whether against the FBI file, state criminal record files, or the state's child abuse/neglect registry. A number of recent surveys of day care licensing practices in the states are available.[9] However, these largely fail to describe the employment screening practices used by the various jurisdictions. Most of the information which follows was collected for this study from discussions with state staff.

All states license at least some child care facilities, usually called day care centers or group homes. Thirty states license family day care homes, 12 states register family day care homes, and three states do both. Five states license only subsidized family day care.[10]

Although only three states use FBI fingerprints to screen day care directors and/or employees, the practice of screening these persons using names, fingerprints or other identifying information against state criminal record files and/or abuse registries is more widespread. Name checks, used alone, miss anyone who has legally changed his name or adopted an alias and generally are far less accurate. Twenty-four states indicated that they currently perform statewide criminal record screens of directors, employees or both. These usually are limited to licensed programs, though not necessarily applied to all licensed day care programs.

[9]*Minimum Standards for Day Care Centers,* National Association for Child Care Management, (1983), 1800 M Street N.W., Suite 1030N, Washington, DC 20036; *Comparative Licensing Study,* Administration for Children, Youth and Families, Office of Human Development Services (1981), Washington, D.C.; *Day Care Centers in the U.S.—A National Profile 1976-1977* (1978), ABT Associates, Cambridge, MA.

[10]D. Adams, "Family Day Care Registration: Is It Deregulation or More Feasible State Public Policy?," *Young Children,* 4 (1984):75.

While virtually all states maintain child abuse and neglect registries identifying abusers within families, only 15 states use the registry as a screening tool for child care employment or licensing. Because some states have not consistently purged their registries, many contain names of people for whom the allegation of child abuse was never substantiated. Since most of the people listed on these registries have not been prosecuted, any expanded use of the registries as a screening tool for employment could result in due process or legal challenges. Besides the state criminal file and the registry, 24 states require other forms of background checks and/or employee certification of criminal history. Only 14 states use none of these screening tools for child care employment or licensing.

This picture is complicated further by variations in employee coverage: 23 states apply screening to day care program directors, 22 states to day care program employees, but only 18 states to both. Ten states use some type of screen for day care volunteers.

Variations exist also within state boundaries. A few states give cities and counties the option to use certain screens. Probably the most significant of these is New York City, where a new city law, effective October 1, 1984, mandates fingerprinting of all day care center directors and staff as well as of all licensed family day care operators and all adults in these homes. The fingerprints will be screened against the state criminal file (not the FBI file). Meanwhile, the state of New York requires screening of daycare staff against the state child abuse registry, but not against the state criminal record file.

Finally, this incredibly complex pattern of screening variations is in flux, with at least 20 states anticipating new legislation to authorize some sort of criminal record screens for day care operators, employees and/or volunteers.

> I am dismayed at focusing such an extreme legal remedy on such a fraction of the problem.
>
> President, Large Day Care Corporation

POTENTIAL SCOPE OF SCREENING

Based on a sample of 60,000 home interviews conducted in 1983, the U.S. Bureau of Labor Statistics (BLS) estimates that 1,041,000 child care workers are employed in the U.S., with another 80,000 unemployed. Of those employed, 408,000 work in private homes. This group is 95% female and includes child attendants, mothers' helpers, nursemaids, day care workers, baby sitters and governesses. The other 633,000 work in other-than-private homes. This group is 97% female and includes day care workers, day care aides, attendants, Head Start workers, house parents, playground monitors and bus drivers in day care centers. These numbers are quite comparable to those projected from informal estimates by state officials in 10 states which were subsampled in this study.

Presuming that most of what the BLS described as "child care in other-than-private homes" means day care centers and group homes, these are virtually all licensed by states.[11] It is more difficult, however, to estimate what portion of in-home child care or family day care is licensed or registered. The 1981 National Day Care Home Study found that of an estimated 1.3 million day care homes, only 137,865 (10.6%) were regulated.[12]

We estimate, therefore, that 633,000 persons work in licensed day care centers or group homes; and 43,200 (408,000 x 10.6%) work in licensed family day care, for a total of 676,200 employees in licensed day care in the U.S.

Family day care workers, babysitters and nannies have, according to BLS, the highest turnover rate of any group of workers in the country, at 58.8% per year, while workers in day care centers, nursery schools and Head Start rank 9th on the turnover list, at 41.7% per year—right up there with dishwashing, peddling and pumping gasoline.[13] Assuming a conservative

[11]ABT Associates, *Day Care Centers in the U.S.*, p. 10.
[12]S. Fosburg, "Family Day Care in the United States: Summary of Findings," *Final Report of the National Day Care Home Study* (DHHS Publication #OHDS-80-30282).
[13]BLS Occupational Projections and Training Data, as quoted in *Day Care USA Newsletter*, 13:9 (September 10, 1984): 3.

turnover-plus-growth rate of 45% per year, an estimated 980,490 individuals will be employed in licensed day care in this country in calendar year 1985, and 1,589,070 persons will be employed in licensed day care during calendar years 1985-1987.

Therefore, if some form of criminal record screening were applied to all operators and immediate employees of licensed day care programs during the period 1985-1987, the nationwide volume of staff to be screened would exceed half a million persons in each of the three years, assuming no repetitive screening. These estimates do not include family members, volunteers or other employees with access to the children, e.g., janitors. They also exclude an estimated 364,000 workers in unlicensed family day care.

> Fingerprinting millions of people will require a massive collection effort. The time and expense of processing the information will be monumental.
>
> ATTORNEY

POTENTIAL COST OF SCREENING

Costs of a criminal record check depend, of course, on the nature of the check being performed, and particularly upon whether the check involves a fingerprint screen. The FBI charges $12 for each fingerprint card submitted for nationwide licensing/employment screening.

State identification bureau officials with whom we spoke agreed that any criminal record screen should include checks against both the state criminal file and the FBI file. Those states using fingerprints to screen against their state files unanimously agreed that two separate fingerprint cards would be necessary to do both a state and an FBI screen. State costs associated with screening vary:

California	$15.50	Kansas	$ 6.00
Florida (counties)	$ 5.00	Nebraska	$ 5.00
Georgia	$12.00	New York (City)	$17.00
Illinois	$10.00	Washington	$10.00

Some of these represent relatively low-volume operations and may not reflect what fingerprinting would cost if large numbers of day care personnel were to be screened. Also, some represent only the state cost for the screen, excluding the local costs of collecting and forwarding the cards, and processing the returns after the screen.

As an example of costs associated with volume operations, one state identification bureau director told us that he can easily process name-check-only data using magcards, but that fingerprint checks would require so much more staff that his facility would have to be moved. The New York City figure of $17 includes a $14 fee paid to the state and $3 to produce the cards. This will allow hiring only eight teams consisting of one fingerprinter and typist to fingerprint the first 60,000 child care workers in the city.

Other hidden costs involve the delays associated with such screenings in the hiring of employees. While the FBI advises that fingerprint checks are completed in less than 10 days, the state identification officials told us that the checks usually take six-eight weeks to process and sometimes take up to three-four months. Moreover, fingerprinting is an exacting process, and large numbers of cards are routinely rejected by the FBI even after the state identification bureaus have approved and forwarded them.

Costs associated with screening against state criminal records files without fingerprinting are considerably lower, ranging from $2 to $5 per check. Some states, like Texas, use a two-step process for license/employment screens, involving a name screen first and a fingerprint later if needed to validate the identity of a specific employee. Other jurisdictions, like New York, believe that the two-step process is less efficient than fingerprinting from the start.

We estimate, therefore, that a nationwide criminal record check involving both a state file and the FBI file, requiring two fingerprint cards, would cost about $25 per employee in a large-volume licensing/employment screening operation. There are precedents for both full government financing of such screening efforts and fee payments by the employing organization or the applicants themselves.

We want and need so desperately to find a solution to the tragedy
of sexual abuse that we seem to be grabbing at the first remedy
that comes along without considering its cost or its effectiveness.
                                    ANNE H. COHN, NATIONAL COMMITTEE
                                    FOR PREVENTION OF CHILD ABUSE

EFFECTIVENESS OF SCREENING

Even the most avid proponents of background and criminal
history checks on day care employees acknowledge that they are
not a panacea for preventing sexual abuse in day care.
Prosecutors, therapists, police investigators and other experts
generally agreed that although none of the screening methods
will catch significant numbers of pedophiles, the FBI's national
fingerprint screen is more effective than any other screening
method. Even the FBI system has significant limitations,
however, which FBI officials acknowledged to Congress:[14]

a. The FBI files are not complete. The information con-
    tained in them is furnished voluntarily by state and local
    law enforcement agencies. (Study participants report
    that some law enforcement jurisdictions are very lax
    about sending in fingerprints, which is the only way an
    arrest or conviction is built into a criminal history. Some
    states send 90% of their arrests and convictions to the
    FBI, but other states send in as few as 15%. The director of
    one state identification bureau indicated that out of 400
    substate law enforcement jurisdictions, over 100 hadn't
    sent in a single fingerprint all year.)

b. The records often do not specify whether the sexual
    assault victim was a child or an adult. (As one prosecutor
    noted, "We find out the accused has been convicted of
    battery, but we don't know if it involved a child or if he
    took part in a barroom brawl.")

c. The FBI file contains no records on juvenile offenders
    unless they were tried as an adult. (Research suggests

[14]McConnell, op. cit.

that 58% of all pedophiles committed their first sexual offense as adolescents.)

d. The Identification Bureau does not disclose for licensing/ employment screening purposes information on arrests for which there is no reported disposition, except for arrests within the previous 12 months.

There are other reasons why screening of day care centers would have limited effectiveness. First, most known child sexual abuse is committed by family members, not by unrelated child care providers. Statistics from Illinois show, for example, that in 1983 the following perpetrators committed child sexual abuse:[15]

Family member, relative	80.7%	Babysitters	6.7%
Adoptive Parent	2.2%	Other Not Related	7.2%
Foster Parent	.8%	Not Identified	1.0%
Institution staff	1.2%		

Based on statistics, day care employees as a group should be expected to have fewer child sexual abusers among their ranks than the general population because 78% to 92% of child sexual abusers are male,[16] while day care workers are 95% to 97% female. The effectiveness of screening, of course, has less to do with who commits child abuse than with who has a record of child abuse (or related crime) which will be discovered in the screening process. For example, the FBI reports that 80-85% of its records are for males, which means the probability of identifying a female child abuser is slim. There are reasons that child sex abusers may be expected to have a very low ratio of criminal records. Dr. Vincent Fontana, a nationally renowned expert on child sexual abuse, maintains that less than 1% of all child sexual abusers have criminal records.[17] Research con-

[15]Illinois Department of Children and Family Services, *Child Abuse and Neglect Statistics, Annual Report—FY 1983*, 22.
[16]78% figure cited by Jane Lapp, American Humane Association, Project Director, *National Study of Child Abuse and Neglect Reporting*. 92% from Illinois Department of Children and Family Services Report, op. cit., 22.
[17]*New York Times*, November 7, 1984.

ducted on sex offenders in Knoxville, Tennessee, found that despite long histories of sexual abuse, only 7% had prior criminal records, usually for offenses other than sexual abuse.[18] Another study involving 659 offenders who had committed a total of 280,000 crimes revealed that fewer than 15% had criminal records, again not necessarily for sex-related crimes.[19] Prosecutors cited case after case in which the perpetrator had no prior record.

There are other reasons why there are so few criminal records for child sexual abusers:

Detection Difficulty: Sexual abuse of children is a crime that is very hard to detect. Other than the victims, there are usually no witnesses. These children are easily manipulated or intimidated into maintaining silence. Some children aren't aware that what is happening to them is wrong or unusual; others are extremely guilty or ashamed. Strong social taboos have kept people from talking about this issue, and even when faced with an abusive situation, many adults deny or ignore the problem.

Low Conviction Rates and Legal Manipulations: The variations which can occur in the course of legal proceedings are endless. The result is that sexual offenders who admit their guilt end up frequently having no record, or the record is for an offense that is not sex-related. When convictions do occur, they are often to lesser charges (e.g., a rape charge is reduced to simple assault). In other cases, prosecution or sentencing is deferred if the perpetrator agrees to treatment. If a convicted sex offender with deferred sentencing completes treatment and meets the conditions of probation, a finding of not guilty sometimes is entered on his record.

There are many reasons why the conviction rate among child sex offenders is so low. Many respondents stressed that court proceedings are simply not geared to children. They make poor witnesses (e.g., can't remember dates, number of assaults, etc.) and can be traumatized by normal courtroom

[18]John Brogden, Director, Institute for Child Sexual Abuse, Ft. Worth, Texas.
[19]Dr. Judith Becker, Columbia University.

procedures. Many parents simply won't allow their children to go through the trauma of testifying. Reportedly, seminars are being held for defense attorneys on how to intimidate children and discredit their testimony in these cases. Furthermore, much of what children tell parents, doctors or therapists is excluded as heresay. Children also find it very difficult to confront the accused, a constitutional guarantee which keeps many courts from allowing the videotaped testimony of young children.

Misdemeanors: Given the difficulty of producing evidence in such cases or of using children's testimony, felony charges frequently are reduced to misdemeanors via a plea bargaining process. For example, a charge of sexual contact may be exchanged for a guilty plea to indecent exposure or "flashing," usually a misdemeanor, which may result in *no* criminal record entry in the FBI system. In fact, state criminal records more frequently contain evidence of such sex-related actions even though they would not have been entered into the FBI file. This is one reason state screening officials urged state-level screens before the nationwide FBI screen.

The FBI reports that on licensing/employment screens generally (for everything from cab drivers to bankers) only 8% of all fingerprints submitted will be returned with any criminal history at all—for any kind of offense. This number is fairly consistent with what the state screening bureaus reported about the frequency of returns in general:

ESTIMATED PERCENT OF PERSONS SCREENED AGAINST
STATE CRIMINAL FILES WHO HAVE A PRIOR RECORD OF
ARRESTS FOR ANY CRIME

California	7.7%
Michigan	3%–5%
New Hampshire	1%
New York	5%–10%
Washington	5%–7%
AVERAGE	5%

Estimated screening "hits" for sexual abuse of children, as opposed to all crimes, of course, are much lower. The FBI Identification Bureau has no statistics on sexual crimes against children. None of the screening systems currently in place has yielded many day care employees with past records of child abuse. For example:

In 1983, a screen of 20,000 employees in New York against its child abuse registry resulted in 7 "hits" (.04%). Only 2.3% of all reports of child abuse and neglect in New York State in 1983 were for sexual abuse.

A county in Florida which conducts statewide fingerprint screens of employees identified 2 people with criminal histories out of 3000 screened (.07%). One was a janitor with previous sex crime convictions, and a second had been convicted of murdering an adult.

Georgia conducts statewide and national fingerprint checks on day care operators and statewide name checks on other day care employees. Thus far, a check of 570 fingerprints has resulted in one "hit" (.2%) and name checks of 2,400 employees had identified 2 others (.08%).

In the course of this study, discussions were held with prosecutors, police officials and other experts familiar with 45 individuals charged with sexual abuse of children in 37 day care facilities (22 family home day cares and 15 centers). Based on the information available on these cases, a national background check as proposed in the law would have screened out only one of these perpetrators—a male operating a licensed facility who had served time in a military prison and lost his nursing license as a result of previous convictions for abuse. The only other person with a prior record was a male who was on probation for similar acts, but because he was operating an unlicensed facility, he probably would not have been caught.

In addition to the fact that so few of these perpetrators had prior records, many probably would not be subject to the new screening mandate. For example:

Eighteen were spouses, sons and other male relatives and friends who would not have been caught unless fingerprinting were extended to family members and friends. Furthermore, the nine sons were all juveniles and would not have a permanent record.

Five were men who had access to children in day care, but were not direct providers of child care. These perpetrators— janitors, the mechanic who worked on the bus, the driver of a delivery van, etc.—would not have been caught unless the required fingerprinting extends to volunteers and other peripheral employees with access to the children.

Four were in unlicensed family day care homes and probably wouldn't have been screened.

Many people argue that the time and expense of fingerprinting are justified, even if only one or two pedophiles are caught. They also maintain that mandatory fingerprinting will deter sex offenders from seeking day care jobs. There is equal concern, however, that a mandatory fingerprint screen will lull the public into complacency and create a sense of false security. Almost all parents said that they would feel more secure knowing that day care employees had submitted to criminal history checks. Countered a child abuse expert, however, "I am concerned that people will think that because an employee's record is clean, everything is o.k. That's simply not the case and can be as dangerous as doing nothing."

Screening needs to be placed in perspective. "Catching" an abuser through screening will not incarcerate him or place him in treatment. Presumably he has been through that. All screening will do will stop someone from getting *that* job *that* day. This is consistent with experts' views that children won't really be any safer overall because pedophiles will just turn to other child-oriented activities such as youth sports, Big Brothers and recreation centers, or the unlicensed day care down the street.

A number of respondents feel strongly that the mandate to fingerprint all day care employees is an over-reaction resulting from publicity over a few very notorious cases of sexual abuse in day care programs. Noted one nationally known expert in the field of child abuse, "Hysteria is not the proper impetus for the formation of solid public policy." Many participants also expressed concern that the current climate will drive dedicated quality employees out of day care, especially males.

Summary: A Possible Screening Scenario
680,000 current employees in licensed child care + 47% turnover/growth = 1 million employees to screen.

1 million state fingerprint checks (@ $13) and FBI checks (@ $12) = $25 million.

About 50,000 (or 5%) will have some criminal record (e.g., shoplifting).

Perhaps 1000 (or 2% of those with records) are child sex abusers.

Firing or not hiring these 1000 would cost $25,000 per "child sex abuser diversion."

"Diverted" child sex abusers could still be employed in unlicensed facilities or volunteer in licensed ones.

Since most child sex abusers don't have any criminal records, they wouldn't have been diverted.

Probably half of the child sex abusers in child care operations aren't employees and would not even have been screened.

States, cities and counties currently involved with screening day care employees all report having had to struggle with many issues to clarify their laws and ordinances. They uniformly advise that in order to minimize the number of due process questions and other legal challenges which may be anticipated, a number of issues will need to be clarified before the federal mandate is implemented:

1. *Which crimes will apply and who will decide whether a person is precluded from employment?* Although most of the states currently screening day care employees for child abuse have fairly specific guidelines as to which crimes would make a

person unsuitable for day care employment, they still find a lot of "grey" areas. Noted one person currently involved with such a system, "We know not to count bad checks, and we know we do count rape, but what about prostitution, a drug bust (marijuana) at a college party 12 years ago, or the murder of a cop? We really have to look at each one on a case by case basis. We've had to make lots of judgment calls." The City of New York is currently developing an entire manual on how to treat records of current or potential day care employees. States stress that there needs to be a specific policy on who makes the final decision (e.g., who is liable?), and how much information is released to the provider. There also needs to be an appeals process and careful attention to privacy issues.

2. *Who will be screened?* Prosecutors and other experts stressed that approximately half the institutional perpetrators of sex crimes are individuals outside the immediate paid staff of the day care facility, but with access to the children. There are many instances of abuse by janitors, bus drivers, volunteers and friends and relatives of day care staff in centers. In home day care settings, the perpetrators are frequently spouses or sons of the operators, and often adolescents. To include everyone with access to the children in a screen will greatly expand the magnitude of what will be a massive undertaking if only the immediate staff are screened.

Also, does a person need a fingerprint check to apply for a job, or as a final condition of employment? Can the person be a probationary employee until the criminal history is verified? Is a new fingerprint check required every time a person changes jobs? Does someone have to be rechecked from year to year, once they are on file?

3. *What is a "background check"?* Legal experts advise that without clear, tight definitions as to what will be used, there will be much litigation, especially in privacy-conscious states. Can a check also include arrest records, consulting the civil child abuse registry, etc.?

4. *What about differences between state laws and jurisdictions?* What happens when a person has been convicted of an act

that constitutes a crime in one state but is not considered to be a crime in the requesting state? How do states deal with the fact that various jurisdictions define crimes differently (e.g., an act which would be considered disorderly conduct in one place would be considered lewd conduct elsewhere)?

5. *Who will pay?* Will the cost of screening be borne by providers, employees and applicants, states, etc.?

6. *Penalties for noncompliance?* Will HHS penalize Title XX if day care providers comply, but corrections officials refuse?

Many offenders have explicitly said they wouldn't abuse kids if they knew the children would tell.

DR. JUDITH BECKER, COLUMBIA UNIVERSITY

PREVENTION: EDUCATION

There are no quick, easy or simple answers to the question, "How can child sexual abuse best be prevented?" Study respondents agreed that current licensing practices and fingerprint screens are by no means the whole answer. Many parents, providers and state officials noted that licensing often means only that a provider meets minimal facility and staff ratio standards, which are monitored infrequently.

Although all states regulate day care, there is great variation among states in their licensing and/or registration requirements. Some study respondents cautioned against federal or state action to increase licensing standards severely. Although they fear that overly stringent licensing requirements would drive many more providers underground, they do urge states to monitor licensed providers more regularly to assure that reasonable standards are met. Furthermore, many study repondents raised the concern that heavy governmental emphasis on fingerprint screens may lull parents into a sense of false security, i.e., into assuming that such checks will guarantee their children's safety from sexual abusers, when, in fact, fingerprinting will divert few child sex-abusers. They urge that fingerprint screens be used as a complement to other deterrent or prevention activities.

There is consensus among those who have worked with both victims and abusers regarding some actions besides screening which will help deter child sexual abuse:

The *key* recommendation is *to educate everyone,* but especially children, parents, teachers and caretakers to the existence of abuse, what abusive behavior is, what to do when faced with an abusive situation and how to avoid abuse.

Next, respondents say we must *teach both parents and children to report,* and to report promptly, when abuse does occur.

Other suggestions aimed at preventing child sexual abuse include:

Required reporting of sexual abuse by teachers, caretakers and medical personnel

Revamping of child protective service programs and retraining of CPS social workers

Increased and improved counseling programs for families at risk

Improved and increased treatment programs for victims and abusers

Judicial reform of the criminal court sytem to reflect the developmental differences between adults and children

More vigorous investigation and prosecution plus imposition of tougher penalties for convicted abusers.

Prevention of sexual abuse in day care settings is easier to define than intrafamilial child sexual abuse. The first line of defense still rests with the parents who *must* become involved: parents should get to know the staff, make unannounced visits, meet other parents and have a roster of other parents' names and phone numbers and, most important, know and recognize the telltale signs of abuse. (For a brief outline of detection signals, see page 355.

Day care providers can prevent sexual abuse by:

Educating staff to be aware of the signals of abuse

Asking for and checking all applicants' references before hiring (both teaching and non-teaching positions); asking on the application form whether the individual has ever been arrested, charged or convicted of crimes against children

Encouraging parents to visit at any time

Imposing a probationary period for all new staff

Never allowing teachers or any other staff to be alone with any child

Never allowing children to leave the premises without parental permission and accompaniment

Fostering, within the realities of the physical structure, as much open space as possible—leaving doors open, eliminating "nooks and crannies" and other places where children can be separated from others, etc.

Teaching the children through repetitive training with proven materials and approaches on sexual abuse curricula

Supervising staff and volunteers carefully.

Since education is the cornerstone of these prevention strategies, study respondents recommended increased federal and state roles in supporting, developing and disseminating information to combat child sex abuse. Education programs must be targeted to each specific audience, e.g., children, parents.

The most commonly mentioned education programs for children are referred to as the "good touch/bad touch" approach. The foundation for many of the available good touch/bad touch materials originated with the Minneapolis Illusion Theater in the 1970s. Essentially this approach tells children (a) what kinds of touching are appropriate and what kinds are wrong, (b) it's o.k. to tell, (c) whom to tell and (d) how to avoid the abuser. Some education programs teach children assertive skills for escaping or resisting sexual abuse, primarily to say "no" to the potential abuser. This emphasis on resistance is, at best, controversial, especially for younger children who are taught to respect and obey the wishes of adults and who would have difficulty sorting the conflicting emotions, needs and expectations during the immediacy of the abusive contact. "The emphasis for children should be on telling rather than on saying 'no.' We'll never prevent sexual abuse by instructing a child to say 'no,' " emphasized Lucy Berliner of the Seattle Sexual Assault Center.

Anti-sex-abuse educational materials and other resources are proliferating. One focal point for cataloguing these resources is the national Committee for Prevention of Child Abuse, based in Chicago. In both government and private efforts to educate the public, it is probably desirable to emphasize the point, one expert contacted in this study put it, that "this is not to be confused with sex education—it is public health and safety education."

STUDY METHODS

During this program inspection, staff from the Office of Inspector General (OIG) and the Office of Human Development Services interviewed by telephone 300 respondents from 49 states and the District of Columbia (New Mexico is the missing state). All telephone interviews were conducted during November 1984. Individual respondents included:

state child protective staff and social workers,
state licensing officials,
state criminal identification system directors,
Congressional staff,
Federal Bureau of Investigation staff,
physicians,
clinical psychologists,
sexual assault therapists,
district attorneys,
police investigators,

a judge,

university researchers,

other experts in child sexual abuse,

parents of children in child care,

providers of child care, including three major proprietary chains which represent more than 1,500 centers, and

representatives of special interest groups.

OIG Region X staff then analyzed all data gathered from the telephone surveys, plus published data provided by study respondents.

APPENDIX IV

COMPUTER-RELATED FRAUD AND ABUSE IN GOVERNMENT AGENCIES AS REPORTED BY THE PRESIDENT'S COUNCIL ON INTEGRITY AND EFFICIENCY [PCIE]

ABSTRACT

At the request of the PCIE, the HHS Inspector General convened a task force of experts in computer security and computer auditing to provide the PCIE with a perspective on the nature and scope of computer-related fraud and abuse in Government programs. The results of this work follow.

INTRODUCTION

The U.S. Government alone owns or operates more than 18,000 main frame computer systems. The applications run on these systems range over such diverse areas as national security, scientific or economic data, benefit payments, and payroll. Without the computer, most of these functions could not be accomplished.

Yet, our almost total dependence on computer systems causes continuing problems for the Government manager. Computer systems process enormous volumes of data with little human intervention, resulting in the concentration of the remaining manual functions into fewer hands, with little separation of duties. Rapid computer technological advances create a dependence on a relatively small number of data processing technical experts. Just as important, the computer itself represents a valuable resource to be protected from accidental or intentional loss of availability.

The vulnerabilities of computer systems to fraud and abuse have been reported for a number of years:

In 1977, a staff study of the Senate Committee on Government Operations cited that ". . . the Federal Government has taken appropriate steps to insure the integrity of those computer systems which process national security data . . . But there are no corresponding safeguards, standards or adequate security procedures in many Federal programs unrelated to national defense."[1]

The former Law Enforcement Assistance Administration's manual on computer crime states that "Unfortunately, . . . businesses, government agencies, and institutions that use computers for technical and business purposes . . . (are) neither adequately prepared to deal with nor sufficiently motivated to report this new type of crime to the authorities."[2]

[1]U.S. Congress, Senate, Committee on Government Operations, *Staff Study of Computer Security in Federal Programs,* (Washington, DC: U.S. Government Printing Office, February 1977), p. 267.

[2]U.S. Department of Justice, Law Enforcement Assistance Administration, *Computer Crime: Criminal Justice Resource Manual,* by SRI International, under Grant No. 78-SS-AX-0031, (Washington, DC: U.S. Government Printing Office, 1979), p. 2.

The U.S. General Accounting Office reviewed Federal systems and found that ". . . executive agencies' automated information systems and the assets they control are exceedingly vulnerable to misuse, abuse and theft."[3]

In the 95th Congress (S. 1766), and again in the 96th (S. 240) and 97th (H.R. 3970), Federal legislation has been proposed which would make computer fraud a Federal offense. On January 31, 1983, Congressman Bill Nelson reintroduced the Federal Computer Systems Protection Act (H.R. 1092). Amidst the debate regarding the need for and provisions of such legislation, several points of consensus seem to emerge:

Computer fraud and abuse do exist. Perceptions about the size of the problem, however, vary widely.

No data exist which define the scope of the problem either in Government or the private sector, although case histories gathered by experts describe a variety of computer-related incidents.

While no computer system can ever be entirely secure, most systems, particularly those with non-defense related applications, lack sufficient controls to afford an adequate level of protection from computer-related fraud and abuse.

The President's Council on Integrity and Efficiency (PCIE), because of its concern over the need for increased computer auditing and computer security expertise and activity within the Inspector General (IG) community, directed the IG of the Department of Health and Human Services to lead a computer security project for the Council. The task force he convened includes experts in computer security and computer auditing from the Departments of Agriculture, Commerce, Defense and Treasury; the National Aeronautics and Space Administration; and the General Accounting Office.

[3]U.S. Congress, General Accounting Office, *Federal Systems Remain Highly Vulnerable to Fraudulent, Wasteful, Abusive, and Illegal Practices*, MASAD-82-18 (April 1982): 7.

OBJECTIVE OF THE STUDY

The PCIE charged the task force to provide the Council with a perspective on the nature and scope of computer-related fraud and abuse in Government programs. Specifically, study objectives were to answer the following questions about computer-related fraud and abuse:

Is there a problem?

If so, what are the characteristics?

What should the Inspector General community do to detect/prevent future instances?

What additional computer security expertise and activity are required in the IG environment?

SCOPE AND METHODOLOGY

To accomplish this objective, the task force undertook a survey of the known computer-related fraud and abuse cases in Government agencies. Although a few other reports of computer-related crime have been published (notably a 1976 study by the General Accounting Office[4]), this PCIE study is the first systematic data collection effort of its kind in the Government.

The study involves a two-phase approach; a survey phase and a followup interview phase. This report presents the findings of Phase I.

The task force decided to include both fraud and abuse in the scope in order to obtain the broadest possible data base and to ascertain the similarities and differences in the two subsets. For this purpose, the following definitions were developed:

Computer-related fraud is any illegal intentional act or series of acts that is designed to deceive or misrepresent in order to

[4]U.S. Congress, General Accounting Office, *Computer-Related Crimes in Federal Programs*, FGMSD-76-27 (April 27, 1976): 2.

obtain something of value. Further, a computer system must have been involved in the perpetration or cover-up of the act, or series of acts. A computer system might have been involved through improper manipulation of: (1) input or transaction data, (2) output or results, (3) applications programs, (4) data files, (5) computer operations, (6) communications, or (7) computer hardware, systems software, or firmware.

Computer-related abuse is the misuse, destruction, alteration or disruption of data processing resources. The key aspects of computer-related abuse are that it is intentional and improper, but it does not necessarily imply the violation of a specific law nor the presence of false representation. Examples of computer-related abuse are (a) unauthorized use of the computer by Federal employees for their personal programming activities, and (b) misuse of computer equipment for revenge against a government agency.

These definitions served both as instructions to respondents and as criteria for later analysis. In the case-by-case analysis stage, the definitions were further refined, specifically in the cases involving theft of computer time. The task force recognized that computer time is often considered an asset and that the unauthorized use of the computer can be discussed in terms of fraud. For analysis purposes, however, the task force, after lengthy debate, decided to classify this type of case as abuse.

To survey the agencies regarding their known cases of computer-related fraud and abuse, the task force developed a questionnaire patterned after a survey instrument designed by the American Institute of Certified Public Accountants (AICPA) for their as yet unpublished study of computer fraud in the banking and insurance industries.

The questionnaire instructed respondents to complete one survey form for each case of computer-related fraud and abuse discovered between January 1, 1978 and March 31, 1982. (The beginning date was chosen to coincide with the advent of most IG organizations.) The questionnaire requested information in the following areas: (1) type of computer-related fraud or abuse,

(2) perpetrator profiles (for up to four perpetrators per case), (3) case description, (4) detection method, (5) computer environment, (6) methods of perpetration and concealment, and (7) effectiveness of controls and audit procedures.

The survey forms were directed to the Inspectors General and other members of the PCIE, plus the Federal Bureau of Investigation (FBI), U.S. Secret Service, and the Chief Postal Inspector. Upon receipt of the completed survey forms, the task force reviewed the cases for completeness and eliminated those cases from the total which did not meet the definitions of computer-related fraud and abuse. Cases were then given a preliminary analysis to categorize and prepare them for computerized statistical analysis.

FINDINGS

The degree to which cases are in fact detected and/or reported cannot be estimated. Although originally charged to discover the scope of computer-related fraud and abuse in Government programs, the task force rapidly became aware that this was not possible. As noted in a 1976 GAO report, agencies do not differentiate between computer-related and other types of white collar crimes. (See note 4) Instead, the task force has to rely on individual memory and/or *ad hoc* information systems which agencies may have instituted. To add to these constraints, neither the FBI nor Secret Service was able to respond to the survey because their case files are all kept in their field offices and would require a prohibitive amount of time to research.

Such problems should decrease in the future, at least for criminal cases. As a result of our survey and their concern for the problem, the Justice Department's newly implemented Fraud and Corruption Tracking System (FACTS) will uniquely identify all computer-assisted fraud cases referred to the FBI and/or the U.S. Attorneys. In response to our inquiry, the U.S. Secret Service has also stated that its information system will now identify computer-related fraud cases.

What Was the Response to the Survey?

The following agencies reported cases to the task force:

Department of Agriculture
Department of Commerce
Department of Defense
Department of Energy
Department of Health and Human Services
Department of Justice
Department of Labor
Department of State
Department of the Treasury
National Aeronautics and Space Administration
Office of Personnel Management
Veterans Administration

Within these agencies, the majority of individual respondents represented the investigative community (70%), composed of both IG investigators (20%) and internal agency investigators (43%) or security officers (7%). The other respondents represented program/functional personnel (7%), data processing personnel (4%) and unspecified job types (18%).

Of the 215 responses to the survey, 43 were eliminated since they did not meet the definitions of computer-related fraud or abuse. The remaining 172 cases comprised 69 fraud and 103 abuse cases.

The fraud cases primarily (93%) involved theft of cash or diversion of other assets, and over three-fourths of these cases entailed a fictitious or unauthorized benefit (59%) claim or an unauthorized payroll payment (21%). Abuse cases primarily involved theft of computer time (57%), theft of data (13%) and/or destruction of alteration of data (17%).

The majority of both fraud and abuse cases involved in-house (agency operated) facilities (80%) and occurred during normal processing (89%). The systems involved employed a variety of different types of computer technology: 48% involved batch processing; 41% involved on-line, real-time processing; 33%

involved on-line inquiry capabilities; 28% involved centralized processing; 22% involved remote batch; and or 16% involved data base management systems (percentages total more than 100% because of multiple answers).

Who Were the Perpetrators of Computer-Related Fraud and Abuse?

Seventy-five percent of the total cases involved only one perpetrator (referred to below as the primary perpetrator). This proportion was somewhat lower for fraud (65%) than for abuse (82%) cases, indicating that collusion either is more common in fraud cases or is at least more investigated or documented.

As shown in Table 1, the most noticeable differences between the primary perpetrators of fraud and abuse are in the areas of salary, job area, and disciplinary or legal action taken:

> While four out of five of the fraud perpetrators earn $20,000 or less, almost half of the abuse perpetrators earn over $20,000.

> Almost two-thirds of the fraud perpetrators are functional users of the system, but almost three-fifths of the abuse perpetrators are data processing personnel.

> Although three-fourths of the fraud perpetrators were subjects of judicial action, only about one in ten abuse perpetrators were subjects of any judicial action.

Since the nature of abuse is characterized by a high proportion of use of computer resources, the higher proportion of data processing personnel, who have access to and knowledge of programming and operations, may be expected. The low proportion of data processing personnel in fraud cases may be understood more fully after presentation in the next section of the techniques employed to perpetrate the fraud or abuse.

The survey data provide the following profile of the primary perpetrators of computer-related fraud and abuse:

TABLE 1
Characteristics of the Primary Perpetrators

Characteristics	Percentage of primary perpetrators[5]	
	Fraud	Abuse
Employer:		
U.S. government	66	79
State/local	22	1
Private sector	12	20
Level of employee:		
Nonsupervisory	77	73
Supervisory	23	27
Annual salary:		
$20,000 or less	81	51
$20,001–$50,000	19	43
Over $50,000	0	6
Job area in relation to the computer:		
Functional user	62	30
Data processing personnel	30	59
Other (outsiders, unknown job types)	8	11
Disciplinary/Legal action received after detection:		
No action	16	30
Judicial action (with or without administrative action)	74	9
Administrative action only	10	61

The difference between fraud and abuse in salary may be understood in terms of motive. In 93% of the fraud cases, the motive was financial gain, as opposed to 6% in abuse cases. The most frequently identified motivation (46%) in abuse cases was the convenience or availability of the computer for entertainment or personal/outside business.

[5]Percentages are given for the total responses present on each item. The proportion of missing responses is less than 10% in all characteristics except salary (fraud). Data were unavailable in 16% of the fraud cases on this characteristic.

APPENDIX IV

The contrast between fraud and abuse cases in the judicial actions taken is not surprising given the survey definition that abuse "does not necessarily imply violation of a specific law." A more interesting finding is that 84% of the fraud cases and 70% of the abuse cases had some disciplinary or legal action taken, implying that a high proportion of perpetrators are indeed sanctioned. This bears closer examination in Phase II, since this finding could also be attributed to better documentation and recall in sanctioned cases.

What Were the Losses Associated with Computer-Related Fraud and Abuse in this Study?

Respondents estimated losses in 58% of the total cases of fraud and abuse, ranging from $0 to $177,383. The responses for fraud versus abuse are as follows:

Fraud

For the 65 cases in which data were provided, the responses ranged from $0 to $177,383 as in Figure 4A.1. Respondents for fraud cases were also asked if they felt the loss figures they provided were lower than actual losses. Of the 61 responses, almost half (48%) stated they had reason to believe this amount was greater. For example:

In one highly-publicized fraud of a benefit funds system, a claims technician created fictitious beneficiaries to obtain benefit payments for her co-conspirators. Although evidence used for prosecution established the amount of the fraud only as $102,000, investigators believe the perpetrator may have diverted as much as $500,000 through such fraudulent transactions.

Losses varied by the type of application system victimized. Almost three-fifths (59%) of the frauds occurred in benefit funds disbursement systems. Within benefit funds system cases, 63

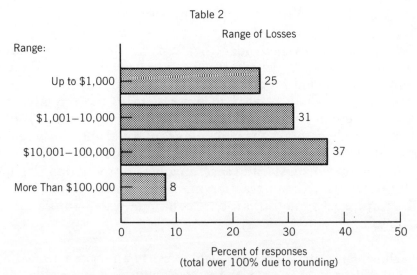

Table 2

Range of Losses

FIGURE 4A.1. Range of losses.

percent of the individual losses were over $10,000. All of the cases with losses over $100,000 occurred in benefit funds disbursement systems. By contrast, payroll systems, which had the second highest (21%) incidence in our fraud cases, had most (78%) of the individual case losses in the range of $10,000 or less. (See below for further discussion of contrasts between the two types of systems.)

Abuse

Only 34 (33%) respondents in abuse cases gave estimates of monetary losses to their agencies, ranging from $0 to $5,214. The 33 percent included 17 percent who estimated no losses ($0), and 16 percent who estimated amounts greater than zero. Only 6 respondents gave estimates greater than $1,000.

Abuse respondents were also asked to estimate the value of any other losses, such as the value of stolen computer time, software, or data. Again, response was limited: 55 percent of the cases gave no estimate, 26 percent estimated $0, and the remaining 19 percent estimated between $2 and $3,500.

How Were the Cases Perpetrated?

The survey requested identification of the one or more techniques used to perpetrate the fraud or abuse. As shown below, respondents selected from 17 different techniques ranging from those related to input data to those related to development of programs or manipulation of processing. Table 3 on page 391 displays the percentages of fraud and abuse cases in which each of the techniques was identified:

As illustrated, most fraud cases involved introduction/manipulation of input and/or creation/manipulation of files. In 70% of the fraud cases, more than one technique was identified. For example:

> Three data entry clerks, through access to a remote terminal, entered fictitious claims and subsequently deleted records of these transactions to obtain over $150,000 in Food Stamps. The techniques employed were manipulation of authorized input data, introduction of unauthorized input data, and manipulation of files/records.

The high incidence of input types of fraud corresponds to GAO's findings in their 1976 report: 62 percent of their cases involved fraudulent record initiation.[6]

Abuse cases identified the techniques of development of programs for improper use and theft of equipment, software, data or computer time in greater proportions than did fraud cases. This corresponds to the predominate nature of abuse cases, i.e., theft of computer time. It also appears congruent with the finding that more data processing personnel than functional users are involved in abuse cases. Data processing personnel are more likely to have the necessary technical skills with which to use the computer facilities and develop or manipulate programs.

Similar to fraud cases, 78% of the abuse cases identified more than one technique to perpetrate the abuse. As indicated by the

[6]U.S. Congress, General Accounting Office, *Computer-Related Crimes in Federal Programs*, FGMSD-76-27 (April 27, 1976): 6.

TABLE 3
Techniques Used to Perpetrate Computer-Related Fraud and Abuse

Technique	Percent Fraud*	Percent Abuse*
Introduction of unauthorized input data	64	50
Manipulation of authorized input data	59	15
Manipulation or use of files/records	36	16
Creation of unauthorized files/records	30	47
Override of internal controls	25	7
Diversion or manipulation of output	20	12
Manipulation of computer programs or documentation	16	8
Manipulation or use of processing	14	29
Manipulation of errors, exceptions, or rejects	9	2
Unauthorized use of passwords or billing accounting codes	9	22
Unauthorized transmission or interception of communications	7	9
Theft of equipment, software, data or computer time	7	55
Manipulation of communications facilities or processing	6	14
Willful damage, destruction or alteration of equipment, software or data	3	8
Development of programs for improper purposes	1	34
Unauthorized use of vendor utility programs	1	14
Willful denial of service	1	5

*Percentages total more than 100% since more than one technique could be chosen.

percentages in the table, abuse cases often showed some combination of unauthorized input, creation of unauthorized files, development of programs, and/or theft of computer time. The following two examples illustrate multiple techniques:

A computer programmer ran football pools on his agency's computer. To do this, he wrote a small program to compute odds, format and print schedules, and record bets; made unauthorized inputs; and created records and files for each pool.

An engineer used his agency's computer facilities to maintain the records of his after-hours business and to transmit data messages to his customers. Upon discovery, the perpetrator was able to delete or encrypt his files, preventing management from determining the extent of his abuse. The perpetrator's techniques included introduction of unauthorized input and files, use of processing, development of programs, use of passwords, un- authorized transmission of communications, and theft of computer time.

How Were the Cases Detected?

In order to determine how well internal control systems detect computer fraud and abuse, respondents were asked to identify the source of detection, and the major factor which triggered detection. For analysis purposes, the sources of detection were grouped as follows:

Sources of Detection

Agency Personnel—senior and middle managers, data pro- cessing personnel, and co-workers.[7] This group also includes two (2) perpetrators who confessed to fraud.

Professional Evaluators—internal agency auditors, external auditors (such as GAO auditors), computer security officers, program or functional evaluators, and agency staff investi- gating computer match "hits."

Other—recipients of Federal benefits, contractor or vendor suppliers, and law enforcement and other investigative staff.

Trigger Factors

Accident—chance occurrences such as complaints, curiosity or revenge of informers, unusual activities of perpetrators.

[7]Respondents frequently characterized coworkers as whistleblowers.

Audit—routine internal audit, routine external audit, non-routine audit, and investigative or computer security reviews.

Controls—internal controls, unusual change in accounting/ management reports, violation of computer security controls, and noncompliance with operating procedures.

Figure 4A.2 displays how the cases were detected, and Figure 4A.3 displays factors which triggered detection.

Most Cases Are Found Accidentally by Insiders

Agency personnel[8] detected more than one-half (55%) of the fraud cases and more than two-thirds (68%) of the abuse cases. Personnel in management positions discovered as many of the fraud cases (24%) as did co-workers (23%). However, co-workers identified more than twice as many abuse cases as did managers. Data processing personnel discovered a small percentage of the cases, but identified almost three times as many abuse as fraud cases. This is probably best explained by the fact that abuse cases involved mostly theft of computer time which data processing personnel would be alert to in conducting day-to-day activities. These personnel would less likely be alert to cases entailing fictitious benefits or unauthorized payroll payments.

In most cases, agency personnel discovered the cases by accident. In fact, an accidental occurrence triggered detection of twice as many cases as did either an audit or a system of control. Of the cases found by accident, most (27% fraud and 31% abuse) were triggered by chance or curiosity of the informer. For example:

A Federal employee, through access to benefit claims authorization and input procedures, fraudulently obtained over $100,000

[8] Agency personnel includes mostly Federal workers (74%).

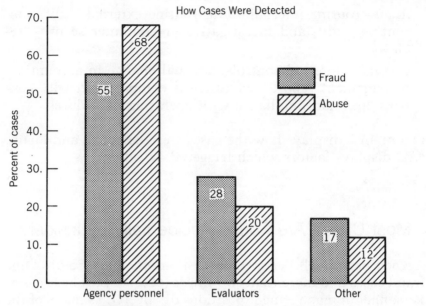

FIGURE 4A.2. How cases were detected.

over 1½ years. He used the computer to reactivate accounts of deceased beneficiaries, and to create fictitious records. The case was detected by a bank clerk who observed the perpetrator opening more than one direct deposit account (in different names) at the same bank. The bank reported the observation to Federal officials.

The survey data show that only one-fourth of the cases (25% of fraud cases and 24% of abuse cases) were detected through internal controls. This finding indicates that agency control systems generally were nonexistent or inadequate to detect the cases at the time they were perpetrated.

Control systems were most effective, however, in detecting fraud cases involving payroll applications. Of the fraud cases entailing payroll, most (46%) were discovered through a control system, generally separation of duties. This contrasts markedly with the finding that only 12% of the cases involving fraud in benefit fund application systems were detected through controls. Most (59%) of the fraud cases involving benefit fund

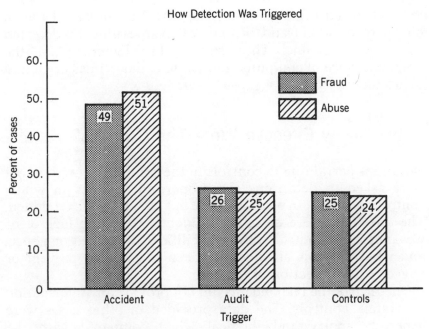

FIGURE 4A.3. How detection was triggered.

systems were discovered by accident. The vulnerability of benefit funds programs to fraud and abuse and the lack of control systems over them bears close scrutiny in Phase II of the project.

Professional evaluators identified about one-fourth of the cases (28% of fraud cases and 20% of abuse cases). Internal auditors comprised the largest percentage of evaluators and discovered most of their cases using traditional audit techniques. Internal auditors identified more fraud than abuse cases, detecting 27% of cases involving unauthorized payroll and 30% of cases involving benefit funds applications.

The survey data on how the cases were detected parallel those documented by other investigators. Parker[9] has reported that most cases of computer crime are detected by persons within

[9]Donn Parker and Susan Nycum, "Computer Crimes: Case Histories and Proposed Legislation," report prepared for the HEW Secretary's National Conference on Fraud, Abuse, and Error, December 1978, p. 6.

the victimized organization. Also, GAO[10] documented that a high percentage of fraud (of all types) in government is detected by agency personnel. These sources also document that the preponderance of computer and white collar crimes are found by accident.

How Effective Were The Controls?

Questions pertaining to controls in the computer environment were asked to determine the proportion of cases in which controls were: not in place, in place but not used, or overridden. The questions were designed to identify how the lack of or weaknesses in control systems facilitated the fraud or abuse, and what controls should have been in place to prevent or trigger early detection of the case.

One-fifth of the respondents did not provide any information on system controls. The data provided in other cases were generally spotty and illogical when compared with the descriptions of the schemes involved. For example, a contractor employee was able to computer generate checks to herself by inputting false claims for medicare benefits. For more than three years, the perpetrator would input beneficiary names and identification data and her own address. Benefit checks were then sent to her home. The fraud was found by accident. Section 8.1 of the survey form indicated that controls were in place, and there were no recommendations with respect to controls that should have been in place or could be implemented to prevent or detect the fraud. It is illogical to believe that controls can be effectively in place and permit a fraudulent act to continue until it is found by accident.

The poor quality of the responses to questions on controls implies a lack of knowledge about computer system controls among respondents. It also implies that information on control systems generally is not documented during investigations.

[10]U.S. Congress, General Accounting Office, *Fraud in Government Programs—How Extensive Is It?—How Can It Be Controlled?*, AFMD-81-57 (May 7, 1981): 20.

Hence, the data which was provided may be based, for the most part, on the respondent's memory of the case, or his ability to deduce the probable status of control systems from a description of the case. Whether or not a review of computer system controls is a part of the investigation of a computer crime is an issue to be explored in Phase II of the project.

Because of the non-comparability of the data requested and supplied, no attempt was made to summarize these responses for analysis purposes.

Many of the reported cases identified controls which were not in place, were not used, or were overridden. This apparent lack of good control systems across Federal agencies seems to explain the finding that most computer fraud and abuse cases were detected by accident, and the low incidence (25% fraud, 24% abuse) of cases detected through controls. A good system of controls would have prevented the cases or have led to their early detection. The following cases illustrate the lack of or weaknesses in control systems.

Controls Not in Place or Overridden

The lack of procedures requiring segregation of duties, and the lack of forms control made it possible for a Federal employee to establish unauthorized benefit claims and divert $24,000 over a 5-month period. The perpetrator was able to change information in a deceased client's file. The perpetrator was also able to correct his input errors because no segregation of duties existed in the edit resolution, and his corrective inputs were not reviewed by a supervisor. After a check was generated, the perpetrator was able to erase erroneous data. Eventually the case was detected by a computer match and subsequent investigation.

In another case, the lack of segregation of duties and the ability to override input controls permitted a Federal employee to redirect program recoveries to his own bank account. The perpetrator was able to clear a systems alert code, delete a notice of recovery, and steal the repayment. There was no system of review to assure proper posting of recoveries. This fraudulent act went undetected until a fellow employee accidently noticed the improper processing of cases and notified management.

Controls Not Used

A caseworker created fictitious applications for Food Stamps. She entered the fictitious information in the computer to generate authorizations to purchase Food Stamps, which she then received and cashed. Although there were procedures to assure supervisory review of new applications and authorization of new transactions, the procedures were not followed. The case was detected accidently by a co-worker. The estimate loss in the case exceeded $12,000.

Three data entry clerks were able to steal Food Stamps, valued at over $150,000, because the supervisor consistently left his key in the issuance terminal. The clerks stole the Food Stamps and used the computer to generate false issuance reports by deleting their personal "transactions" from the file. Written procedures requiring authorization of transactions, management review, and input controls were not used by the supervisor. The supervisor's failure to control access to the issuance terminal also violated agency policy.

In addition to identifying general controls in the computer environment, respondents were asked whether agency computer systems were subject to any type of audit or review. Also, they were asked whether a formal risk analysis/vulnerability assessment program had been implemented in accordance with OMB Circulars A-71 and A-123. Transmittal Memorandum No. 1 to OMB Circular A-71 (July 27, 1978) requires Federal agencies to establish automated security programs, and A-123 requires each agency to establish and maintain adequate systems of internal controls.

Responses to these questions were very weak. In more than three-fourths (78%) of the cases, respondents were unable to answer the questions concerning a system audit or review, and over two-thirds (68%) lacked knowledge about the implementation of A-71 and A-123. These data support our earlier finding that the lack of and weaknesses in controls exist in computer environments. Further, the paucity of responses to these questions indicates a general lack of awareness among respondents about internal controls or where to turn for information about those controls.

CONCLUSIONS AND RECOMMENDATIONS

Despite the constraints mentioned in the Findings Section, the data do provide a picture of the type of computer-related fraud and abuse which is known to and reported by the Inspector General community. The frauds are characterized by low level employees in functional areas committing input types of frauds in Government payment systems. The abuses usually involve higher paid, technically sophisticated employees using computer resources. Both types of acts are usually detected accidentally by insiders.

Further Survey Work

Although this picture is possible from the data, we cannot determine the scope of the problem of computer-related fraud and abuse in Government. In addition to the problems regarding lack of a systematic case identification, other factors work against a complete picture of computer-related fraud and abuse. The literature discusses both the weaknesses in controls (and therefore in detection capabilities) and the reluctance of officials of victimized systems to report computer-related fraud or abuse once detected. Such factors may account for the relatively low number of responses, given the existence of over 16,000 computerized systems.

In addition, certain portions of the survey responses are incomplete, particularly in the areas of loss estimates, knowledge of prior audits or reviews, and systems controls. Nevertheless, because this survey is the first of its type in

Government, we need to refine and maintain it as a unique source of information for the IG community. Therefore, because we must assess the limits of the survey data, and build upon it as an ongoing source of information and analyses, we recommend the following:

The Computer Security Task Force should conduct Phase II to identify and analyze the causes of the survey data limitations, the extent of computer security awareness and activity within the IG organizations, and the state of controls in victimized systems. The specific objectives of Phase II should include the following:

To identify cases which were not identified or reported in the survey and assess reasons for unreported cases.

To ascertain the reasons for incomplete responses in such areas as controls, prior audits and reviews, and loss.

To determine why no cases were reported by some agencies (e.g., because of better controls, lack of investigative jurisdiction, etc.).

To collect best practices in the vulnerability/risk assessment programs implemented per OMB Circulars A-71 (Transmittal Memorandum No. 1) and A-123.

To determine agency and OIG experience with detection and investigation of computer-related incidents.

Once Phase II is complete, the task force should conduct periodic survey updates to build upon the initial survey data and experience, to maintain awareness in the IG community, and to keep the Council informed of the extent of the known problem. This update should utilize the new FACTS and Secret Service information systems, as well as sources identified through Phase II.

Training and Awareness

The incomplete responses on systems controls and prior audits or reviews point to the likely explanation that the respondents, who were mostly investigators, had no knowledge of these areas. Investigators, whether in the IG environment or in agency integrity/security functions, are not usually as involved as auditors in the identification of internal controls. Similarly, investigators may not be as aware of documented systems control weaknesses, if in fact such audits or reviews exist.

Conversely, however, investigators should be aware of exploited vulnerabilities through their investigations, and should be recommending systemic improvements based on their case experience. This integration of investigative experience into program improvement recommendations is becoming increasingly common in IG organizations. It appears from our survey responses, however, that investigators are not aware of the state of internal controls in their agencies' computerized systems, nor possibly about the types of controls necessary to automated systems in general. While this lack of awareness needs confirmation through the Phase II followup, such conclusions are reinforced by anecdotal information. A number of respondents commented that the PCIE survey had heightened their awareness of computer weaknesses and the need to know more about controls.

From these preliminary findings and conclusions, then, it would appear that training of investigative staff on controls in automated systems (particularly payment systems) and in the findings of any specific computer audits, vulnerability assessments, or security reviews in their agencies would improve both the investigative process through recognition of known vulnerabilities and the investigators' input to recommendations for systems improvements. Any such training and awareness programs should be integrated with the PCIE Computer Audit Council curricula now being developed for auditors and investigators. Therefore we recommend that:

IG's should provide training, such as the curricula being developed by the PCIE Computer Audit Council, to investigators, as well as auditors, on the internal controls in automated systems.

Investigators should be made aware of the documented vulnerabilities of the agencies' computer systems, including the results of EDP audits and internal control reviews.

Controls in Automated Systems

Although the PCIE survey responses provide insufficient data to identify specific control weaknesses in the victimized systems, the findings, especially those regarding detection, do imply that systems and management controls are inadequate, as has been discussed in numerous prior reports. Individual cases do show that controls can be effective in the detection of computer-related fraud and abuse. The aggregate data, however, show that half of the cases were detected by accident. The finding is alarming because of the implications for both control weaknesses and undetected fraud and abuse.

Cases in the survey data base occurred during the time frame from 1978 to 1982. While the concern about the vulnerabilities of computerized systems has not lessened since then, the requirements of OMB Circulars A-71 (Transmittal Memorandum No. 1) and, especially, A-123, which was only issued October 28, 1981, were not fully implemented at the time these computer-related frauds and abuses occurred. The requirements for computer security and internal controls provide the framework and processes through which agencies can identify the types of systems and management control weaknesses which were exploited in many of the survey cases. Therefore, although we cannot address either specific or current control weaknesses without further review, we do recommend the following:

Agencies, in their A-123 internal control reviews, should give particular emphasis to assessments of the internal controls in automated systems. In light of the survey findings on computer-related fraud, payment systems appear most vulnerable and should be given especially close scrutiny.

The PCIE should establish a system to alert all IG and related organizations to generic computer system control weaknesses and vulnerabilities found during investigations, audits or reviews. Such a system would serve in concert with the ongoing data collection and internal training and awareness recommendations to focus the IG community on common systems weaknesses and enable them to devise common prevention strategies.

APPENDIX V

COMPUTER-RELATED FRAUD IN GOVERNMENT AGENCIES: PERPETRATOR INTERVIEWS

Report of Inspector General
Richard P. Kusserow,
Department of
Health and Human Services

ABSTRACT

The President's Council on Integrity and Efficiency directed the Inspector General of the U.S. Department of Health and Human Services to follow up on its 1983 study, "Computer-Related Fraud and Abuse in Government Agencies," by interviewing the perpetrators of computer-related fraud cases. Staff from HHS/OIG interviewed 46 perpetrators regarding how and why they committed their crimes. Although not a statistically valid sample, these interviews provide the following information on computer-related fraud among government agencies.

1.   The perpetrators were insiders, that is, they were federal employees, or employees of state, local, and private agencies administering federal programs. In general, they were young, good employees with an average of five years employment with the agency. Most had above average performance ratings, and most had been promoted at least once. Just over one-fifth had a prior criminal record.

2.   They held a wide variety of positions within the agencies ranging from senior program manager to entry level clerk. The more common positions were caseworkers, clericals, and data entry technicians. Most were in a position to cause checks to be issued, although many did not have direct access to the computer.

3.   Typically, the perpetrators committed their crime by manipulating input data to cause funds to be issued, and most were aided by co-conspirators. They generally used one of three schemes: modifying existing cases in a benefit or payroll system; creating false cases in those systems; or creating false claims in a reimbursement system. Many destroyed the paper or electronic evidence of their crimes.

4.   On the average, the period of criminal activity took place over six months. The number of illegal transactions per case ranged from 1 to 200 with a median of 8. The reported average loss per case was $45,000, but about one-fifth of the cases exceeded $100,000.

5.   Three-quarters of the perpetrators reported that they stole money in response to a situational stress. Most commonly it was a personal financial problem or disgruntlement with the job. Others, not motivated by stress, had discovered vulner-abilities in the system and could not resist that temptation.

6.   Nearly half reported that they did not even think about the consequences of their actions when they committed the crime; others assessed the risks of getting caught as minimal. Many reported that they were personally aware of crimes like theirs or had heard of such crimes.

7.   Most perpetrators were aware of computer security controls but assessed them as weak. They described ID numbers

and passwords as simplistic, edits and screens as known and therefore avoidable, and supervision as lax or naive regarding automated systems. They pointed out that access to or within computer systems was often not restricted. The perpetrators also made a number of recommendations on how to strengthen government computer systems.

In order to address the vulnerabilities noted in this study, it is recommended that:

Computer fraud perpetrators be routinely debriefed

Automated system controls be strengthened

Security and system control guidance to state, local, and private agencies be reevaluated

Line managers receive training on internal and system controls

Personnel security procedures be reviewed

INTRODUCTION

In 1982, the President's Council on Integrity and Efficiency (PCIE) concerned about the apparently growing incidence of computer-related fraud and abuse, commissioned the Inspector General of the Department of Health and Human Services (HHS/IG) to study the problem. PCIE's charge was to provide a perspective on the nature and scope of computer-related fraud and abuse and on what the IG community should do to upgrade its audit and investigative skills and activities to deal with the problem.

In response, the HHS/IG surveyed the federal agencies to gather all cases of computer-related fraud and abuse identified from the period January 1978 through March 1982. That survey obtained 172 cases (69 fraud and 103 abuse) which were analyzed for perpetrator characteristics, techniques of perpetration, losses, methods of detection, and controls. The June 1983 report of this study, "Computer-Related Fraud and Abuse in Government Agencies," included the following findings:

1. Fraud cases primarily involved theft of cash or diversion of assets, usually through input manipulation in benefit or payroll systems. Most abuse cases involved use of computer time for outside business or entertainment.

2. Most perpetrators were federal, nonsupervisory employees. Four out of five of the fraud perpetrators earned $20,000 per year or less. Two-thirds of the fraud perpetrators were functional users of the computer system, rather than data processing personnel.

3. Confirmed losses ranged up to $177,383 per case, although actual losses were thought to be higher in many cases.

4. Operating personnel found over half of the frauds and over two-thirds of the abuses. More importantly, half of the cases were detected by accident, which was twice the incidence of detection by either controls or audits/reviews.

The report recommended that the IG community upgrade its expertise through computer training and awareness programs, and also that controls in automated systems be given especially close scrutiny. Because the survey responses were incomplete in some areas, the PCIE felt that more study was called for. Specifics about the controls in the environment of the victimized systems were thought to be a particularly vital area for further inquiry.

Objective of the Study

The PCIE therefore asked the HHS/IG to expand upon the original study by interviewing the perpetrators identified in the original study. The objective was to determine what the perpetrators would tell us about their crimes and the vulnerabilities in government computer systems. Specific study questions included:

Who were the perpetrators?
What jobs did they have?
How was the crime committed?

Why was the crime committed?
What was the work environment?

Scope and Methodology

To accomplish this objective we first had to identify perpetrators involved in the 69 computer-related fraud cases from the original study. That study, to preserve confidentiality and encourage cooperation, had not identified individual perpetrators, and therefore used only data descriptive of the crime. Upon our request for identifying and locating information for each perpetrator, the agencies were able to identify perpetrators from 60 of the original 69 cases.

Because most of the crimes had been committed over three years earlier, much of the locating information was no longer correct. In addition to using traditional field work techniques to locate the perpetrators, we were assisted by two other agencies: the Bureau of Prisons at the Department of Justice located those who were in federal correctional institutions or in pre-release programs; and the Division of Probation in the Administrative Office of the United States Courts assisted by locating perpetrators under the supervision of federal probation officers. Overall, we were able to locate perpetrators for 39 of the original cases. The primary reason for failing to get such locating information on the others was that many of the case files had been archived. This was particularly true of Department of Defense cases where the perpetrator had been discharged from military service.

We were able to interview 29 perpetrators from 21 of the original cases. We were unable to interview the others because perpetrators in nine cases were not prosecuted, seven perpetrators refused to be interviewed, and two cases were still open.

Because more cases had occurred since the original study two years earlier, we requested that IGs identify all computer-related fraud cases occurring after the original request for cases. That request yielded 18 additional perpetrators of which we interviewed 17 (one refused). We were able to interview three of these newer cases during their pre-sentencing period.

In total, we interviewed 46 perpetrators (29 original and 17 new) who were involved in 39 cases of computer-related fraud. These cases involved seven federal agencies.

Department of Agriculture

Department of Defense

Department of Health and Human Services

Department of Justice

Department of Labor

Department of the Treasury

Veterans Administration

The findings of this study are based largely on discussions with these 46 perpetrators. In addition to the data gathered during the discussions, other sources of information, such as case files, FBI "rap" sheets, and the survey questionnaires from the original study, were used in the analysis. The 46 discussions do not represent a statistically valid sample of government computer-related fraud cases. They represent the voluntary comments of perpetrators identified for this study, and are presented to add new insights to our understanding of this relatively new type of crime.

WHO WERE THE PERPETRATORS?

When I got out of the Navy I was job hopping. I took the necessary test to find a secure government job and was hired as a casework representative. I was promoted and knew I had a career.

A FEDERAL CASEWORKER.

Perpetrators Were Employees, Not Outsiders

Persons using computers to defraud the government could be anywhere given today's technology. However, as was found in the original study, virtually all perpetrators were employees of an agency administering a Federal program. With virtually all of the computer-related frauds being committed by employees, two related points can be made: (1) since none of the perpetrators who had gained access to the government computer system was from outside the agency, none was a beneficiary, client, or hacker; (2) all of the perpetrators were authorized users, that is, it was a necessary part of their job either to query, enter, or modify data in the computer system or to direct the operation of the computer system.

Just over half of the perpetrators were federal employees, while the remaining employees represented state (16 percent), local (16 percent), and private (12 percent) agencies. The private sector employees were under contract to a government agency to administer a federal program or manage an automated system; all acted independently, rather than as part of a corporate scheme. It should be noted however that many of the perpetrators had coconspirators who were not employees, but none of those personnel gained direct access to the computer (discussion of coconspirators in Section III of this Appendix).

The one perpetrator who was not an agency employee was a health care provider. A terminal was placed at his facility by the fiscal intermediary to expedite the submission of state Medicaid claims.

Perpetrators Were Young, Good Employees

In general the perpetrators appeared to be the younger employees of the agency. While those contacted during the study ranged in age from 20 to 50, their median age was 30 at the time they committed the crime. In comparison, the average age of federal employees is about 40.

Three-quarters of the perpetrators told us that they had attended college. A third of those attained at least a bachelor's degree, with some doing post graduate work. The other two-thirds reported spending between one and four years in college, with some attaining an associate degree. Even among those who did not attend college, many had attended classes in business or computer academies.

During our meeting with the perpetrators, we asked them about their job performance ratings. In general, they reported that they were good employees; only two noted unsatisfactory performance appraisals. Two-thirds noted that they had received above average, excellent, or outstanding ratings and one-third reported that they got average or satisfactory performance evaluations. It was not uncommon for the perpetrators to be considered one of the better employees in the office—the one to whom other employees went to with problems. Many were also "students of the computer system," and were called upon to assist others. Additionally, a quarter of the perpetrators told us that they had received awards for their performance. Ironically, four of those award recipients received their award for designing or implementing the computer system they ultimately stole from. For example, a programmer with a federal agency working on a payroll system got a cash award in 1981 when he set up the electronic funds transfer for his agency's payroll system. In 1982, he used that same system to steal to support his cocaine habit.

Another indicator of the perpetrators' success with the agencies is the fact that about three-quarters had been promoted or advanced in job responsibilities while at the agency.

Based on our discussions with the perpetrators, it appeared that most of them had sought out permanent, government employment. For example, for a third of the perpetrators this was the job they sought after getting out of school. For another third, they had consciously sought out a permanent, government job after having worked elsewhere.

Although they were among the younger employees of the agencies, the computer-related fraud perpetrators had spent an average of over five years with the agency before they began to commit the crime. Time on the job before the crime ranged from one year to 20 years, and varied by type of employer. While federal employees had been with their agency for an average of six and a half years when they committed their crime, this figure dropped to five years for state employees and three for employees of local public agencies.

Some Had Criminal Records

One of the most surprising findings that resulted from our discussions with the perpetrators was that almost one-quarter of them had prior criminal records when they were hired by a government agency. While a few admitted that they had hidden that fact from their employer, others reported that they were hired under special programs for ex-felons or that their employment was an acknowledged condit;on of their probation. The earlier crimes of the perpetrators ranged from rape an armed robbery to white collar crimes of embezzlement and forgery. For some, the computer-related fraud was their second crime, but for others, it was but one in a series of criminal activities. It is also noteworthy that while 18 percent of the federal employee perpetrators had previous criminal records, this figure was as high as 43 percent for state and local employees. None of the private employees had a former criminal record.

Time on the job before the fraud was committed varied between those with a criminal record and those without one. For example, only 14 percent of those without criminal records committed their computer-related fraud within one year of being hired, as compared to 40 percent of those with a criminal record. Similarly, the median length of employment with the victimized agency for ex-offenders was only three years, in contrast to six years for those without a criminal record. And, two-thirds of the ex-offenders were in the specific job from which they committed the crime for less than one year, compared to only one-third of those without prior records. Apparently the opportunity to commit fraud was seized more quickly by those with prior records. Carla and James are two such perpetrators.

> When we talked to Carla it was in a federal prison. This was her third time in jail. In the early 1970s, she was sentenced to three years in a state prison for forgery and was later convicted of welfare fraud in the mid-1970s. In fact, she was on probation for welfare fraud when she was hired by a county welfare agency as a

clerk-typist in their data center. An A.A. degree in accounting, hard work, and good evaluations won her a data center supervisory position within one year.

At about this time, she met James, a data input technician working on the same program. James had been hired under a special program for ex-offenders. He had been arrested and convicted at least five times in the six years prior to being hired. The charges included theft of government property, credit card theft, forgery (27 counts), and fire arms violations. During our interview, he readily admitted that he was a career criminal. During his first year on the job, he too had been promoted, but he also acquired a drug addiction that could not be financed by his $10,000 per year salary.

Together, James and Carla developed a plan to steal to support his drug habit and supplement her salary. Four months, 50 cases, and $120,000 later they were caught by a computer match.

WHAT JOBS DID THEY HAVE?

I did not need to sit at a terminal to do my job. I just filled out forms. In keypunching, they never check anything. They just entered what was on the form.

A FEDERAL VOUCHER CLERK

Perpetrators Had a Broad Range of Jobs

The perpetrators held a wide variety of jobs at the time they committed the crime. The positions ranged from secretaries to senior program managers and from entry level clerks to highly trained systems analysts.

The most commonly occupied job type (35 percent) was that of caseworker. This is a relatively discreet group of employees in entitlement programs who determine eligibility and the amount of the payments to be made to program beneficiaries. Most of these employees met directly with the public, but some made decisions based upon the case files. None were in supervisory positions (see Table A).

TABLE A:
Perpetrator Jobs

Job	Total Number	Percentage Supervisors	Percentage With Direct Computer Access
Caseworker	16	0%	12%
Technician	13	38%	100%
Clerk	12	1%	67%
Other	5	100%	80%
Total	46	24%	59%

The next most frequently held job type (28 percent) was that of computer support or technical personnel. These are both professional and support staff whose *raison d'etre* was the computer system itself. About half could best be characterized as data entry technicians, that is, non-supervisory employees who sat at video terminals and entered data into the system. More often than not they made no evaluation of or decision on the data; they just entered it. The remaining technicians were more involved with the overall operation of the computer. Three were computer professionals who either designed and wrote programs, or supervised the operation of large management information systems. The others were support personnel working in the data center doing such things as loading decks of cards, hanging tapes, or managing the hard copy output.

The third most common position (26 percent) was held by persons with clerical titles. This category included employees whose primary responsibility was to review and process paper, such as case files, payroll forms, or vouchers and bills for goods or services rendered to the agency. As a normal part of their job they were functional users of the computer, but they would not spend all of their time at a terminal.

Of the remaining five perpetrators, four were line managers

heading up major management information systems or financial operations, and one was a health care provider.

Direct Computer Access Not Universal

In order to perform their jobs, all the perpetrators needed to modify data in the system or have access to the computer itself. However, not all actually sat at a terminal or worked on a computer. Just under half of the perpetrators performed their jobs through the creation of input documents away from the computer (see Table A). These documents would occasionally be reviewed and then were submitted to technicians who would enter the data. This is particularly true for the caseworkers. Only two of the 16 caseworkers loaded data directly into the computer as a normal part of their job. However, many caseworkers did have "query-only" access to the computer system to review the status of cases.

Typical of this are benefit program field offices where caseworkers have "query-only" computer terminals they can go to in order to review the status of specific cases. However, when they want to make a change in a case they must complete a form. That form is reviewed by one technician and submitted to another technician to be entered into the computer system.

Most Worked for Benefit Programs

Just over three-quarters of the perpetrators worked for benefit programs that issued funds, and were in a position to issue those funds. About half of these employees worked for federally administered entitlement programs such as Social Security or the Black Lung program. A third worked for state or locally administered grant programs such as Food Stamps or Unemployment Insurance. The remainder were employees of private companies managing financial transactions for the Medicaid or Medicare programs.

The remaining perpetrators worked in administrative or staff positions, most often in various parts of payroll operations.

HOW WERE THE CRIMES PERPETRATED?

I brought the screen up with a phoney ID. I created a phoney
beneficiary and a phoney claim using my mother's Social
Security number. I just keyed it in.

A PRIVATE AGENCY CLERK

Most Perpetrators Issued Funds

The 46 perpetrators interviewed for this study were involved in
39 different criminal cases. In four instances we interviewed
two perpetrators per case and on one case we were able to reach
four. Accordingly, the analysis of how the specific computer-
related frauds were committed will be based upon 39 cases.

In 85 percent of the cases, the perpetrators caused negotiable
financial instruments to be issued. Most frequently U.S.
Treasury checks were issued, but checks were also caused to be
issued against state agencies and private financial organizations. In addition to checks, a few cases involved Food Stamp
coupon issuances. The stamps were usually converted to cash at
about 75 cents for a dollar's worth.

The cases that did not involve negotiable financial documents
included:

1. Restoration of annual leave.
2. Modification of income tax deductions.
3. Keeping funds returned to the agency.
4. Sale of false ID cards.
5. Sale of information.

Virtually All Were "Data Diddlers"

"Data diddling" is a commonly used term to describe those
computer crimes where an employee commits the crime by
manipulating data before or during the input process, or during

output from the computer system. Examples are: changing the name, address, or bank account of a beneficiary to that of the perpetrator or the perpetrator's coconspirator; or erasing the history of a payment so that a duplicate check is issued.

Over 90 percent of the cases involved data diddling. This is consistent with the finding in the original study that most cases involved manipulation of data. Almost all the cases involved manipulating input to the data system, but a few involved the manipulation during both the input and output processes. These cases involved food stamp issuance, and output data manipulation was necessary to bypass controls, such as separation of duties, and to conceal the fact that illegal stamps were issued.

As noted earlier, not all of the perpetrators had direct access to the computer, nor did they require direct access to the computer system to commit their crimes. In fact, half of the cases of input manipulation were not committed with "hands on" access to a computer. In these instances the perpetrators, based on their substantial knowledge of the system, were able to create documents that were later entered into the system by another person. When entered, they modified data in the system to cause the illegal transaction.

The three cases that would not be described as data diddling were all committed by computer experts. In one instance, data from a criminal justice information computer system was sold. The two other cases were technical computer crimes often referred to as "Trojan Horses" which occur when a person with programing expertise places a small, illegal computer program within a larger normal operating program. The small program is difficult to detect and generates the illegal transactions when the larger program is run.

In one of these cases, the names and addresses of three friends of a federal programmer were inserted in place of three employees in the agency's payroll. After the program was run, the sub-program was deleted so that the check went to the perpetrators' friends; but a review of the computer tape showed that checks were issued to the employees. The second "Trojan Horse" case was quite similar. A technical consultant from a private company working on a federal benefit program caused his wife's name and address to be inserted in place of a beneficiary when the program to issue the entitlement check was run.

Three Schemes Predominate

The crimes committed by the perpetrators were dictated by the purpose of the computer system on which the perpetrator worked, and in virtually all cases involved the manipulation of data in either on-going payment systems or one-time payment systems. On-going payment schemes occur on benefit *program* systems where a person or family is eligible for a specific benefit such as Social Security, unemployment insurance, or a paycheck.

Once eligibility is established, funds are issued on a regular basis. One-time payment schemes occur on *financial* systems designed to issue funds to a vendor, provider, or beneficiary in response to a specific bill or voucher for goods or services. With regard to data in these payment systems, perpetrators had two options. They could either create unauthorized files or records, or manipulate existing files or records. This leads us to the three predominant schemes used by the perpetrators that account for 35 of the 39 cases (see Figure 5A.1).

The most common scheme, accounting for almost half of the crimes, was the manipulation of data on existing cases in an on-going payment system. This type of crime occurred in such programs as Social Security or other entitlement programs. In such instances, the beneficiary already existed in the program data base as a valid case. Then, seizing upon an opportunity when the beneficiary died or lost eligibility for example, the perpetrator redirected the check to himself or a coconspirator. In other instances, perpetrators have caused duplicate payments to be issued to relatives who are valid cases on the system. A third way of taking advantage of existing cases was to identify and reactivate dormant cases and to have the benefits sent to a coconspirator. The following is a common example of this scheme.

Predominant Schemes

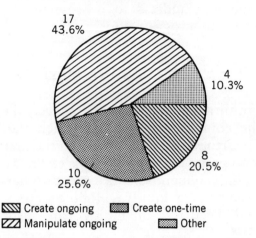

17
43.6%

4
10.3%

8
20.5%

10
25.6%

⬚ Create ongoing   ⬚ Create one-time
⬚ Manipulate ongoing   ⬚ Other

FIGURE 5A.1.   Chart 1—predominant schemes.

Bill, a caseworker, got a notification that a beneficiary had died. Instead of terminating that person's eligibility, he went to a bank and opened up an account in that beneficiary's name (and social security number). He then simply completed an input form that changed the address so that the check would be sent to his bank via direct deposit. Bill then periodically drew money out of that account. Bill did not have to do very much modification to the case file in the computer. All he did was change the routing of the check.

With the second scheme, the perpetrators created false claims in a one-time payment systems and had the payments go to coconspirators. This accounted for about a quarter of the cases. Most frequently they authorized a payment to a coconspirator for bogus bills such as would be received on a purchase order or for reimbursement to beneficiaries for medical services. For example:

Tom was a voucher examiner. His job was to review bills for completeness and then give them to data entry technicians to be loaded into the system so that a payment could be made. One day Tom started submitting bogus bills to the technicians. They were just like real bills from doctors and physical therapists because there was MD or PT after every name. That was one of the edits in the system. However, the names and addresses were not real medical professionals, they were Tom's friends. Over 18 months they stole $250,000.

In the third common scheme, false records were created and added to files in on-going payment programs. This was more difficult to accomplish than other schemes because of the documentation required to establish eligibility. In some of these cases the perpetrator used the identity of coconspirators, while others went through the process of creating false identities.

Some employees used both versions of this scheme with a food stamp program. First they had friends come to the office and apply for food stamps. They needed real Social Security numbers and matching names because that was a control in the system. Once they had the real name and number, they put false income data on the application and their friends become eligible for benefits.

Then when the Cuban and Haitian boat lift people began arriving, the eligibility system broke down. The newcomers become eligible for benefits but didn't have Social Security numbers. In order to bypass the Social Security number control, the program officials adopted a system of pseudo-Social Security numbers, that could be issued in each office. The perpetrators did not need their friends' names or numbers now; they could just create false beneficiaries with pseudo-numbers. And they did.

In the schemes that involved on-going payment systems, it was not uncommon for the perpetrator to periodically terminate their illegal cases or claims. This was done to prevent detection. For example, cases were terminated to avoid a quality control audit of cases or a programmatic requirement for a periodic, face-to-face recertification of the case. Other perpetrators, would keep a bogus case going for only a specific number of months—usually three to six.

It was also common, when creating or modifying a case in an entitlement program, for the perpetrator to initiate the periodic payments with a large payment. These payments are typical of adjustment in benefits caused by retroactive eligibility or accounting for previous underpayments. This was often not a separate act but was done by the perpetrator at the time the case was initially modified or created.

Most Took Steps To Cover Up Their Crime

As would be expected with a white collar crime, most of the perpetrators took specific steps to cover up their crime. In almost half of the cases the perpetrators destoyed the hardcopy evidence of their crime. This occurred most often when the perpetrator, such as a caseworker, did not have direct access to the computer. In such cases they would destroy the input document they had given to the input technician. But some perpetrators also had to destroy computer output evidence of their crime, such as printouts or alerts produced when their crime was picked up by a screen or edit in the system. A perpetrator who had worked for a federal agency said, "At first I was really nervous. I had to put the case file in my brief case and walk out of the building. When I got home I burned it. When I did it and realized how easy it was, I knew how bad the system was."

A few perpetrators reported that they did not have to worry about destroying evidence of their crime. Instead they relied on virtually nonexistent filing systems or on routine, periodic destruction of hardcopy to cover up their crime for them. Some perpetrators also used the computer to cover up their crime. For example, they reported that they were able to delete the record of their illegal transaction from the system, or they relied on routine purging of transactions from the system to cover up the crime.

Most Used Coconspirators

In the original study, the survey data indicated that most of the perpetrators (75 percent) acted alone. However, based on interviews with the perpetrators we found that three-quarters of the computer-related fraud cases involved coconspirators. Beyond the psychological value of providing moral support, coconspirators served other specific needs. Most frequently the perpetrators use coconspirators who were outside the agency. These persons were often used to provide a false ID and address and/or receive and cash checks. In some cases, fellow employees conspired in the crime. In such cases, this was usually necessary to bypass controls such as separation of duties. In only a few cases, did a perpetrator use both internal and external coconspirators.

Most of those who did not use coconspirators felt very strongly that this was the only way that they could commit the crime. One senior level manager summed it up for this group when he said, "I couldn't have done it if I had had to involve someone else." These perpetrators were generally older employees, and interestingly, 60 percent of those who had acted alone had received awards, compared to only 20 percent of those who used coconspirators. All but one of the perpetrators with a former criminal record used coconspirators.

Only a Few Had To Bypass ID and Password Controls

Almost half of the perpetrators told us that the computer systems did not require them to use an identification number and/or password to get data into the system to commit their crime. This occurred for two reasons. First, as already noted, many perpetrators did not need direct access to the computer sytem to commit their crime. (However, some of these perpetrators did have to forge a supervisor's signature on the data entry document.) Secondly, some perpetrators worked on systems that simply did not require ID or password controls for each user. This situation would typically occur where a bank of terminals would be brought on line at the beginning of the day and shut down in the evening. During the day any number of staff would have access to the system.

In the remaining cases, nine perpetrators used their own ID and/or password to commit the crime, while only 11 had to make up or steal an ID number. Usually when perpetrators used their own ID/password it was on systems that did not record the users identification number with the transactions, so there was no permanent record of who made the data entry.

Those who needed another ID/password identification to commit their crime did not seem to have too much difficulty getting it. Some just sat at the terminal during their free time and made up possible identifying combinations until they found a valid one. In two cases *any* three alpha characters would serve as an identifier and all the employees knew it. So it was not very difficult to get into the system in that office. In three other offices, the ID number was simply an employee's initials. In these cases the perpetrator just stole another worker's ID.

Frequency, Duration, and Loss
Varied Greatly

The number of times the perpetrators committed their criminal act ranged from one to 200. This was dictated in part by the type of scheme they used. For example, if the perpetrator created or manipulated data in an entitlement program, that one criminal act would yield a monthly check as long as the perpetrator kept that case active. However, if the perpetrator created false bills in a voucher payment system that crime would usually yield only one check. To illustrate this fact, one perpetrator only made four unauthorized entries into a benefit program computer and got over $100,000. Another entered 55 false bills into a state bill payment system and only got $1000. The median frequency for committing the criminal act was only eight times, which serves to demonstrate the potential efficiency of using a computer to commit a crime and how infrequently the perpetrators needed to exploit the vulnerabilities in the system.

The duration of the crime also affected the number of times the illegal act was committed. The time from when the first illegal act was committed until the perpetrator was caught, or voluntarily stopped prior to being caught, ranged from one month to 72 months. The median duration of the crimes was six months.

The reported amount of direct financial loss to the government agency ranged from no loss to $350,000. The average loss per case was $45,000. Eighteen percent of the cases involved losses greater than $100,000, which is somewhat higher than the seven percent reported in the original study. There were two cases of no dollar loss. One was selling of information and the other was issuing false ID for immigration purposes. Although none of the perpetrators admitted to stealing more than had been identified in their case as submitted to the court, some implied during the interview that more was stolen.

WHY DID THEY COMMIT THE CRIME?

I had personal problems because I was $20,000 in debt. But I had also worked my butt off for them and they passed me over for a promotion. I was good and deserved more. I decided to get back at them.

A Federal Program Manager

Perpetrators Stole Under Stress

Because eight perpetrators refused to admit committing a crime, we were not able to discuss their motives during the interview. Consequently, analysis of motives is based on 38 discussions. Three-quarters of the perpetrators reported that they were responding to or were influenced by a specific situational stress when they committed their crime. Most of these perpetrators stole money because of a specific family problem such as medical bills, potential eviction or loss of a home, or loss of spousal income. Others reported that specific debts caused them to steal, and a few said they stole to support a drug habit.

Still others in this group reported that their primary reason for committing their crime was because they were disgruntled. Some were mad at the organization, while others were seeking revenge on an immediate supervisor. A systems analyst for a private company confided: "I had given my soul to that company and I got burned. That company ended up being my life and I got caught in the stigma of this lousy contract with the government. They wouldn't transfer me out. I had to show them." Furthermore, a third of those who stole because of a specific personal problem noted that they were also unhappy employees and that fact made it easier for them to commit their crime.

Although most perpetrators started stealing to meet a specific need or in response to other stresses, few voluntarily stopped once that need was met. Only one in six of the perpetrators voluntarily stopped.

Temptation and Boredom Influenced Others

A quarter of the perpetrators reported committing their crime because an opportunity presented itself rather than because of some driving problem. In some cases it was a specific event such as funds being returned to the office, or the accidental discovery of a vulnerable procedure in the system. However, for others it was the result of boredom or free time. In such instances the perpetrator, often sitting at a terminal, would play with the system or play "beat the system" in idle time until they won the game. For example:

> Connie, a terminal operator for a state program, enjoyed exploring the system. She worked in the reimbursement section and found out that there was an emergency payment program with no screens for payment under $1000. "When it started I was playing with the terminal on a break. I typed in my friend's name and then I hit return; it was processed. I could have cancelled it, but I didn't."

Only Some Feared Being Caught

Perpetrators reported that a factor that significantly contribut-
ed to their committing a crime was that they didn't fear being
caught or punished. Over half said that they did not even think
about the consequences of their actions. They reported that they
acted on impulse, or that they just did not care. One
programmer said, "the drugs were in control. I didn't even think
about being caught."

Most of the other perpetrators who said that they realized that
they might lose their job, go to jail, or be forced to pay
restitution, felt that the chances of being caught were minimal.
The primary factor here was that most felt management was not
sensitive to crime from the inside, so they were not being
watched.

WHAT WAS THE WORK ENVIRONMENT?

Everyone had an ID number and there was a password to bring
the system up. But the codes and ID numbers were on the wall, so
everyone and anyone could see them. No one cared.

A State Claims Examiner

Controls Seen As Weak

Not surprisingly, most perpetrators rated computer security
and internal controls in their offices as weak and not a
significant barrier to their crime. While over 80 percent of the
perpetrators were able to identify specific examples of
computer security, three-quarters of these said it was weak.

The most common examples of security noted by the
perpetrators were various types of access controls. Most
systems required personal ID codes and/or passwords. However, as mentioned earlier, perpetrators easily found ways to
bypass the ID and password controls, or did not need direct
access to the system. Usually however, the access code gave the

user full access to the system. In only a few cases was the user limited to specific files or types of transactions.

Other common controls noted by the perpetrators were screens, edits, or alerts that were built into the system. Generally these features would limit the amount of checks that could be issued or would send a hardcopy message back to the office that a specific, atypical transaction had been initiated. A third form of control noted by the perpetrators was separation of duties. In such instances people who made eligibility or payment decisions were not permitted to do data entry.

While access controls, screens, and separation of duties were designed into most computer systems, poor implementation at the user level often undermined their intent. Access controls were often simplistic, or were bypassed in daily practice in the interest of productivity. For example, it was not uncommon for ID numbers to be the users' initials or any three digits. Also, passwords and operating codes were often issued in memos or manuals. Terminals, once brought on-line by an authorized operator, were often left on when the operator left the terminal. Edits and screens in the system were well known to all system users and the perpetrators usually just steered clear of them. A few perpetrators reported that it was not uncommon, when a backlog or special event arose, for managers to lift the edits or screens to speed-up the input process.

The security intent of separation duties would be breached when, due to staffing changes, a person was trained in both input and output duties or simply when terminals were left unattended after being brought on-line. For example, some offices have separate terminals for query-only and input. A number of caseworker perpetrators, who had query-only authority, said it was easy to just walk in and sit down at an input terminal under the guise of doing only a query and then to enter an illegal transaction.

Perpetrators Were Aware Of Other Crimes

Another factor that influenced the perpetrators was their perception that the system was vulnerable. Two-thirds of them reported that they were aware of other crimes "like theirs." Half of these said they knew of specific crimes, while the others said they had heard of such crimes. In the wake of a computer crime, it was common for the *modus operandi* of the perpetrator to be spread by rumor. In a few instances the crime seemed to pervade the office. This was particularly true when supervisors were part of the scheme. For instance, a supervisor in one food stamp office recruited workers to be part of a crime by showing them how to commit the crime. We were able to interview four perpetrators from one case, but it was estimated by one that as many as 30 people were involved. In another office, the number was estimated at 14.

Perpetrators Said Supervision Was Weak

The perpetrators frequently volunteered that "no one was watching me," when discussing how and why their crime was committed. These reports of weak supervision fell into two categories.

First were weaknesses associated with more traditional forms of supervision. Perpetrators reported that supervisors did not review their work either because they were a trusted employee, because their supervisor was too overloaded to review everything, or simply because work generally was not reviewed. If and when work was reviewed, it was reviewed for productivity and for errors. Employee crime appeared to be a low priority at best.

The second form of weak supervision was of a more technical nature. Some perpetrators reported that their supervisor knew what their job was, but did not know how they did their job at the computer terminal. This is because supervisors often came up through the program when the job was done manually and had never learned how the job is done on the automated system. Accordingly, perpetrators were able to take advantage of such supervisory naivete. One perpetrator told us, "One of the largest problems you have is that managers have no knowledge of the systems. I finished my project three months ahead of time and

my supervisor didn't know." Another perpetrator who was
paying bogus bills to friends said, "My supervisor didn't know
anything about the system. Those old ladies watched me all day
and never caught me."

HOW WOULD PERPETRATORS STRENGTHEN THE SYSTEMS?

I would impress people with the idea of computer security or any
security. We knew no one was watching.

A FEDERAL CASEWORKER

During the discussions with the perpetrators we asked what
could have prevented them from committing their crime or how
they would eliminate the vulnerabilities in the computer
system they had exploited. What follows are their more
commonly cited recommendations.

Random Case Validation

Perpetrators who modified existing cases or created false cases
said they exploited the fact that cases were not verified. They
said that when case files were reviewed, it was just a paper
review. No one actually spoke to the beneficiary. In fact, one of
the major problems perpetrators had in concealing their crimes
was dealing with periodic case recertifications. It was common
for a perpetrator to have to terminate a false case when a
recertification notice went out. Perpetrators recommend that
supervisors randomly, openly, and on an ad hoc basis contact
beneficiaries to verify their existence and the status of their
case. It appears that a very small sample, with only a telephone
inquiry, would have raised the risk of detection sufficiently to
preclude some of the crimes.

Rotate Caseload

Some perpetrators were able to conceal their crime and control their bogus cases because they were permanently assigned a specific caseload. Case assignments are often based on alphabetical order or the end digit in the beneficiary's ID number. Perpetrators recommended rotating caseloads to assure that one person does not have permanent control of a case.

Identify Workers With Their Transactions In The Database

Perpetrators noted that they were able to anonymously enter bogus data into the system. Most systems which the perpetrators worked on did not identify the input technician and/or caseworker with the transaction. Consequently, the perpetrators felt that the system "wasn't being watched." The perpetrators recommended that the system identify the persons who authorizes and/or inputs each transaction.

Limit Access Within The System

Perpetrators noted that they were often able to commit or cover-up their crime by using override or force codes in the system. Such codes give the perpetrator the opportunity to delete data from the system or to bypass edits and screens. Perpetrators recommended that system users' access be limited to only the codes or types of transactions they need to do their job and suggest that this be controlled by each user's ID and password.

Enforce Security Features

Some perpetrators were able to commit their crimes despite computer security features specifically designed to prevent such crimes. Sometimes computer controls were bypassed to promote office efficiencies, while in other situations they were not in effect because of benign neglect. Perpetrators recommend that the purpose and value of computer system controls be stressed to first line managers and that persons in charge of computer security periodically evaluate the implementation of specific controls.

CONCLUSIONS AND RECOMMENDATIONS

Investigations of computer-related fraud cases are generally limited to the facts necessary to prosecute the alleged perpetrator. The findings from interviews with perpetrators described in this report add to earlier findings reported by Inspectors General which were based on data in their files. For example, interviews reported the involvement of coconspirators in many more cases than IG files suggested. Similarly, interviews provided more descriptive information on how the crimes were perpetrated and the effectiveness of system controls.

Debrief Perpetrators Routinely

Law enforcement officials and criminologists often interview persons convicted of economic crimes to identify the characteristics of a subset of perpetrators. Because computer fraud is a relatively new area of economic crime, we believe that interviewing these perpetrators will add to the growing body of knowledge in this area; and that findings from interviews can be used by management and Inspectors General to prevent additional fraud cases. We recommend, therefore, that:

1. Inspectors General routinely debrief perpetrators of computer fraud to identify the specific vulnerabilities in their computer systems.

2. Inspectors General provide feedback to management on the findings from perpetrator interviews and assure that controls are instituted to correct vulnerabilities.

3. Inspectors General, program managers, and systems security officers include perpetrator case histories in training on computer crime and computer security, both to heighten awareness and to act as a deterrent.

Strengthen Automated System Controls

Perpetrators reported that the existing controls in the victimized systems were weak and easily bypassed. IDs and passwords were simplistic and/or public knowledge and gave the user access to the whole system, rather than only the applications or transactions necessary for the user's job. A number of the victimized systems did not identify or maintain a record of the specific individual who authorized or input the data, creating the atmosphere of anonymity and severely hampered later review or investigation. Screens and edits were easily circumvented by users or lifted by management in the interst of productivity. These findings suggest the need to implement additional controls to strengthen the integrity of automated systems and prevent the perception that "no one is watching." We therefore recommend that:

1. All payment systems be capable of enforcing personal accountability, by including such features as personal identification and authentication, and audit trails.

2. Access controls in such systems limit user access to only the programs, records, or transactions required by the user's job responsibility.

3. Management periodically review the adequacy and implementation of all automated systems controls and security features, as required by OMB Circulars A-71 (TM-1) and A-123.

Guidance to State, Local, and Private Agencies

Federal agencies have a substantial investment in state, local, and private computer systems, both because the federal government finances most of the development and maintenance costs of such systems, and because those systems control the allocation of federal funds. Yet these systems appear to be vulnerable. About half of the perpetrators worked for state, local, or private agencies that were administering federal programs. It is recommended that:

> Federal agencies re-evaluate their guidance to state, local, and private administering agencies regarding computer security and controls.

> Vulnerabilities in state, local, or private agencies computer system be addressed with the same vigor as those in federal systems.

Training and Awareness of Line Managers

The original study observed IG investigators were not fully aware of internal control procedures for automated systems. Nor were they aware of specific vulnerabilities in their agency's computer systems. Training in these areas was recommended. It appears that a similar lack of sensitivity to controls and potential vulnerabilities exist among line program managers. The potential for employee crime has not been stressed and some managers see system controls more as impediments to productivity than necessary security features. It is recommended that:

> IGs and/or system security officers provide training and awareness programs targeted to line program managers.

> Procedures be established for "advertising" the existence of internal and system controls to indicate that "someone is indeed watching."

Review Personnel Security Procedures

In the course of locating the perpetrators we learned that one in five had a prior criminal record. Some were hired by the agencies under special placement programs for ex-felons. In light of our findings it is recommended that:

Inspectors General and management re-evaluate agency personnel security policies and clearance practices for persons in positions of trust, including all positions with access to payroll, benefit records, and other payment data.

A PERPETRATOR TELLS HIS OWN STORY

As a follow-up to our discussion with one of the perpetrators, he wrote down his own views of how and why he committed his crime. He has given us permission to include it in the report in the hope that it may help prevent other individuals and agencies from finding themselves in similar situations.

I am 44 years old and married. I am a formerly admitted lawyer and former claims examiner in a benefit program in a federal regional office.

From June of 1980 to November 1981, while employed as a GS-11, I manipulated financial disbursement computers in such a way as to cause the computers to issue about 40 checks totalling about $54,000 to recently deceased beneficiaries. I had the checks mailed to my home. I forged the beneficiary's signatures and then deposited the checks in my personal checking account.

A more alert personnel security system, coupled with improved computer security would have made my crimes more difficult to perpetrate. However, the personnel security system was not designed to detect or flag likely violators. As for computer security procedures, they were virtually nonexistent. Password controls were lax. Audit trails were not examined by officials with any eye to detecting crime. The computers were not safeguarded adequately and, as a consequence, any number of us who had access to the ADP systems could have initiated the same crimes that I initiated.

The scheme I used was basically foolproof. I could have gone on with it indefinitely. In fact, 18 months went by from the time I quit my job until the government, capitalizing on a simple and stupid mistake that I had made, detected my crimes and caught up with me.

Before recounting the details of my experience as a federal employee, I would like to provide background of my own past. In a very real sense, my past played an important role in what I did. I grew up in a middle class home. A reasonably good student, I attended Penn State for two years and then transferred to the University of Pittsburgh where I completed my studies and graduated with a Bachelor of Science degree in Psychology. In 1969, I enrolled in law school, graduating in May of 1973 and being admitted to the Bar in May of 1974. It took me a total of 10 years to graduate because I worked to finance my own way.

It is also noteworthy that somewhere in my high school and college career I developed a serious drinking problem. I would continue to drink excessively and regularly until, at the age of 35, I brought my habit under control.

My alcoholism did not prevent me from obtaining a security clearance when I was in the Air National Guard, where I served from 1966 to 1971, including the period of May of 1968 until December of 1968, when as a result of the Pueblo incident, my unit was activated.

While still in law school, I started a private investigations business, in a small town, near a major eastern city. Most of my business involved injury claims due to product malfunction and car accidents and law enforcement related cases in which defense lawyers retained me on behalf of their clients. I had the investigative business from 1971 until 1975.

In the mid-1970s, I began to suffer from frequent bouts of depression stemming, I believe, from too much studies, too much outside work, and too much alcohol. In addition, my family was suffering because we were constantly short of cash. And I had another family problem. It was my mother, who, like me, had a drinking habit of equally self-destructive proportions. Eventually, she literally drank herself to death. I tried to encourage her to give up drinking and failed in my efforts, leaving me emotionally drained from seeing someone destroying herself, while caught up in the same trap that I was in.

My investigative work also had become a source of emotional difficulty for me. I was retained on one particularly grisly murder case that endangered my physical well-being and that ultimately led me to decide that I wanted to get into a more conventional pursuit. It was that decision that caused me to apply for a federal job. That was in 1974.

I made another important decision in the year 1975 and I quit drinking.

I was somewhat idealistic about my government job. I felt I could do some good for my program beneficiaries and their families. At the same time, I hoped that change of scenery and pace would be good for myself and my family.

Unfortunately, I was soon to be discouraged with government service. I had been promoted a couple of times and had outstanding ratings on my performance. However, when a promotion that I wanted and felt that I clearly deserved was denied me, I became an enraged, disgruntled employee.

As I look back, I realize that I grossly overreacted to the lost promotion. I was in a rage—over what I will leave to psychiatrists to explain. It was one thing to be angry over what I perceived to be an unjust personnel action. It was quite another to experience the rage that I experienced.

For a time, I was able to channel my rage, by involving myself in union work. I became president of a local union for federal employees representing employees in four agencies. I also served as a substitute for a national representative, when there was no such representative in my area for a time.

I found the union work to be very satisfying. I didn't get paid for it, but I felt that I was able to help people to get a fairer shake than they were getting.

However, the emotional problems that I mentioned still remained within me and I made a scapegoat out of my agency. By now my family was living better than I ever lived. My wife and I were both bringing home good salaries. So we didn't really need more money. Yet for reasons to this day that I am unsure of I began to devise a scheme to steal through my agency's computer system.

Having grown up with traditional middle class values, I had never stolen anything before in my life. Also, as the product of a middle class environment, I had always been astonished at the criminals I had known in my investigative business because of their lack of fear of getting into trouble. Yet now, for the first time in my life, I found myself plotting a crime—and, if that wasn't unpredictable enough, I found myself not fearing getting caught or getting incarcerated. I know from my own experiences that career criminals do not feel humiliation when they are apprehended. They, in most cases, don't seem to be deterred by the prospect of going to prison. For about a year and a half, I was in that frame of mind myself. For lack of a better term, I would describe myself, during the time period in question as burnt out. I was obsessed with one objective—and that was to beat my agency illegally and to get away with it.

My scheme went like this:

I would note the death of a beneficiary who had been receiving a monthly entitlement check. I would be alerted to the death because I would receive a computer message that a check had been returned with this notation, "Possible Death of Payee."

Next, the office would send out a letter to the beneficiary's address asking for information as to the beneficiary's status. We would receive a response confirming the death. I would then ascertain that there were no other possible claimants. I would then proceed with my scheme.

First, I would remove the entire case file from the office. I took it home and destroyed it.

Second, I would enter into the computer a message that the beneficiary had undergone a change in financial circumstance— a large number of medical bills, for example. I would make a retroactive benefit totalling less than $5000. Anything under $5000 I was authorized to process without another section's participation. In theory, two persons' computer access cards were necessary to create the benefit checks that I created by myself. However, there was no security regarding those cards, as the cards of other employees who may have been absent from the office, were just left lying around, totally unsecured. Additionally, each employee had a personal ID number to be used to log on to the computer when the access card was put in the terminal. I was able to steal another employee's ID number by standing behind them as they logged on. I simply watched their fingers as they typed their ID number.

Third, I would alter the beneficiary's address. Instead of sending the check to the beneficiary's home, I directed it to my address. However, because you needed two employees to complete such a transaction, I first used my own access card and ID to initiate the change and then I used another employee's card and ID to confirm the change. It was easy.

Fourth, I would terminate the beneficiary's case on the computer a month later. In six months, I knew the computer would erase all memory of the case and its history. That is why I call this a fool-proof scheme.

The checks would come to my house. I would sign the beneficiary's name, then endorse it myself and then deposit it in my personal account. I quit committing the crimes in November of 1981. Four months later I resigned, and about a year and a half later, the crimes were detected.

The mistake I made was that around the first of the year, I inadvertantly misdated the date of a beneficiary's death. This, when caught in a computer match led auditors to make a routine inquiry and they discovered several checks going to one address. It wasn't long before they realized that a violation may have occurred. The Secret Service was called in. My checking account was subpoenaed. Further inquiry established that the beneficiaries had all died earlier than I had listed them. The authorities put together a solid case against me.

I was indicted on many counts of mail fraud and forgery in April of 1984. I plead guilty and was sentenced to one month in a half way house, two three-year suspended sentences and five years of probation and ordered to make restitution of the $54,000. I was also fined $2000. I was also suspended from the practice of law.

It was not money that motivated me in my crimes, it was

irrational rage caused by emotional exhaustion, the sources of which were my long time excessive drinking, my overwork, disappointment with government service and the anguish of watching, but being unable to help, as my mother drank herself to death.

I made as much and more money than I earned with the government. All these factors are evidence that money or greed was not my primary motivation.

I have asked myself many times if my agency could have done anything to predict that I, and people like me, would initiate fraud against its computer. The answer is, yes.

The computers capable of disbursing dollar instruments were not properly protected against abuse. They were like unlocked bank vaults waiting to be invaded. Security around these machines was almost nonexistent. So the first thing I would say is that plant security must be considered an essential function of personnel security. If the bank vault has money in it and if nobody is watching, somebody, for whatever reason, is likely to steal from it.

The problem is also one of attitude. For example, one of the jobs that I had before was as a claims examiner for a private insurance company. There was a totally different approach to money there. Security was important to the managers. Conversely, this attitude seemed to be lacking at the Federal agency.

Along with improved physical security, I would point out that a more alert personnel security system might have flagged me or someone like me for two or three reasons.

I was a practicing alcoholic. I had a twenty-year history of heavy drinking.

My anger and rage at the agency—most of which was unwarranted and irrational, was not something I tried to conceal. If a trained investigator would have interviewed me, I would have revealed my feelings, thereby calling attention to the possibility that I was a risk.

ACKNOWLEDGMENT

This report represents another step forwad in our effort to better understand computer-related fraud in government agencies. But this step could not have been taken without the support of others both within and outside of the Inspector General community. I want to recognize the efforts of staff from IG offices who reviewed their files to identify new cases and to provide locating information on old ones. The Department of Justice's Bureau of Prisons and the Probation Division within the Administrative Offices of the U.S. Courts provided valuable assistance in locating perpetrators and setting-up interviews.

I would also like to acknowledge the help of the 46 perpetrators who voluntarily met with us during the study to discuss "their side of the story." This report could never have been written without their cooperation.

Finally, I would like to thank the members of my staff—Jack Molnar, Project Manager, Gail Shelton, Jane Tebbutt, Lois Terry, and Denise Washington—for their many efforts in support of this project.

ACKNOWLEDGMENT

APPENDIX VI

REPORT OF THE TASK FORCE ON THE CRIMINAL IMPLICATIONS OF FALSE IDENTIFICATION

The Problem

For thousands of years, people lived in small hamlets and dealt with their neighbor. Everyone knew intimately those with whom they did business.

A couple of hundred years ago, the industrial revolution changed all that. People have been migrating in ever increasing numbers to larger towns and cities. We now deal with strangers, whose identity and reputation are unknown to us.

We have, therefore, come to depend on written substitutes (paper or plastic documentation) to attest to who we are. These documents include checks, credit cards, and signed applications. They, in turn, depend on what are commonly called foundation or breeder documents that establish the basic identity, such as birth certificates, social security cards, or drivers' licenses.

Discussion

Identification documents are myriad and are issued by federal, state, local, and private entities. False identification can be easily acquired through an assortment of fraudulent techniques, including the manufacture or purchase of counterfeit or altered documents, imposture, and misrepresentation in document issuance processes. Indeed, a variety of false identification is available on virtually any street corner or through mail order identification kits.

The use of false identification, which was not a federal crime in itself until the passage of The False Identification Crime Control Act in 1982, is a multibillion dollar problem affecting government and business. False identification is the primary *modus operandi* in such criminal activities as fraud against business or government, illegal immigration, passport fraud, drug smuggling, terrorism, and flight from justice. In fact, if there is one common denominator among the welfare cheat, illegal alien, smuggler, terrorist, bad-check artist, and fugitive from justice, it is probably that they all used some form of false identification in one or more of the following categories:

1. That which had been fabricated or counterfeited.
2. That which had been altered.
3. That which had been acquired fraudulently or under false pretenses from issuing agencies.
4. That which belonged to another person (imposture).

It is difficult to quantify accurately the losses to the public and private sector, but it is clear that the American public is the ultimate victim. In 1976, the Federal Advisory Committee on False Identification (FACFI), in its report, "The Criminal Use of False Identification," estimated that crimes involving false identification cost the American public and business $15 billion annually.[1] In 1982, the staff of Senator William V. Roth's

[1]U.S. Department of Justice, *The Criminal Use of False Identification: The Report of the Federal Advisory Committee on False Identification* (November 1976): xiii–xiv.

Permanent Subcommittee on Investigations, updated that estimate in excess of $24 billion.[2] Whatever the figure, it is a horrendous price tag.

Recognizing that the subject of false identification and its impacts is both vast and complex, the Task Force limited its deliberations to the three types of federal identification documents (Social Security cards, immigration documents, and passports) and the impacts of false identification-related crimes involving these documents on large state and locally administered programs.

The Task Force also recognized that the evolutionary changes in ways people transact business with one another are taking on a different dimension as a result of the information explosion that arises from computerization. We are witnessing a phenomenon unparalleled in human experience. More information is being collected, stored, manipulated, and retrieved in our lifetime than all other lifetimes of mankind combined. Virtually all segments of our society now depend on computerized transactions in order to conduct business. Within our generation, there will be a virtual disappearance of all hard-copy documents, replaced by data bases of electronic impulses.

Access to that information, then, becomes all that more critical. Limiting that access properly is the aim of the recommendations of our task force.

Birth Certificates

The task force recognizes that the foundation, or breeder, document for almost any other kind of identification for citizens is the birth certificate. Over 7000 state and local vital records offices issue birth certificates with no uniform standards for issuance processes, controls, or quality of documents. In some

[2]U.S. Congress, Senate, Committee on Governmental Affairs, Permanent Subcommittee on Investigations, Staff Statement submitted at hearings on Fraudulent Use of Federal Documents to Penetrate Benefit Programs (June 15, 1982): 1.

jurisdictions, birth certificates are easily counterfeited, obtained through imposture, or created from stolen legitimate blank forms. Likewise, the reporting of deaths within the states is another loophole by which impostors can create reestablished identities. Public Law 98-21, passed by the Congress April 1983 as part of amendments to the Social Security Act, addresses this concern.[3] The task force recognizes that vital records are under state and local jurisdictions, but makes the following recommendations as an initial point of improving this vulnerable link in the identification chain of documents.

Task Force Recommendations

1. We recommend a review and comparison of best birth record systems and practices, looking towards developing minimum standards in dealing with the issuance, formatting, processing, and quality of documents. This should be done at least on a statewide basis, if not nationally (Addendums I, II).

2. We recommend that issuing agencies not issue certified copies or replacement documents without proper verification procedures.

3. We recommend that all federal and state agencies issuing identification documents immediately adopt a policy to validate all evidentiary documents presented at application, prior to issuance of any new or replacement ones.

INVESTIGATION AND PROSECUTION OF FALSE IDENTIFICATION CRIMES

The False Identification Crime Control Act of 1982 (Public Law 97-398) referred to in the introduction by the three co-chairper-

[3]Public Law 98-21 allows states, under voluntary agreements with the Secretary of Health and Human Services (HHS); to furnish information concerning individuals on whom death certificates have been officially filed.

sons of this task force to illustrate the problem, was passed in recognition of this growing problem of false identification and the need for specific legislation to deter crimes involving false identification. The act has two primary purposes: (1) it allows prosecution and conviction for offenses involving federal identification documents, including counterfeiting and trafficking in counterfeits; and (2) it creates certain federal offenses specifically relating to counterfeiting and trafficking in counterfeit or stolen state, local, or foreign identification documents.

The intent of this legislation, however, cannot be fully realized without strong enforcement priorities and innovative and cooperative techniques on the part of federal law enforcement agencies.

Task Force Recommendations

4. We recommend that the Attorney General emphasize the seriousness and negative impact on our society from the criminal use of false identification and direct his United States Attorneys to prosecute aggressively under the new False Identification Crime Control Act of 1982, as well as other existing statutes (Addendum III).

5. We further recommend that the Attorney General actively encourage all investigative agencies to investigate such cases within their purview (Addendum IV).

6. We recommend that federal and state investigative units emphasize the development of improved techniques in the investigation of false identification-related crimes.

7. We recommend that federal investigative agencies establish a policy of cooperation to share intelligence and engage in joint investigations of identification fraud schemes and profiles.

IDENTIFICATION DOCUMENT PRODUCTION

The Task Force found that some existing documents are very easily counterfeited or altered and that many identification documents in use today do not contain sufficient techniques to identify the bearer of the document uniquely. The Task Force recognizes that technology does exist both to secure documents sufficiently from most counterfeiting or tampering and to provide positive personal identification techniques.[4] The Task Force also recognizes, however, that thorough risk assessments and cost-benefit analyses must dictate the optimal amount of document security and personal identification techniques to be employed in the production of identification documents.

Task Force Recommendations

8.   We recommend a full dissemination of information on existing technology to better protect benefit programs and payment systems from false identity frauds. For example, materials on (1) tamper-resistant cards, (2) systems of personal identification/verification, and (3) machine readable and automated control techniques, need to be shared.

9.   We recommend that, to the extent possible, and where cost-effective, current state-of-the-art technology should be employed in the production of these identification documents.

10. We recognize that no added improvements to document issuance or eligibility determination processes will be meaningful unless the public is alerted to the false identification problem and is trained to recognize a legitimate from a false document. We therefore recommend that the federal government, as well as the private sector, engage in a campaign to so educate program managers and the public to deal with the problem.

---

[4]Such techniques are discussed in depth in two reports provided to the Task Force: Health and Human Services Inspector General's Report, "False Identification: The Problem and Technological Options" (April 1983), and the American Bankers Association Report on the ABA Counterfeit and Altered Card Fraud Project (September 1983).

COMPUTERIZED VERIFICATION TECHNIQUES

The Task Force recognizes that one of the most effective tools in ensuring the integrity of benefit programs, passport processes, and payment systems against false identification is the use of automated verification techniques, such as computer matching, edits, and screens and the use of online data bases. Cited as top examples among these innovative approaches are (1) the Immigration and Naturalization Service's (INS) Systematic Alien Verification for Entitlements (SAVE) project which identifies illegal aliens who are, or might be, improperly receiving benefit payments. The SAVE project stresses cooperation between the INS and other state and federal agencies to prevent such payments. The program will complement other enforcement efforts to curtail the employment of illegal aliens, and to reduce the ability of illegal aliens to support themselves from the fruits of criminal enterprises. These efforts reduce the "pull" factors which encourage illegal immigration. The SAVE project provides automated access by the states to the INS Service's Alien Status Verification System. When an alien applicant is checked against the system and there is no record on the system, or if a questioned record appears, the applicant is referred to INS for a formal status verification check. Information about the alien applicants with valid legal status is expeditiously returned to state authorities to allow continued processing of the pending application. Specific steps taken to date: Implementation of pilot projects in California, Illinois and Colorado, which have resulted in $40 million in cost avoidance over the past six months. INS is now prepared to expand this service to other states. (Addendum V.) And (2) the Department of Health and Human Services Inspector General's Project Clean Data, which identifies false and erroneous Social Security numbers being used to obtain benefits (Addendum VI).

Task Force Recommendations

11. We recommend that state and federal program managers make it a policy to maximize the use of matching

technology to prevent, surface, and eliminate individuals from the system who are applying for or receiving program benefits as a result of false identification.

12. We recommend the development and dissemination of primers and instructions as practical guidance to state and federal managers to instruct them in the applicability of various matching techniques to their systems.

13. We further recommend the development of a framework for assessing costs and benefits from computer matching as a way of demonstrating to the American public the value of using these techniques.

BENEFIT ELIGIBILITY PROCESSES

Fraudulently obtained identification is deemed to be a front-end problem that requires proper eligibility verification *before payment or issuance,* whether for a government benefit, passport, credit card, or driver's license. We recognize the need to foster and facilitate an increase of front-end eligibility verification processes in order to prevent improper access to public benefit programs at all levels of government. (Addendum VI.)

Task Force Recommendations

14. We recommend and advocate that all significant eligibility factors common to federal and state benefit programs be identified.

15. We further recommend and advocate that current front-end computerized state and federal techniques be catalogued and exchanged among appropriate agencies at all levels of government.

16. We recommend improved security of existing documents both in their issuance in the application phase and in their use.

Conclusion

In making these recommendations, the Task Force acknowledges that responsibility for action falls primarily to the very federal agencies represented on the Task Force—the departments of Health and Human Services, Justice, and State. These departments, and their program and enforcement agencies, have already begun to act in many areas, through such initiatives as improvements to the Social Security Number issuance system and card, the Immigration and Naturalization Service's automation of its files and pilot projects with states, and the Passport Service's systems improvements, document security, and training programs. The President's Council on Integrity and Efficiency (PCIE) is also actively pursuing initiatives involving computer matching and front-end eligibility verification and is involving state program managers in these efforts. The HHS Inspector General, through his co-chairpersonship of the PCIE Long-Term Computer Matching Project, will strongly advocate the principles and actions recommended by the Task Force.

The Task Force recognizes, however, that support for these recommendations is necessary not only at federal, state, and local levels, but also among the public at large. Public awareness of the scope and impact of false identification, and support for measures to counter the problem are essential if we are to check the pervasiveness and cost of false identification-related crimes.

ADDENDUM I

As an outgrowth of the recommendations made by the Task Force on Criminal Implications of False Identification at LAW's Conference on the Judiciary, LAW was asked by the Governor's Office to conduct a workshop at the Second Annual Governor's Training Conference on Crime Victims, April 8, 1985.

LAW's Workshop, entitled "Victimization Through the Use of Fraudulent Documents," had as its purpose to educate the public about the problem and assemble authorities from several state offices in which the problem of false identification is pervasive, damaging and costly.

The meeting was moderated by Doris Dolan and led by a panel of four, namely: David W. Mitchell, Chief, Office of State Registrar; Steven J. Mullen, Regional Fraud Coordinator, Passport Services, U.S. Department of State, San Francisco; Roy Lundgren, Assistant Chief, Investigative Services, Department of Motor Vehicles (DMV); and David D. Davis, Assistant Chief, Post Licensing Services Division of Driver Safety, DMV.

Problems and possible solutions were discussed with the issuance of birth certificates surfacing as the first priority issue to be resolved. All available research was reviewed at a follow-up workshop held July 31, 1985. With the cooperation of Governor Deukmejian's Office and the panelists, a procedure will subsequently be developed and implemented to serve as a model for replication by other states.

ADDENDUM II

Following the May 1984 Conference, HHS Inspector General Richard Kusserow initiated a study of birth record systems and issuance practices as recommended by the delegates serving on the Criminal Implications of False Identification Task Force. Since birth certificates are primary evidence of U.S. citizenship, Passport Services, U.S. Department of State, has a linked interest and is providing input and assistance to this project.

The survey is being conducted in nine states to document what vulnerabilities exist and the best practices now in existence. The objective of this study is to determine both short-term and long-term solutions to the problem of fraud involving birth certificates.

ADDENDUMS III AND IV

As a follow-through to the recommendations of the Fifth Conference on the Judiciary, Edwin Meese III, Attorney General of the United States, has issued directives to all U.S. Attorneys and federal and states investigative units to prosecute aggressively under the False Identification Crime Control Act of 1982 and has encouraged them to emphasize the development of improved techniques and share intelligence in the investigation of fraud schemes involving false identification.

ADDENDUM V

Alan C. Nelson, Commissioner, Immigration and Naturalization Services (INS) as an update to the May 1984 conference, reports in this addendum that the cost avoidance has resulted in a $95.3 million savings to taxpayers in the three states designated in the SAVE pilot project for the federal fiscal year ending September 30, 1984.

In addition, Commissioner Nelson has continued to initiate specific steps to implement Project SAVE in the following areas:

1. Contact governors, beginning with states with the largest entitlement programs to inform them of the programs and obtain a memorandum of understanding to being operations in the unemployment compensation area.

2. Allow computer systems in appropriate state offices access to the Alien Status Verification System.

3. Implement referral procedures to verify the status of questioned applicants.

4. Expand program to include all entitlement programs in participating states.

5. Use results to enlist remaining states in the project.

ADDENDUM VI

The HHS Inspector General will continue to promote matching technology and provide guidance to states through standardized-format pilot tests in eight states and through a compendium of front-end automated verification techniques which will be published in the near future.

In July 1984, President Reagan signed into law the "Deficit Reduction Act of 1984" (Public Law 98-369). The "Income and Eligibility Verification" provisions include requirements for use of Social Security numbers for record keeping and information exchange and for standardized formats and procedures in computer matching in the Aid to Families and Dependent Children, Food Stamp, Medicaid, Unemployment Insurance, and Supplemental Security Income programs. These provisions are a direct outgrowth of the work of the PCIE Computer Matching project and will greatly facilitate implementation of the Task Force's recommendations under "Computerized Verification Techniques" and "Benefit Eligibility Processes."

BIBLIOGRAPHY

American Bar Association. *Report on Computer Crime* (June 1984).

American Institute of Certified Public Accountants. *The Study of EDP-Related Fraud in the Banking and Insurance Industries* (April 1984).

American Institute of Certified Public Accountants. *Warning Signals of the Possible Existence of Fraud, CPA Letters.* (March 12, 1979).

Burroughs Corporation. *Magnetic Techniques Study* (August 1977).

Comptroller General of the U.S. *Standards for Audit of Government Organizations, Programs, Activities, and Functions,* Washington DC: U.S. Government Printing Office, 1981.

Clinard, Marshall B. "Criminological Theories of Violations of Wartime Regulations, *American Sociological Review,* 11:3 (June 1946): 258–270.

Cressey, Donald. "The Theory of Differential Association," *Social Problems,* 8:1 (Summer 1960): 2.

Federal Advisory Committee on False Identification. *The Criminal Use of False Identification* (November 1976): xii.

Geis, Gilbert, "Sociology and Crime," in *Sociology of Crime.* Edited by Joseph S. Roucek, New York: Philosophical Library (1961), pp. 7–33.

Glaser, Daniel, "Criminality Theory and Behavioral Images," *American Journal of Sociology,* 61 (1956): 433–455.

Glueck, Sheldon and Eleanor. *Delinquents in the Making.* New York: Harper and Bros., 1952, pp. 88–90.

Hanson, Walter E. "Focus on Fraud," *Financial Executive* 43 (1975).

Health and Human Services. *Preventing Sexual Abuse in Day Care Programs.* National Program Inspection, Office of Inspector General, Region X (November 1984).

Health and Human Services. *Study of Convicted Providers in Medicare and Medicaid.* Office of Inspector General (1984).

Health and Human Services. *"False Identification: The Problem and Technological Options."* Office of Inspector General (April 1983).

Housing and Urban Development. *Security Planning for HUD—Assisted Multifamily Housing.* Washington, DC.

International Civil Aviation Organization. *Working Paper on Passport Travel Document* (April 1974).

Kropatkin, Philip. *Audit Logic.* New York: Ronald Press, 1984.

Kusserow, Richard P. "Program Inspections," *Government Accountants Journal* 23:1 (Spring 1984).

Mathyer, Jacques. "The Problem of Security and Identity and Authorization Documents," *International Criminal Police Review* (March 1980): 66–79.

Montgomery, Robert H. *Auditing Theory and Practice.* 8th ed. New York: Ronald, 1957.

National Institute of Law Enforcement and Criminal Justice, Federal Security Code.

National Police Agency, *White Paper on Police,* Japan.

Post, Richard S., and Kingsbury, Arthur A. *Security Administration: an Introduction.* Springfield, IL: Charles C Thomas, 1970, p. 5.

President's Council on Integrity and Efficiency, *Computer Related Fraud and Abuse in Government Agencies* (1984).

Reid, *The Reid Report.* John E., and Associates (1967).

Samenow, Stanton E. *Inside the Criminal Mind,* New York: Times, 1984.

Sandia National Laboratories. *Entry-Control Systems Handbook* (September 1980).

Sutherland, Edwin H. "Critique of the Theory." In *The Sutherland Papers.* Edited by Albert Cohen, Alfred Lindemuth, and Karl Schuessler. Bloomington: Indiana University Press 1956, pp. 30–41.

Sutherland, Edwin H. *Principles of Criminology,* 5th edition. Revised by Donald R. Cressey. New York: J. B. Lippincott, 1955, pp. 74–81.

Sherrick, Inspector General Joseph. *Indicators of Fraud in the Department of Defense Procurement,* Department of Defense (May 1984): 1, 3–9, 13–14, 17–19.

INDEX

Access:
  controlling by mechanical means:
    entry control system tapes, 146
    fraud and abuse, susceptibilities to,
      148
    photo ID cards, 145, 168
  defined, 105
  denying, 105
  employee, 119
  illustrations of unauthorized, 107
  mechanical controls against, 145
American Institute of Certified Public
      Accountants, 200
Audit:
  ADP systems, 303
  fraud and defalcation, auditor's re-
      sponsibilities, 200
  internal auditors, role of, 214
  Montgomery, Robert, 200
  planning of, 215
  public accountants, role of, 214
  qualifications of auditors, 214
  responsibilities and objectives of, 199
  types of audit, 216

Banking industry, denying access, 195
Bribes, 230

Common Law, English, 9
Computers:
  access control through physical secu-
      rity, 288

auditing existing systems, 303
auditor/investigator concerns and
    uses, 260
fraud and abuse of, in government
    agencies, A-IV
fraud perpetrator, characteristics of,
    280
hackers, 260
micros, minis, PC's, security rules for,
    295
optimal systems security, conclusions
    on, 301
record matching, automated, 315
systems integrity, ensuring, 299
vulnerabilities:
  case studies:
    Japan, 277
    U.S., 272
  rating ADP:
    environment for, 263
    risk assessments of, 293
Corporate criminality, detecting, 230
Crime and punishment:
  evolution of, 6
  industrial revolution, impact on, 8
Crimes, prohibited, 11
  ABSCAM investigation, 12
  prosecution, reluctance to enter
      into, 13
  white collar crimes, cost of, 14
Criminal equation, 5
Criminality, theories on, 59

Criminal proclivity, 6, 69

Document security:
  coded credentials, 154
  counterfeiting, protecting against, 150
  lamination techniques, 152

Employees:
  pre-employment screening of, 120
  troubled:
    management's responsibilities, 80
    types of, 78
Executive protection, denying opportu-
    nities from attacks, 193

False identification:
  criminal use of, 160, A-VI
  definitions for, 162
  examples of use, 163
Fraud:
  contract/procurement, 238
  warning signals, 98
Fraud and abuse:
  Japanese study on ADP, 277
  PCIE study, A-IV
  perpetrator profile, 280
  U.S. studies, 272

Hackers, 260

Identification cards, 145
  adequate design for, 168
  standards for, 165
Indicators of criminal activity:
  bribes, hidden in accounting records,
    230
  business, corporate criminality, indi-
    cators of, 233
  defense procurement, lessons learned,
    238
Inspections, concept of:
  inspectors general, 207
  program, 217
Internal control systems, 175
  concerns about, 179
  front end controls, 184
  fundamentals of, 181
  management's role in, 178

on-line reviews, 184
responsibilities for, 184

Maluum prohibitum, 11
Management, rules for, enlightened, 91
Motivation:
  defined, 49
  espionage, in, 55
  external forces, 73
  internal forces, 57
Muckrakers, 12

Opportunity, defined, 175

Physical security:
  components of, 135
  defined, 135
  environmental security, 137
    alarm systems, 137
    doors and windows, 140
    fire protection, 143
    lighting considerations, 140
    identification procedures for employ-
      ees/outsiders, 141
President's council on integrity and
    efficiency, 208
Providers, convicted, in Medicare and
    Medicaid, A-II

Retail sales operations, 249
  bad check considerations, 253
  credit card considerations, 254
  motivating employees towards hon-
    esty, 250

Security:
  ADP, 272
  document, 167
  executive protection, 193
  information, 108
  physical, 135, 288
Sexual abuse in day care programs, 41,
    A-III
  screening against offenders, A-III
  sexual abuse, signals of, A-III
Stress, situational (motivation), 53
Sutherland, Edwin H.:
  theory of differential association, 60

Targets:
  children as targets, 41
  cost considerations, of target protection, 32
  executives as targets, 37
  protecting against criminality, 19
  rating environment's, against attack, 20

Unauthorized access, security against:
  employee access implications, 119
    credentialing checks, 120
    employment applications, essential elements of, 124
    ensuring, 111
    honesty tests, written, 131

  psychological stress tests, 128
  screening, preemployment, 124
  sensitive positions, implications of, 120
information security, defined, 109
personnel security:
  defined, 109
  executive protection, 114
  steps to ensure, 37

Vulnerability assessments, traditional, 32

White collar crimes, 11
  costs of, 14
  prosecution of, 13